Media Hoaxes

MEDIA HOAXES

Fred Fedler

Iowa State University Press / Ames

MEDIA HOAXES

Fred Fedler

Iowa State University Press / Ames

Fred Fedler is Professor of Journalism, School of Communication, University of Central Florida, Orlando.

© 1989 by Iowa State University Press, Ames, Iowa 50010

Manufactured in the United States of America
⊗ This book is printed on acid-free paper.

First edition, 1989

Library of Congress Cataloging-in-Publication Data

Fedler, Fred.
    Media hoaxes / Fred Fedler. — 1st ed.
        p. cm.
    Includes bibliographical references.
    ISBN 0–8138–1117–1
    1. Mass media — United States. 2. Practical jokes. I. Title.
P92.U5F44   1989
071′.3 — dc20   89–15568

CONTENTS

⬜⬜⬜ Common Themes

PREFACE

Most people will be able to read this book in a few hours, yet it took nine years to complete—five years to research, three years to write and rewrite, and one year to publish.

The research became an enjoyable hobby. I began by trying to uncover all the media's old hoaxes, but discovered that it was an impossible goal. The media created thousands of hoaxes, and most have been lost or forgotten.

The task of finding and learning more about the hoaxes would have been easier if every newspaper compiled an index that listed all the stories it published each year. More than 1,650 daily newspapers are published in the United States, yet only one—the *New York Times*—is fully indexed, from its establishment in 1851 to the present. Other major dailies have begun to publish an annual index, but only for their current editions.

Researchers might page through old newspapers, looking for their hoaxes. But paging through all the editions published by even a few newspapers would require too much time. Also, researchers would fail to notice the newspapers' best hoaxes. The hoaxes were too clever, deliberately written to deceive even careful readers. As a result, researchers who found a story about an earthquake in Chicago, or about the wild animals escaping from a zoo, might not realize that the story was a hoax.

Other stories are obviously fictitious: stories about ghosts, mermaids, or a dangerous crack in the moon, for example. After the Civil War, a newspaper in Chicago also described a new technique for shipping cattle to markets in the East. The newspaper reported that the cattle were frozen, then loaded aboard railroad cars. Butchers in the East supposedly thawed and revived the cattle, then slaughtered the live animals several days later. As a result, the meat they sold was always fresh.

Today, anyone reading those stories would know they were fictitious. But to fully understand them, readers would need more information — the "inside" story about their creation and publication. To learn more about the stories' creation, I consulted reference books that list magazine articles published since 1802. Magazines have published thousands of articles about journalism, and some describe the media's hoaxes.

I found hundreds of other hoaxes by scanning the books written about famous journalists and famous newspapers. Journalists are prolific writers, and thousands have written books about their careers. The books are fascinating — entertaining as well as informative. They describe the journalists' most exciting stories, but also describe life during earlier periods in our country's history.

Not all the books are reliable, however. Journalists writing their memoirs discuss events that occurred during their youth, often forty or fifty years earlier. Some details are vague. Others are exaggerated. Still others are mistaken. The journalists may have forgotten their escapades as young writers. Or, while writing their memoirs, the journalists may have avoided anything that would make them seem foolish or irresponsible. An extreme example, the book written by a famous editor, describes only his work in New York. Other sources revealed that the editor murdered his wife.

Similarly, newspapers often publish books about themselves, usually on their one-hundredth anniversary. Employees asked to write the books emphasize their newspapers' most wonderful achievements. Few mention their newspapers' biases, errors, or other acts of irresponsibility. The problem is not always deliberate, however. Employees may not know about the hoaxes their newspapers published fifty or one hundred years earlier. The participants are dead, and their stories forgotten.

After learning about a hoax, I still had to obtain a copy of it — and that was the most difficult task of all. The books and magazines that mentioned a hoax often failed to reveal the date it was published. Other books and magazines failed to tell where the hoaxes were published — to identify the newspaper, city, or state. Even when a source provided that information, some publications were no longer available. Too many old newspapers have been thrown away, especially the weeklies published in mining towns in the West. In some cases, the entire towns have disappeared. Other newspapers have been destroyed by fire. During the 1860s, for example, Mark Twain worked as a reporter for the *Territorial Enterprise* in Virginia City, Nevada, and many of Twain's stories have been lost because no one saved copies of the *Territorial Enterprise* published during that period. A few of Twain's stories have survived, but only because they were reprinted by other newspapers in California and Nevada.

Famous dailies, especially those published in big cities, are more likely to have been preserved, but no library has copies of all of them. Instead, researchers are forced to travel from one library to another and may be disappointed by the results. Some editions are missing, and some pages are crumbling, torn, or blurred. Even researchers using a powerful magnifying glass are unable to decipher some key words, sentences, and paragraphs.

Because of all the problems, it was impossible to determine the truth about every hoax. Too many details were inconsistent or unavailable. While writing about those hoaxes, I tried to present the sources' conflicting claims. Or I used words indicating that their claims are questionable: words such as "supposedly," "reportedly," and "allegedly."

Many of the best hoaxes were created by the nation's best writers: Benjamin Franklin, Edgar Allan Poe, and Mark Twain, for example. To be included in this book, their longest hoaxes had to be condensed and edited. Originally, some were hundreds of pages long. I tried to retain the hoaxes' original language and flavor, but I modernized their spellings and used a consistent style of abbreviations, capitalization, and punctuation. Similarly, several newspapers have changed their names. For consistency, and so readers will recognize them, I used only the newspapers' current names.

Thousands of hoaxes remain lost or forgotten in the pages of historic newspapers and magazines. Occasionally, someone looking at one of those publications may uncover a hoax, but the evidence is being destroyed. Old newspapers and magazines are deteriorating, and editors are discarding their old files. The files are too expensive to store, maintain, or microfilm. Other files are lost when newspapers fail. A few newspapers have donated their files to libraries or universities, but few of the recipients have enough money to catalog the files, or enough space to make them easily available to the public.

Similarly, more and more newspapers are being microfilmed. Yet large newspapers publish several editions every day. To save money, some microfilm only a few of the editions. Even major dailies, such as the *Chicago Tribune,* have failed to keep copies of all their old editions.

If you know about a forgotten hoax—any hoax lost in one of those old newspapers or obscure editions—I would like to hear about it. I would appreciate receiving as much information as possible, particularly the name of the medium that created the hoax and the date of its broadcast or publication. Some readers may also be able to provide a copy of the hoax or some details about its creation. My address is

> Fred Fedler
> School of Communication
> University of Central Florida
> Orlando, FL 32816

Many people helped me write this book. After learning about a hoax, I often wrote to total strangers, asking for more information. Journalists and librarians were especially kind. Most answered my letters, and some spent hours digging out the details I needed.

Typically, Gayle Garrick at the *Boston Globe* said my letter about a hoax involving the *Globe* "tickled her curiosity." In 1883, an editor at the *Globe* wrote about a volcano, and other writers have insisted that the editor's stories were inspired by a drunken dream. Garrick found several stories the *Globe* published about the volcano. She also provided information suggesting that the previous accounts were mistaken. There were no drunken dreams.

While traveling in England, I spent a day at the Written Archives Center maintained by the British Broadcasting Corporation. When I arrived there, I found that its staff had already gotten out everything I needed. Moreover, someone had gone through all the material, marking the pages I wanted. While the material was being duplicated, I spent an hour chatting with the staff. As the conversation continued, they recalled other hoaxes created by the British media.

Francis J. "Skip" Muzik, Jr., a graduate student at the University of Wisconsin, has been especially helpful (and shares my enthusiasm for research). Skip uncovered hoards of valuable material, much of it in hundred-year-old newspapers and magazines. He traveled to Chicago to find the hoaxes published by newspapers there.

Since 1971, I have taught at the University of Central Florida in Orlando, and three librarians at the university— Leonie Black, Wava Tibbits, and Cheryl Mahan—helped me borrow hundreds of magazine articles and old books from other libraries across the country. Several graduate students also helped: Shari Hodgson, Karen Quinn, Susan McKinney Andersen, Christina Mayers, and Susan Braman.

Ed Brady was another inspiration. I met Ed after he retired. He was already in his sixties, but remained more curious and adventuresome than most twenty-year-olds. For years, Ed sent me copies of every hoax that he could find.

Other friends and colleagues also helped: Richard Cole at the University of North Carolina, Randy Murray at California Polytechnic State University, and Dan Pfaff at The Pennsylvania State University. Dick Norbraten, a former colleague at the *Sacramento Bee,* sent me clippings about a radio program in Northern California. Other friends and acquaintances who provided some additional information include Donald R. Browne, Tom Eveslage, Max K. Hall, Aralynn Abare McMane, Raymond B. Nixon, Sam G. Riley, Steve Valdespino, and Paul Wehr.

They will never know it, but I would also like to thank the wildlife that entertained me as I wrote, edited, and rewrote this book on a back porch overlooking a woods in Oviedo, Florida.

What's a Hoax and Why Did

OURNALISTS have published thousands of hoaxes, but rarely try to define or describe them. Some journalists think that definitions are unimportant. Other journalists think that definitions are impossible: that the hoaxes they publish are too diverse to describe. Thus, journalists are placed in the position of Supreme Court Justice Potter Stewart. While ruling on a case that involved hard-core pornography, Justice Stewart confessed that he could not define the term. But, Stewart added, "I know it when I see it."

Journalists, too, rely on their intuition—their instinct, experience, or professional judgment. For most journalists, the process becomes automatic. They look at a story and, instantly, recognize it as a hoax.

The *Random House Dictionary* defines a hoax as "something intended to deceive or defraud." *Webster's* adds that a hoax is an act "intended to trick or dupe." Other dictionaries agree that a hoax involves deception: that it deludes, fools, hoodwinks, or misleads its victims.

Like other hoaxes, the media's are often deliberate fabrications, created to fool the public. But the hoaxes published by newspapers and broadcast by radio and television stations possess several additional—and unique—characteristics.

First, the media's hoaxes are usually created to entertain—not cheat—the public. Thus, the hoaxes are a form of practical joking, but on a grand scale. Journalists who create the hoaxes never think of themselves as liars or cheats, nor even as fakers. Unlike criminals, they rarely intend to defraud the public: to gain some unfair or dishonest advantage. The

They Do It?

journalists only want to amuse people: to give them something to talk and laugh about.

Second, as part of the fun, journalists often admit that their stories are fictitious. While writing the stories, journalists include clues that reveal they are fictitious. But most readers are so excited by the stories' other details that they fail to notice—or understand—the clues. A day or two later, the journalists often publish a second story admitting that it was all a hoax. The journalists may explain why they created the hoax—and brag about its success.

Third, hoaxes broadcast by radio and television stations are sometimes unintentional. The nation's broadcasters rarely try to fool anyone, but the public is more gullible than most people realize. In 1938, for example, Orson Welles never expected anyone to believe his drama, "War of the Worlds." Yet, by the time the program ended, some Americans were preparing to defend their homes. Other Americans wanted to flee, but did not know where they would be safe. Thus, the public—not broadcasters—labeled some of their stories "a hoax."

Journalists create another type of hoax to beat their rivals. If journalists suspect that a rival is copying their stories, they are tempted to set a trap. Typically, the Associated Press transmitted a story about Siht El Otspueht, a rebel leader in India. Another news agency, United Press, copied the story. The Associated Press waited until several newspapers published the story, then revealed that, spelled backward, the rebel's name was "The UP stole this."

Nonjournalists create other hoaxes to fool everyone—
the media and the public. The nonjournalists usually want to
obtain some publicity for themselves or for a cause they
favor. Or the nonjournalists may want revenge—to embarrass the media.

In 1872, for example, the *Daily Bulletin* in Portland,
Oregon, complained that the police seemed unable to solve or
prevent crime in the city. For revenge, the police gave
Portland's other newspapers a fictitious story about some
sailors who, while pulling up their ship's anchor, also pulled
up a man's body. The man had supposedly been murdered,
and his body horribly mutilated—his skull fractured, his
throat cut, and his body punctured by eighteen bullet
wounds. As expected, the *Bulletin* copied the story. Its rivals
promptly revealed that the *Bulletin* was guilty of plagiarism—that it had copied a hoax.[1]

A few of the media's hoaxes cause some harm, but it is
rarely intentional. In the past, fooling the public was considered a challenge—a test of journalists' ability. Journalists
seemed to think only about the fun—not the danger—involved. Moreover, the results were unpredictable. No one
knew how the public would respond. Some hoaxes failed, but
others were more frightening than anyone expected. The
most frightening hoaxes disrupted the lives of thousands of
people. Some people feared that their friends or relatives had
died. Others feared that their own lives were in danger.

A radio program in South American caused the most
serious tragedy—a riot that killed twenty people. Yet few
journalists ever went to jail because of the hoaxes. The police
wanted to arrest some journalists, but were unable to find
any laws that the journalists violated—laws that made it illegal to fool the public.

When Americans realized that they were fooled, many
were embarrassed—but not angry. Most people were frightened for only a moment or two, and some actually enjoyed it,
just as millions of Americans continue to enjoy the frightening movies produced by Alfred Hitchcock and the books
written by Stephen King. Moreover, readers continued to talk

about the hoaxes for years. They also continued to buy copies of them, so the sale of some stories actually increased after they were exposed as hoaxes.

Other journalists—not the public—were most critical of the hoaxes. Some journalists seemed to be jealous of their rivals' success. Other journalists, like the public, were embarrassed by their gullibility. Some believed and even reprinted their rivals' hoaxes. But the journalists were reluctant to admit that they copied their rivals. Instead, most claimed that they found the stories themselves. Then, when the stories were exposed as a hoax, the journalists were humiliated—exposed as both liars and plagiarists.

Why were the hoaxes so successful? To fool the public, journalists made their stories as realistic as possible. They selected topics likely to interest the public, often topics that had recently been in the news. Journalists also reported that famous people—individuals their readers knew and trusted—were involved in the stories. Other hoaxes described events that occurred years earlier, or that occurred in distant countries. As a result, it was difficult for anyone to prove that the stories were fictitious. A hundred years ago, no one could easily travel to distant countries, nor even communicate with them. In 1835, for example, it was difficult for editors in the United States to prove that a Dutchman had not sailed to the moon in a balloon.

Also, each time journalists created a hoax, something peculiar happened. Other Americans swore that the stories they created were true. Strangers claimed that they witnessed every event the journalists described, or that they possessed other evidence proving that every detail was true. Even respected scientists verified the stories' authenticity.

A few hoaxes were never exposed or corrected. Instead, they continued for weeks, exciting or frightening millions of Americans. Even today, some Americans continue to believe them.

One of the most successful hoaxes libeled Mrs. O'Leary's cow. In 1871, a fire destroyed 17,500 of Chicago's 60,000 buildings. The fire became a continuous sheet of flame, two miles long and one mile wide. To improve his story about the fire—to make it more interesting—a reporter accused Mrs. O'Leary's cow of starting the fire. The reporter claimed that the cow kicked over a lantern in the O'Learys' barn.[2]

A Baltimore journalist, H. L. Mencken, became alarmed when one of his hoaxes became too successful. Mencken had written a fictitious tale about the White House bathtub, and everyone seemed to believe it. Other writers quoted Mencken's story, and it reappeared in publications everywhere, even in scientific journals. Mencken wrote two more articles, both admitting that the tale was a hoax. Typically, not everyone who had read Mencken's hoax saw (or believed) his retractions. As a result, Americans continue to believe, quote, and reprint his hoax.

Other stories that appeared in the media—rumors and tall tales, for example—were also fictitious, but not hoaxes.

Before the invention of the telegraph, people heard sensational rumors about the events occurring in distant areas. Editors published the rumors because they seemed important. Several weeks or even months might elapse before anyone learned whether they were true. Unlike hoaxes, journalists did not create the rumors, nor publish them to entertain the public. Many of the rumors concerned serious problems, such as shipwrecks and Indian massacres. Moreover, stories about the rumors often began with the words "IMPORTANT—IF TRUE."

Editors in the West also printed tall tales. They wrote the tall tales to amuse, not fool, their readers. In addition, the tales helped fill their newspapers when the editors had no news. Unlike hoaxes, the tall tales were preposterous—so obviously false and exaggerated that the editors never expected anyone to believe them, only to be entertained by them.

An editor in Arizona wrote about a Wampus Cat, a ferocious beast that was "a cross between a wild cat, a badger, and a lobo wolf, with fangs two inches long and claws that could peel the bark off a mesquite tree."[3] Another editor described an unusual bird. To hide from its enemies, the bird swallowed itself.

The tall tales claimed that everything in the West was

bigger and better, even its mosquitoes. In 1859, a Denver paper described several men traveling in a stage. In the distance, they saw what appeared to be the frame for a log cabin. When they got closer, they discovered that it was the skeleton left by a mosquito.

Editors in the South published similar stories, called "folk tales." Many of the stories described the region's wild people and animals, including snakes. Southerners believed that snakes lived in human bodies, and some people feared that they might swallow small snakes while drinking from rivers or lakes. Or, larger snakes might crawl down their throats while they slept at night. Folk tales also described the terrible operations needed to cut the snakes from people's bellies.

Unlike hoaxes, the folk tales were not created by journalists. Rather, editors in the South printed the tales being told by their readers. Some editors even believed them.

Judged by modern standards, all the stories discriminate. Reflecting our society and its beliefs at the time, the stories ignore women or emphasize their traditional role as wives, mothers, and sex objects. The stories also portray women as the weaker sex, as ignorant and immature. In a crisis, they seemed to become hysterical and faint. Other stories contain statements critical of Asians, blacks, Indians, Italians, politicians, Texans, Easterners, Westerners, Southerners, doctors, chiropractors, and every resident of Cincinnati.

Portions of this book may also offend some journalists. Journalists may dislike a book that exposes so many of their hoaxes. Journalists also may fear that a book about their hoaxes will encourage other Americans to create new hoaxes intended to fool today's reporters and editors.

Most hoaxes appeared during the 1800s. Everything was different then—newspapers, their reporters, publishers, and readers. Many of the differences encouraged journalists to create hoaxes. The differences in our society also encouraged more practical joking among nonjournalists, so the hoaxes did not seem unusual at the time. It was a wilder era, and practical joking—including hoaxes—became a form of popular entertainment.

The first hoaxes appeared in England, and journalists in America imitated them. Many of England's most famous writers—Addison, Swift, and Steele, for example—turned to satire, but pretended that someone else had written it. Their satire entertained readers, but also poked fun at their beliefs and behavior. In addition, a pamphlet written by Swift predicted that a quack—a famous astrologer—would die. Later letters and pamphlets described the astrologer's death and ghost. The astrologer tried to deny that he was dead, but readers throughout Europe began to laugh at him and his unusual predicament.

Another hoax involved the *Leicester Herald.* Just before the newspaper's deadline one evening, an employee upset several columns of type, scattering them over the floor. There was not enough time to reset the type. Instead, an editor swept it up and simply dumped it back into the columns. He titled the mess "The Dutch Mail," and added a note explaining that, because the mail arrived late, he did not have enough time to translate it. Some readers, including Dutch scholars, responded that the mail used an unusual dialect, a dialect they had never seen before.

A Boston postmaster published America's first newspaper in 1704. No one knows who published America's first hoax, but Benjamin Franklin published some of the best. Franklin began publishing the *Pennsylvania Gazette* in 1729 and, like England's famous satirists, created several hoaxes to amuse himself and his readers. During the Revolutionary War, Franklin created other hoaxes to ridicule the British and their policies in America.

Hoaxes became more common during the 1830s, and newspapers on the East Coast published the most famous.

Until the 1830s, newspapers appealed primarily to the upper classes—to the rich and well educated. Newspapers were expensive and emphasized serious articles about business, politics, and foreign affairs. As a result, even the newspapers published in big cities attracted only a few thousand readers. Then editors discovered that they could earn more money by appealing to the masses — to the millions of workingmen on the East Coast. To appeal to the masses, editors lowered their newspapers' prices to a penny and changed their content. The editors began to publish more sensational stories about crime, sex, scandal, and sports. They also published larger headlines, more pictures, and a never-ending series of stunts, crusades, and hoaxes.

It was a time of explosive growth and intense competition. During the 1860s, for example, about four hundred daily newspapers were published in the United States. By 1900, the number had jumped to two thousand. Cities such as Philadelphia and New York had more than a dozen English-language dailies. As recently as 1933, Washington, D.C., had five. Only one, the *Washington Post,* has survived.

Six or seven daily newspapers were published in Denver. The *Denver Post* prospered because it provided more news, excitement, and features than any of its competitors. One of the *Post*'s owners advised an editor, "You've seen a vaudeville show, haven't you? It's got every sort of act — laughs, tears, wonder, thrills, melodrama, tragedy, comedy, love, and hate. That's what I want you to give our readers."[4]

Newspaper jobs were also much different: less respectable, but more adventuresome and carefree. They were low-level, white-collar jobs that attracted the upwardly mobile — immigrants, their children, and the youths raised on farms and in small towns. Newspaper jobs rarely attracted gentlemen.[5] The upper classes thought of newspaper people as drifters and drunkards who led exciting lives but pried into other people's private affairs.

Few of the journalists were well educated. Many had not graduated from high school, and some believed that it was a disadvantage to have graduated from college. Journalists who had attended college sometimes tried to hide that fact "as though it was a stretch in prison." An editor at the *Chicago Tribune* also discouraged marriage, fearing that it would interfere with his staff's work. If a reporter wanted to get married, the editor might threaten to cut the reporter's salary, or even to fire him.[6] The editor at another Chicago daily bragged, "Two of my men are ex-convicts, 10 of them are divorced . . . and not a single one of them is living with his own wife."[7]

Reporters learned their work through on-the-job training, usually in a small town. Ambitious reporters dreamed of moving on to a metropolitan daily, but there never were enough good jobs for everyone. Instead, the newcomers in some big cities were asked to work "on space." The system gave editors an opportunity to test the newcomers' ability—and to save money.

The newcomers, usually called "stringers," reported for work every day but were sent home if it was quiet and there were no stories for them to cover. At the end of the week, the stringers pasted or strung all their stories together and presented them to a cashier. The cashier measured the stories with a ruler and paid the stringers a few dollars for each column (about twenty inches). Stringers might be paid more for a good story, or for an exclusive story they found themselves. But to save money, some editors cut the stringers' stories before publishing them.

Job security was nonexistent. Journalists could succeed while they were still young, and one became the managing editor of a New York daily at the age of twenty-one. The system was more difficult for older employees. The older reporters and editors at some papers were fired if they were unable to keep up with the competition. Some publishers fired dozens of other employees each time their profits fell. On a whim, a publisher in New York reportedly walked into his newsroom and fired everyone seated on the right-hand side. Publishers said the shake-ups kept their staffs alert.

The system encouraged faking. After being given an assignment, reporters were reluctant to return empty-handed. Some would not make up an entire story; however, they might add a few unimportant or descriptive details. For example, before the invention of telephones, reporters were tempted to guess at minor facts that no one could obtain before their deadline. Reporters called the practice "filling in," and they considered it different from ordinary lying.

If a source was dull, other reporters might invent more interesting quotations. If a source was uncooperative, reporters might invent an entire interview. If reporters were unable to find a source, they might invent both their source and interview. Reporters seemed willing to fake anything— even Sunday sermons. A Chicago reporter, angry because he was assigned to cover the Sunday sermon at a small church, created his story in a saloon that Saturday night. Colleagues say the minister was so pleased with its eloquence that he called the newspaper to thank its editor.[8]

For years, scoops were considered the path "to prestige, circulation, and prosperity."[9] A Chicago journalist recalled that a murder delighted him. "One human being had killed another," he said, "and I was happy because this was what I had been training for; reporting murders was my business. Now I could get a story into the paper, get recognition."[10]

Journalists were also expected to obtain good pictures. Some journalists stole them. When a gangster was killed, a reporter for the *New York Mirror* visited the mother of a girl involved in the case. During her interview, the reporter noticed a picture on a table in the parlor. Knowing that her editor might want it, the reporter slipped it under her coat and walked out. Another story involved a young bride killed on her wedding day. A reporter went to the bride's home, and the bride's father found her there, searching several rooms for a picture. The father chased the reporter with a knife, threatening to kill her as a thief.[11]

Some editors encouraged the deception. The editors wanted good stories—colorful human-interest stories—and seemed unconcerned about how their reporters obtained them. At the time, editors were more interested in selling newspapers than in journalism's ethics and responsibilities. If their reporters seemed hesitant, editors might assure them that "Everyone is doing it." Or, they might give the reporters' stories to rewrite men and instruct them to "Hype this up."

Because of the pressure to come up with good stories, reporters began to stretch the truth, to stress their stories' most sensational angles, to invent more interesting details, and to exaggerate until some stories became works of fiction—hoaxes. The more sensational their hoaxes became, the more their editors liked them.

A new group of publishers began to emerge during the 1830s, and many of the publishers encouraged—or at least accepted—the hoaxes. Like other journalists, the publishers may have enjoyed fooling the public. They also realized that a clever hoax would increase their newspaper's circulation (and profits).

The publishers, called "press barons," dominated American journalism for 100 years.[12] Many were geniuses—energetic, perceptive, and innovative. Because of their success, the publishers became tremendously rich and fiercely independent. Some acted responsibly, using their newspapers to help their readers and improve their communities. Other publishers were eccentric and selfish. Readers complained that the newspapers they established were irresponsible—superficial, biased, and sometimes even dishonest. Yet because of their of wealth and power, the publishers were free to do as they pleased. If they wanted to create a hoax, no one could stop them.

One of the publishers, James Gordon Bennett, Jr., took over the *New York Herald* when his father retired in 1867. Bennett was twenty-five, bright, and charming, with the potential to become an excellent journalist. Instead, Bennett became a playboy. Spoiled and dictatorial, he seemed to stumble from one drunken escapade to another.[13] For forty years, Bennett squandered all the *Herald*'s profits on himself: about $1 million a year.

Bennett lived in Paris and, for sport, enjoyed racing a coach and horses through the city's streets. After midnight, he reportedly stripped, except for a top hat and cigar. Once, forgetting to duck for a low bridge, he was knocked off the coach and almost killed. An amateur magician, Bennett also enjoyed walking through the finest restaurants in Paris and trying to pull their table cloths out from under their settings. Everything on the tables usually fell to the floor, smashing the dishes and ruining the food. No one complained, however. Bennett pulled out wads of money and paid for everything.

Under Bennett's leadership, the *Herald* became as wild as his personal life, publishing some of journalism's most famous stunts and hoaxes. In 1874, for example, a single story filled the *Herald*'s entire front page. The story reported that all the wild animals had escaped from the Central Park Zoo and that the animals were attacking residents of the city. The story was fictitious—a hoax—but caused a panic.

For years, other differences in our society encouraged journalists to create more of the hoaxes. First, people were more isolated during the eighteenth and nineteenth centuries. Communication and transportation were difficult, especially in winter. Yet editors needed something—anything—to fill their papers. If there was no news, they had to invent some. Then, because of their isolation, readers were unable to prove that the stories were fictitious.

Second, editors exchanged papers with one another. Before the invention of the telegraph, it was an inexpensive, yet efficient, way of obtaining the news. Thus, if the editor in one city concocted an interesting story, the editors in other cities were certain to copy it, not knowing—or perhaps caring—that it was fictitious. Readers talked about the stories, so they were also spread by word of mouth. Other readers clipped the stories and mailed them to friends. Eventually they reappeared in books and magazines, so a single story might be repeated thousands of times. A week or two later, the editor who created a story might admit that it was fictitious. Other editors who reprinted the story might fail to notice—or reprint—the retraction. As a result, millions of Americans would continue to believe it.

Third, the people living 100 years ago were easier to fool. People were poorly educated, yet it was an age of exploration and discovery. Scientists were developing exciting new theories and inventing wonderful new machines. Newspapers informed the public about all the discoveries, and readers believed them. Thus, readers were also inclined to believe the newspapers' hoaxes—their stories about other exciting new discoveries.

Nonjournalists were also having more fun during the eighteenth and nineteenth centuries. Other Americans staged a variety of practical jokes, often on a grand scale.

One of the most famous jokes amused all of England. In 1810, Berners Street was a quiet London neighborhood, inhabited by well-to-do families. After breakfast one morning, a wagon loaded with coal stopped at the home of a widow there. It was followed by a van loaded with furniture, a hearse with a coffin, two doctors, one dentist, and six men with an organ. A grocer sent a load of potatoes, and a brewer sent several barrels of ale. They were followed by coach makers, clock makers, wig makers, and opticians, all carrying samples of their wares. Unemployed coachmen, footmen, cooks, and maids—all looking for jobs—added to the congestion. The procession continued all that day and night, and police officers found the street jammed with traffic. Spectators enjoyed the ale, but the tradesmen became angry. They wanted revenge—to learn who was responsible for the hoax.

Theodore Hook, a famous practical joker, had noticed the quiet street and bet that he could get everyone in London talking about it. To win, Hook spent three days writing letters that attracted the mob.

Similarly, youngsters in the United States temporarily stole cows, horses, and outhouses. Adults sent out bogus wedding cards. That type of practical joking became especially common in the West. People in the West used the jokes to initiate newcomers and tourists there. Westerners might arrest the newcomers, send them on fools' errands, or arrange bogus Indian attacks.

Other stunts and practical jokes continued to entertain Americans for the next one hundred years. In 1938, for example, "Wrong-Way" Corrigan wanted to duplicate Charles Lindbergh's flight but was refused permission to fly alone—from New York to Europe—in a dilapidated plane. Disappointed, Corrigan announced that he would return to California. Twenty-four hours later, he landed in Dublin.

"Is this Los Angeles?" he asked.

Corrigan insisted that his compass, the only instrument aboard his plane, had gotten stuck, and that he had accidentally flown in the wrong direction. The flight made Corrigan famous. He was given a ticker-tape parade down Broadway, and a movie was made about his life. On the twentieth anniversary of his famous flight, someone asked Corrigan whether his compass had really gotten stuck.

"That's my story," he said. "I've been telling it so long that I'm beginning to believe it."[14]

Americans no longer seem to enjoy hoaxes, nor that type of stunt and practical joking. People have changed, and so have the conditions that, for years, encouraged journalists to create the hoaxes. Yet, when someone does create a hoax—no matter how silly—some Americans always believe it. Even journalists who create the hoaxes are surprised that so many Americans, often millions, are so easy to fool.

America's Greatest Hoaxers: Franklin, Poe, Twain, and De Quille

Thousands of journalists created a hoax or two. More successful journalists created several hoaxes, and their most exciting stories were reprinted everywhere: in books, newspapers, and magazines throughout the United States. The stories fooled millions of readers — and, each year, continue to fool a few more of them.

America's first great hoaxer, Benjamin Franklin, imitated England's early satirists. Franklin created a half-dozen whimsical tales that amused his readers — but that also conveyed a message. Franklin's tales poked fun at Americans' beliefs and behavior, often trying to reform them. In addition, Franklin often pretended that someone else had written his stories.

During the American Revolution, Franklin created other hoaxes as a weapon — as propaganda that portrayed the British as cowards and killers.

America's second great hoaxer, Edgar Allan Poe, adopted a much different style of writing. Poe wrote long adventure stories, and some were horrifying, filled with blood and other gruesome details.

Poe was desperately poor and needed the money that his stories might earn. But some of Poe's stories failed because readers were disgusted by his gruesome details. Other stories failed because readers were bored by his minor details. In addition, Poe was a victim of bad timing. Another journalist published an exciting hoax about the moon at the moment that Poe was writing a similar story. When it and several of Poe's other stories failed, he immediately abandoned them — never writing their final installments.

Two of America's other great writers, Mark Twain and Dan De Quille, perfected the American hoax. The European satirists whom Franklin imitated used a sly, gentle wit to poke fun at their readers' beliefs and behavior. Americans, led by Twain and De Quille, wrote more exaggerated, even preposterous, tales about discoveries in the fields of science and exploration. Americans also wrote more frightening tales, often about monsters or Martians.

Twain's and De Quille's stories reflected their personalities and the life around them. People in the West told tall tales and created elaborate (and sometimes dangerous) practical jokes. The Westerners' sense of humor helped them forget the danger and drudgery in their lives. Thus, most enjoyed the hoaxes written by Twain and De Quille, even when they were fooled by them.

Twain's hoaxes were wilder than De Quille's, bloodier and more horrifying. Many were created for revenge, to embarrass the people Twain disliked. Twain seemed to forget that Westerners were more violent than other Americans, and that the readers upset by a story might attack the reporter responsible for it. One of Twain's stories called another editor a coward and fool, with "a groveling disregard for truth, decency, and courtesy." As the feud between the two men escalated, they apparently became involved in a duel. Then, to avoid arrest, Twain was forced to flee. Thus he left Nevada famous — but a fugitive.

1 English Traditions: Ben Franklin's Satire and Hoaxes

F the editors of your local daily want to expose a problem, they can launch a crusade. The editors can assign a team of reporters and photographers to gather all the details. They can also publish a series of cartoons and editorials that urge you to act, to help them eliminate the problem.

Journalists who worked during the eighteenth century published satire rather than editorials. Their satire was gentle and good humored, and it included the publication of several hoaxes. Journalists used the satire to entertain—but also to influence—their readers, to change their beliefs and behavior. After originating in England, the satire was copied by editors throughout America.

One of England's first hoaxes embarrassed a shoemaker. The shoemaker, a man named John Partridge, also worked as an astrologer and published his predictions in an almanac. Jonathan Swift, one of England's most talented writers, was irritated by Partridge's quackery. Swift also may have wanted to have some fun. He began by attacking all of London's astrologers, calling them imposters who, each year, published a lot of nonsense and lies. Moreover, their predictions seemed timid and vague.

Swift then issued his own predictions for 1708—but attributed them to "Isaac Bickerstaff," a name he had noticed on a blacksmith's sign.

Unlike London's other astrologers, Bickerstaff was bold and specific. He began with "a trifle." After consulting the stars, Bickerstaff predicted that Partridge would die at about 11 p.m. that March 29.

On March 30, Bickerstaff wrote a letter admitting that he erred, but by only four hours. Bickerstaff explained that Partridge had become ill two or three days earlier. Then, at about 4 p.m. on the 29th, Bickerstaff learned that Partridge was dying. He immediately went to see Partridge, partly out of sympathy, but also out of curiosity.

As he lay dying, Partridge admitted that his predictions were nonsense, believed only by the poor, ignorant, and vulgar. Partridge said that he invented the predictions to help sell his almanac. He had a wife to support and did not earn enough by mending old shoes. Now, as he lay dying, he was troubled by the thought that his predictions may have hurt the readers who believed them.

Bickerstaff left, but learned that Partridge died at 7:05 that evening. Thus, his prediction was mistaken by almost four hours.

Swift's friends immediately continued the hoax, describing the problems that Partridge encountered after his death. Partridge supposedly heard church bells tolling for him. An undertaker called, and a sexton inquired about his grave. When Partridge left home, he was accused of sneaking about without paying for his funeral. Other people stared at Partridge as though he was a ghost.

Partridge was furious and, in his almanac for 1709, denied that he was dead.

Swift, still posing as Bickerstaff, wrote a new article that defended his predictions. He declared that Partridge was obviously dead, since no living man could have written the rubbish that appeared in his new almanac. Bickerstaff added that even Partridge's wife admitted that he had "neither life nor soul." It was not his fault, Bickerstaff continued, if some ill-informed carcass was walking around and calling itself Partridge.

One of Swift's friends, Richard Steele, began to publish *The Tatler* in the spring of 1709. By then, Bickerstaff had become famous throughout Europe, and Steele pretended that Bickerstaff published his newspaper. Steele described Bickerstaff as sixty-four and "a philosopher, a humorist, an astrologer, and a censor." *The Tatler* became an instant success. It was an entertaining paper—good humored and well informed. In addition, its pages were filled with satire that poked fun at its readers' dress and manners.

Steele abandoned *The Tatler* but began to publish another newspaper, *The Spectator,* with Joseph Addison. They pretended that the paper was published by another elderly gentleman. Like Bickerstaff, the man was educated, witty, and good-humored. Moreover, he promised to publish *The Spectator* every morning to "improve and divert his countrymen."

The Spectator attacked swindlers, disliked Italian opera, and denounced drunkards and dueling. Like *The Tatler,* it also poked fun at its readers' dress and manners.

Benjamin Franklin copied the London papers. Like Addison, Swift, and Steele, he published satire and hoaxes to entertain his readers. Moreover, he often pretended that someone else had written his stories.

Franklin's early satire tends to be gentle and witty, slyly poking fun at his fellow Americans. In addition each of Franklin's hoaxes conveyed a message. Like modern editorials or crusades, his hoaxes attacked witchcraft, slavery, and religious intolerance. Ironically, Franklin's later hoaxes—copied from the London papers—were aimed at the English, portraying them as murderous thugs.

Franklin began to work as a journalist at the age of twelve. He was apprenticed to an older brother, James, a printer who published the fourth newspaper in America. To compete with two other newspapers in Boston, James tried to amuse as well as inform his readers—to discuss current issues and publish clever essays (including satire).

Benjamin contributed his first essay to the *Courant* when he was sixteen. While writing it, he pretended to be a middle-aged widow named "Silence Dogood." Benjamin may have realized that readers would be more likely to respect the opinions of a widow than those of a sixteen-year-old boy.[1] But the disguise also made his essays more interesting.

During the next seven months, Benjamin wrote thirteen more essays, all remarkable for a sixteen-year-old boy. The essays poked fun at pride, drunkenness, and hoop petticoats. They also discussed issues of particular interest to women, including their need for insurance. Mrs. Dogood complained that, after her husband's death, she had nothing to live on "but contentment and a few cows."

She seemed to be a dignified woman—modest, courteous, serious, and sensible. She also exhibited a sly humor. But her name, "Silence," must have seemed comical for anyone so talkative.

Mrs. Dogood said she was born on a ship sailing from London to New England, and that her father was washed overboard moments after her birth. Because of her mother's poverty, she was apprenticed to a county minister, "a pious, good-natured young man, and a bachelor." He taught her everything a woman needed to know—needlework, writing, and arithmetic.

The minister began looking for a wife and, after several fruitless attempts, pursued Silence. It was easy for him to conquer her heart, Silence admitted, although "whether it was love, or gratitude, or pride, or all three that made me consent, I know not." Their marriage astonished their neighbors, giving them something to gossip about for a long time.

Silence and her husband lived happily together for nearly seven years and had three children. Then her husband died, and Silence admitted that widowhood was a state she never much admired. She could be easily persuaded to marry again, provided that she was assured "of a good-humored, sober, agreeable companion. . . . "

Her fourth essay, perhaps her best, ridiculed Harvard. Silence said she was thinking about sending her own son to Harvard. During an afternoon nap, she dreamed that she visited the place. It was a citadel of conservatism, she found, open only to the wealthy, and full of corruption and bad manners. Silence accused the students at Harvard of being idle and ignorant. She explained that rich parents sent their sons to Harvard because they could afford to do so, not because any of their sons were great scholars. Thus, most failed to learn a thing. Instead, they wasted their college years and emerged as great blockheads as ever, but prouder and more conceited.[2]

After running out of topics to write about, Silence abandoned the essays that fall. They apparently fooled several young bachelors in Boston. The bachelors wrote to Silence—and may have proposed to her.

On October 22, 1730, Franklin published a hoax titled "A Witch Trial at Mount Holly." By then, he had acquired his own paper, the *Pennsylvania Gazette* in Philadelphia, and the hoax appeared as a news story from New Jersey. Typically, Franklin hoped to do more than entertain the public. He also wanted to ridicule the Americans who believed in witchcraft and who accused their neighbors of being witches.

The story reported that nearly three hundred people had gathered at Mount Holly, about eight miles from Burlington, to watch two experiments used to test a man and a woman accused of being witches. The man and woman were charged with "making their neighbors' sheep dance in an uncommon manner, and with causing hogs to speak and sing Psalms, etc., to the great terror and amazement of the king's good and peaceable subjects in this province. . . . "

Their accusers were very positive that, if the witches were placed on one side of a scale, and a Bible on the other, the Bible would weigh more than either one of them. Their accusers also believed that, if the accused were tied and placed in a river, they would be able to swim despite their bindings.

The accused were anxious to prove their innocence and voluntarily offered to undergo the tests, but insisted that the most violent of their accusers, another man and woman, should be tested alongside them. The time and place were agreed upon, and all four were searched before being placed upon the scale. A huge Bible was placed on one side of the scale, and the man suspected of witchcraft was placed on the opposite side. To the spectators' great surprise, he easily outweighed that great and good book. The other three were also tested, and all their lumps of flesh were too heavy "for Moses and all the Prophets and Apostles."

Not satisfied with this experiment, the accusers and the rest of the mob demanded the trial by water. They proceeded to a pond, where both the accused and the accusers were stripped (except for the women's dresses), bound hand and foot, and placed in the water. The accused man, being thin and spare, began to sink with some difficulty, "but the rest, every one of them, swam very light upon the water."

When told that she did not sink, the woman who had accused the others of witchcraft asked to be dunked again. She swam as easily as before and complained that she had been bewitched to make her float. She wanted to be thrown into the water a hundred more times, she said, to dunk the Devil out of her.

Some spectators decided that the women's garters and dresses helped support them, so they would have to be tested again— naked— when the weather was warmer.[3]

Readers everywhere accepted Franklin's most successful hoax, "The Speech of Polly Baker," as a factual account of a real event. Even scholars quoted the hoax, treating it as a serious sociological document.[4]

Once again, the hoax conveyed a message. Laws in colonial America prohibited sexual intercourse except by married couples. If an unmarried woman became pregnant, her baby was considered evidence that she had violated those laws.[5] As punishment, the woman might be whipped, fined, or imprisoned. But the man responsible for her pregnancy often went free. Franklin used Polly Baker to question the law and to demonstrate the unfairness of punishing a child's mother, but not its father. Thus, Franklin portrays Polly as a sympathetic character—an apparently innocent and sensible woman, betrayed by the men she knew.

Polly told the judges that she was a poor, unhappy woman, with no money to hire a lawyer. She would not trouble the judges with long speeches, but hoped that they would not order her to pay another fine. "This is the fifth time," Polly explained, "that I have been dragged before your court on the same account. . . . " Twice she had been ordered to pay heavy fines, and twice she had been punished because she did not have enough money to pay the fines.

Polly argued that the law was too severe and unreasonable, especially as applied to her. She had never wronged any man, woman, or child, and could not understand her offense. "I have brought five fine children into the world at the risk of my life," Polly said. "I have maintained them well by my own industry, without burdening the township, and would have done it better if it had not been for the heavy charges and fines I have paid." Can it be a crime, she asked, to add to the number of the king's subjects in a new country that needed more people?

Polly insisted that she had not seduced another woman's husband, nor corrupted a young boy. Because she had never been charged with any of those crimes, no one had any reason to complain about her conduct except, perhaps, the ministers of justice, since she had given birth to five children without first getting married and paying them a wedding fee.

Polly thought she would be a good wife—hard working, frugal, and fertile. Moreover, she would have preferred the state of wedlock. "I always was, and still am willing to enter into it," she said. "I defy anyone to say I ever refused an offer of that sort; on the contrary, I readily consented to the only proposal of marriage that ever was made me, which was when I was a virgin. . . . " Then, she had been too trusting. After making her pregnant, the man abandoned her.

Polly revealed that the man was now a magistrate. She had hoped that he would appear in court to help her. Since he did not, she complained that it was unfair that the man who betrayed her—the cause of all her problems—had been promoted and honored by the very government that punished her.

Polly admitted that she had violated laws of religion, but insisted, "If mine is a religious offense, leave it to religious punishments. You have already excluded me from the comforts of your church communion. Is that not sufficient? You believe I have offended heaven and must suffer eternal fire. Will not that be sufficient? What need is there, then, of your additional fines and whipping?"

Polly also urged the judges to correct a more serious crime: to consider the great number of bachelors, many of whom—afraid of the expense of a family—never sincerely and honorably courted a woman in their lives. By failing to marry and have children, she said, the bachelors left unproduced (which is little better than murder) hundreds of their potential descendants. "Is not this a greater offense against the public good than mine?" Polly asked. She urged the judges to force every bachelor to get married, or to pay double the fine of fornication every year.

"What must poor young women do . . . ?" Polly wondered. Customs and nature did not allow women to approach men. Young women could not force men to marry them. Thus the law failed to provide women with husbands, but severely punished them if they did their duty without one.

By having five children, Polly explained, she simply fulfilled the first and great command of nature and God: to "increase and multiply." Instead of being whipped and disgraced, she said, a statue should be erected in her honor.[6]

Impressed by her arguments, the judges found Polly innocent. One of the judges married her the very next day.

"The Speech of Polly Baker" became Franklin's most famous hoax but, for thirty years, no one knew that he had written it. While living in France years later, Franklin heard two acquaintances arguing about its authenticity. Franklin interrupted them, admitting: "Sir, I am going to give you the facts. When I was young, at times I lacked materials to fill the pages of my gazette, so I amused myself by writing stories, and the yarn about Polly Baker is one of them."[7]

No one knows exactly when Franklin wrote the speech, nor where it first appeared. Franklin admitted writing it—apparently while editing the *Pennsylvania Gazette*—but the speech never appeared in his newspaper.[8] A London paper, the *General Advertiser,* published the speech on April 15, 1747, but it may have appeared in other papers before then. After April 15, other publications in Europe reprinted the speech, and ships carried the publications to America. Polly's speech was immediately reprinted here, and accepted as fact. An entire book has been written about its use.[9]

As newspapers and magazines reprinted the speech, some changed its punctuation, wording, and facts. Some added that Polly had fifteen legitimate children after marrying the judge. Others warned of the law's horrid consequence: that the practice of punishing unwed mothers would encourage them to abort their helpless offspring.[10]

To attack a rival, another of Franklin's hoaxes copied one of England's most famous stories. Many of the homes in colonial America contained only two books: a Bible and an almanac. For printers, the almanacs were a profitable sideline. They contained a variety of useful facts and figures — calendars, recipes, poems, and jokes. Almanacs also predicted the weather and foretold the future, and some readers consulted them before making any important decisions.

Franklin decided to publish an almanac for 1733 but pretended that it was written by someone else: Richard Saunders, a poor scholar who often squabbled with his wife. Franklin called his almanac *Poor Richard's,* and the first edition predicted that a rival, Titan Leeds, would die. *Poor Richard's* predicted the exact time of Leeds's death — 3:29 p.m. that October 17. Poor Richard insisted that Leeds knew he would die, but that Leeds calculated the date of his death as October 26. It was a small difference, Poor Richard said, only nine days. Now, only time would tell whose prediction was most accurate.

Before publishing the second edition of *Poor Richard's,* Franklin waited to see Leeds's reply. Leeds insisted that he was still alive — and attacked Poor Richard's folly and ignorance. The attack delighted Franklin; it helped publicize his new almanac.[11] Also, the more that Leeds insisted he was alive, the more foolish he seemed.

In his own almanac for 1734, Poor Richard said he could not be certain that Leeds was dead. He had intended to be with Leeds in his last moments "to receive his last embrace, to close his eyes, and do the duty of a friend." Family matters kept him away. Nevertheless, there was the strongest probability that Leeds had died. Leeds's name still appeared on his almanac, but it called Poor Richard "a conceited scribbler, a fool, and a liar." Poor Richard quoted all the criticisms in his own almanac to prove that Leeds was dead. Poor Richard explained that Leeds must be dead, since his good friend would never treat him so unkindly. Leeds was too well bred to use such abusive language. Thus, Leeds's almanac must have been written by someone else, and that person put into the mouth of a gentleman words "which the meanest and most scandalous of the people might be ashamed to utter, even in a drunken quarrel. . . ."

For the next eight years, Poor Richard continued to insist that Leeds was "defunct and dead." Poor Richard added that everyone who read Leeds's almanacs could plainly see that they were not as well written since his death.

Leeds actually died in 1738, and Poor Richard reported that even the men who published Leeds's almanac finally acknowledged his death—but pretended that he had not died until that year.

Benjamin Franklin wanted Americans to be more tolerant of other people's religious beliefs and wrote several articles critical of religious hypocrites. Franklin also added a chapter to the Bible—the 51st chapter of Genesis. The chapter said that God punished Abraham because he refused to help a stranger who worshiped a different God. While entertaining guests, Franklin enjoyed placing the chapter in a Bible as if it really belonged there. Franklin then read the chapter out loud and asked his guests to identify it. Because he imitated language actually used in the Bible, few of his guests detected the hoax.[12] (If you want to try the same trick, a copy of the 51st chapter of Genesis, exactly as Franklin wrote it, appears in the Appendix. Read the chapter to your friends, and ask them to identify it.)

Another of Franklin's hoaxes attacked slavery, slyly trying to convince Americans that the practice was immoral and unchristian. A newspaper that Franklin read, the *Federal Gazette,* reported an emotional speech given by a Georgia congressman. The congressman, James Jackson, urged Congress not to interfere with the slave trade. Franklin sent the *Gazette*'s editor a letter saying that Jackson's speech reminded him of a similar speech, made a hundred years earlier, by Sidi Mehemet Ibrahim of Algeria. Franklin explained that the Algerians had been asked to stop capturing and enslaving the Christians aboard ships in the Mediterranean. Jackson had not quoted the earlier speech, Franklin said, perhaps because he had not seen it. But the two speeches contained surprising similarities. Franklin then took Jackson's arguments defending the enslavement of blacks in the South and used the same arguments to defend the enslavement of Christians in Algeria.

As translated, Franklin said, the African speech of Sidi Mehemet Ibrahim warned that, if the Algerians stopped attacking Christians, they would be unable to obtain commodities the Christians produced. And if the Algerians stopped making Christians their slaves, Ibrahim asked, "who, in this hot climate, are to cultivate our lands? Who are to perform the common labors of our city and of our families? Must we not then be our own slaves?"

The Algerians had enslaved more than fifty thousand of the Christian dogs, and Ibrahim warned: "This number, if not kept up by fresh supplies, will soon diminish and be gradually annihilated. If, then, we cease taking and plundering the infidel ships, and making slaves of the seamen and passengers, our lands will become of no value. . . . " No one would be available to cultivate the land. Property would lose its value, and the government would lose its revenue—And for what?

If the Algerians freed their Christian slaves, Ibrahim wondered, who would pay their owners for the loss? Would the government do it? Did it have enough funds? Or, to help slaves, would the government do a greater injustice to the slaves' owners?

Besides, if the Algerians set their Christians free, what would happen to them? Ibrahim said that few Christians would return to their native countries, since they suffered greater hardships there. Instead, they would become beggars in the streets.

And what was so bad about the Christians being slaves in Algeria, he asked? Were they not slaves in their own countries? Ibrahim said that Spain, Portugal, France, and the Italian states were governed by despots who held all their subjects in slavery. Even England treated her sailors as slaves. Whenever it wanted, Ibrahim explained, the English government seized and confined sailors in ships of war, condemning them to work and fight for small wages. Thus, by falling into Algerian hands, the Christians only exchanged one slavery for a better one. For in Algeria, they were exposed to the religion of Islamism "and they have an opportunity of making themselves acquainted with the true doctrine, and thereby saving their immortal souls." The Christians who remained at home did not have that happiness. Thus, if the Algerians sent their slaves home, they would be sending them out of light and into darkness.

Some people proposed setting the Christians free in the wilderness, where they might establish a new state. Ibrahim doubted that the proposal would work. He explained that Christians were too ignorant to govern themselves, and too lazy to work unless forced to do so.

"While serving us," he continued, "we take care to provide them with everything; and they are treated with humanity." They were better fed, lodged, and clothed than the laborers in their own countries. Also, in Algeria, they were not required to become soldiers "and forced to cut one another's Christian throats, as in the wars of their own countries."

Finally, Ibrahim warned that, if Algeria freed its Christian slaves, the country's lands and houses would become less valuable. There would be universal discontent and insurrections, endangering the government and producing general confusion. Surely, the government had an obligation to protect the comfort and happiness of its own citizens before that of Christian slaves.[13]

After retiring from the printing business, Franklin spent much of his time abroad, serving as an American diplomat. While in England, he noticed that the newspapers there often published articles critical or mistaken about America. In 1765, he wrote a satirical letter that seemed to defend the newspapers' errors. He signed the letter "A Traveler."

The "Traveler" insisted that a story the British papers had published the previous week was true. Canadians fished for cod and whale in the Great Lakes. "Ignorant people may object that the upper lakes are fresh, and that cod and whale are salt-water fish," he wrote. But when attacked by their enemies, cod flew into whatever water was safest. Whales ate cod and pursued them wherever they flew. Americans who watched whales chasing the cod—even leaping up Niagara Falls together—considered it "one of the finest spectacles in nature."[14]

Franklin lived in Paris during the American Revolution and continued to write hoaxes, but now used them to attack the British and their policy of hiring Germans to fight with them. General Washington had just defeated the Hessians at Trenton, and news of their defeat reached Paris. Europeans also knew that a Prussian count named "Schaumburg" was trying to recruit more Hessians to fight for the British.

Franklin's hoax appeared as a letter that a count named "Schaumbergh" had written to the Hessians' commander in America. The British supposedly paid Count Schaumbergh for each Hessian soldier killed in America. While safely in Rome, the count complained that not enough of his soldiers were being killed. Thus, Franklin's hoax portrays the count as "a moral monster, trafficking in human flesh."[15] His hoax was titled "The Sale of the Hessians." In it, Count Schaumbergh said he had learned, with unspeakable pleasure, of the courage his troops exhibited at Trenton. He was overjoyed when told that, of the 1,950 Hessians engaged in the fight, only 345 escaped. The count praised his commander for sending an exact list of the 1,605 dead to London. The English had listed only 1,455 dead and, if their error was not corrected, he would be cheated out of all the monies to which he was entitled.

London complained that one hundred Hessians wounded in the battle should not be included in the list, nor paid for as dead. But Count Schaumbergh trusted that his commander would do nothing to save their lives. "I am sure," he said, "they would rather die than live in a condition no longer fit for my service." The count insisted that his commander should not assassinate the wounded; however, he might tell his surgeons "to let every one of them die when he ceases to be fit to fight."

The count added that he was about to send new recruits to America — and that his commander should *not* use them carefully.

Count Schaumbergh reminded his commander of a historic battle from which no one returned. He would be happy, he said, if the same thing could be said about his brave Hessians. It was true, the count admitted, that a king had perished in the battle with his men, but he did not feel that he should have to die in America — only his Hessian troops. "Things have changed," Count Schaumbergh explained, "and it is no longer the custom for princes of the empire to go and fight in America for a cause with which they have no concern." Besides, to whom should the British pay the thirty guineas per man if he did not stay in Europe to receive them? The count insisted that he also had to remain behind to find new recruits to replace the men killed in battle. "It is true," he admitted, "grown men are becoming scarce there, but I will send you boys."

The count added that his recent trip to Italy had been enormously expensive, and that he needed more dead soldiers to help pay for it. "You will therefore promise promotion to all who expose themselves," he wrote, "you will exhort them to seek glory in the midst of dangers. . . . Finally, prolong the war and avoid a decisive engagement on either side, for I have made arrangements for a grand Italian opera, and I do not wish to be obliged to give it up."[16]

In the summer of 1782, Franklin circulated another of his hoaxes: propaganda he considered necessary for an American victory. It was a masterpiece that shocked all Europe.[17]

Franklin created a fictitious newspaper, supposedly a supplement to the Boston *Chronicle,* and filled it with gory details critical of the British and the Indians who fought for them. After printing the paper in England, he sent copies to a friend in Holland and instructed him to "make any use of them you think proper"—but to keep their source a secret. Soon, copies were circulating in all of Europe, including England.

The supplement began with a letter that a Captain Gerrish of the New England militia had supposedly written on March 12, 1782. Captain Gerrish reported that his troops ambushed some Indians and captured their supplies. "The possession of this booty at first gave us pleasure," Capt. Gerrish said, "but we were struck with horror to find among the packages eight large ones, containing scalps of our unhappy countryfolks, taken in the three last years by the Senneka Indians from the inhabitants of the frontiers of New York, New Jersey, Pennsylvania, and Virginia. . . . " The Indians had intended to give the scalps to the governor of Canada and wanted him to forward the scalps to England.

Letters captured from the Indians explained that marks they had painted on each scalp indicated the victim's identity and the way the victim had died. The first packet contained the scalps of 43 soldiers killed in skirmishes; their skin was painted red "with a small black spot to note their being killed with bullets." The first packet also contained the scalps of 62 farmers killed in their houses, "painted brown and marked with a hoe." The Indians said that other scalps were marked with a little yellow flame "to denote their being of prisoners burnt alive, after being scalped, their nails pulled out by the roots, and other torments."

The fifth packet contained the scalps of 88 women. Their hair was long and braided to show they were mothers. A small box, made of birch bark, contained "29 little infants' scalps." There were 954 scalps in all, including 88 of women, 193 of boys, and 211 of little girls.

At first, Capt. Gerrish wanted to bury the scalps. Then a lieutenant, who was planning a trip to Ireland, proposed carrying them to England. The lieutenant wanted to "hang them all up in some dark night on the trees in St. James' Park," so the king and queen could see them from their palace the next morning.

Wagons carried the scalps to Boston, and another story reported that thousands of people flocked to see them. But the lieutenant's plans were rejected. The scalps would not be hanged on trees in St. James' Park. Instead, they would be wrapped in decent little packets. One packet, containing a sample of every sort, would be sent to the king for his museum. Another, with the scalps of women and little children, would be sent to the queen. The rest would be distributed to members of Parliament, except for larger packets sent to England's bishops.

The supplement outraged people throughout Europe, helping to turn public opinion against the English and their policies in America. To friends, Franklin admitted that the stories were not totally true; nevertheless, he believed that their "substance" was true. Franklin knew that the British paid Indians to fight for them, and he believed that the Indians scalped nearly 2,000 Americans.

Moreover, America was at war, and Franklin felt that its war against England justified the use of his most powerful weapon: the satire he learned by reading London's most famous newspapers.

2 To the Moon in a Balloon: Poe's Horrifying Hoaxes

EDGAR ALLAN POE wrote six hoaxes during his brief and apparently miserable career. The hoaxes reflect his life—a dark, unhappy, perhaps frightening existence.

Poe always seemed to enjoy deceiving the public, and he was remarkably skillful at it. He had a vivid imagination and a keen interest in science. Thus, many of his stories described imaginary discoveries in the fields of science and exploration. Poe created an illusion of reality by studying the topics and by filling his stories with minor details that, because they were accurate, made the entire stories seem accurate.

Poe's hoaxes also involved unusual adventures, with their heroes in constant danger. The details were exciting—but also horrifying. Many involved tales of crime, death, terror, and decay.

The stories' gruesome details disgusted some readers. Other readers were bored by Poe's minor details. When the stories failed to excite the public, Poe abandoned them, leaving their heroes in dangerous and distant places.

Poe sold most of his stories to newspapers and magazines, but was rarely well paid for his work. Thus, he lived in poverty, drifting from job to job and living in drab surroundings, often cheap boarding houses.

Some editors may have been reluctant to hire Poe because he was too eccentric and quarrelsome.[1] In addition, he was often sick and depressed. Critics said that he was a drunkard, possibly even a drug addict. Acquaintances agreed that a single glass of wine was enough to make Poe act "like a crazy man."[2] Yet some experts insist that Poe's drinking problems were greatly exaggerated, that he was not a drunkard and often went several months without a drink.[3]

One of Poe's first hoaxes involved the moon. He wanted to describe the scenery that he imagined might exist there. At first, he planned to write about an astronomer who used a powerful new telescope to observe the moon. He abandoned the idea after discussing it with friends. The idea seemed too ridiculous. Poe feared that no one would believe his story because it was impossible for anyone to build a telescope that powerful.

Instead, he decided to pretend that an aviator described the moon after flying there in a balloon. Typically, he began by learning everything he could about the topic. As a result, his story seemed logical, even realistic. Poe's hero was a murderer who barely survived a series of dangerous accidents. He described all their bloody details. In addition, he included a clue—a single clue—that informed his more observant readers that the story a hoax.

The story was titled "The Unparalleled Adventures Of One Hans Pfaall," and the first installment appeared in a magazine, the *Southern Literary Messenger,* in June 1835. It reported that Rotterdam seemed to be in a high state of excitement. About noon, from behind a cloud, a queer substance slowly emerged. What could it be? No one knew; no one could imagine. The object came lower and still lower toward the city. In a very few minutes it arrived near enough to be accurately discerned. It appeared to be—yes! It *was* undoubtedly a balloon; but no *such* balloon had ever been seen in Rotterdam before. For who had ever heard of a balloon manufactured entirely of dirty newspapers?

The balloon descended to within one hundred feet of the Earth, allowing the crowd below to see its occupant. It was a man not more than two feet in height. His hands were enormously large. His hair was gray. His nose was long. His chin and cheeks were wrinkled with age— and he had no ears of any kind. The little old gentleman proceeded to throw out a letter. Then, apparently having no further business in Rotterdam, the aeronaut began to reascend. His balloon arose like a lark, drifted quietly behind a cloud, and disappeared forever.

The letter was addressed to Rotterdam's mayor and to Professor Rubadub in their capacity as president and vice president of the Rotterdam College of Astronomy. They opened it on the spot.

The letter was written by Hans Pfaall who, with three companions, had disappeared from Rotterdam about five years earlier. Pfaall's letter complained that, for forty years, he had been a successful bellows mender. Then people began to use newspapers to fan their fires and no longer required his services. Pfaall continued, "I soon grew as poor as a rat, and, having a wife and children to provide for, my burdens at length became intolerable, and I spent hour after hour in reflecting upon the most convenient method of putting an end to my life." From morning till night, Pfaall's house was besieged by creditors—three in particular. "Upon these three," Pfaall said, "I vowed the bitterest revenge."

One day Pfaall happened to read a small pamphlet about astronomy. The next morning, he spent all his remaining money on more books about the topic, and devoted every spare moment to reading them.

Then, acting with the greatest secrecy, Pfaall sold all his remaining property and borrowed a considerable amount of money. He proceeded to buy everything necessary to build and equip a balloon of extraordinary dimensions—a balloon capable of containing more than forty thousand cubic feet of gas. At night, Pfaall took his equipment to a location east of Rotterdam and dug a series of holes on the spot where he intended to inflate the balloon. He filled the holes with canisters containing, in all, four hundred pounds of cannon powder.

"Everything being now ready," Pfaall said, "I extracted from my wife an oath of secrecy." He promised to return as soon as possible and gave her what little money he had left.

"It was the first of April," Pfaall continued. The night was dark and drizzling. Pfaall took with him the three creditors who had given him so much trouble. His creditors worked with great diligence but asked Pfaall what he intended to do. To pacify them, Pfaall promised to repay all his debts as soon as he could. In about 4½ hours, the balloon was fully inflated. Pfaall attached a wicker basket beneath it and put all his equipment and supplies inside.

It was now nearly dawn, and Pfaall dropped a lighted cigar on the ground, as if by accident. While stooping to pick it up, he ignited a fuse on one of the canisters of cannon powder, then jumped into the basket and cut a single cord holding him to Earth. The balloon shot upward, and Pfaall said: "Scarcely, however, had I attained the height of 50 yards, when, roaring and tumbling up after me in the most tumultuous and terrible manner, came so dense a hurricane of fire, and gravel, and burning wood, and blazing metal, and mangled limbs, that my very heart sunk within me, and I fell down in the bottom of the car, trembling with terror. Indeed, I now perceived that I had entirely overdone the business. . . . "

Afterward, Pfaall attributed the extreme violence of the explosion to the fact that he was directly above it. His balloon whirled round and round, reeling and staggering like a drunken man. The explosion hurled Pfaall out of the basket, and he was left dangling by a slender cord tangled around his left foot. Pfaall gasped for breath, felt a horrible nausea, and lost all consciousness.

Pfaall regained consciousness at dawn. "But, strange to say," he said, "I was neither astonished nor horror-stricken. If I felt any emotion at all, it was a kind of chuckling satisfaction at the cleverness I was about to display in extricating myself from this dilemma. . . . " Never, for a moment, did Pfaall doubt his success. He climbed back into the basket, examined the balloon "and found it, to my great relief, uninjured." His equipment and provisions were safe. Pfaall then explained his goal: Harassed beyond endurance by his miseries on Earth, he had decided to leave, yet live—to leave the world, yet continue to exist—in short, "to force a passage, if I could, *to the moon.*"

The moon was about 237,000 miles from the Earth—not a very extraordinary distance. Pfaall added that: "Traveling on the land has been repeatedly accomplished at the rate of 60 miles per hour . . . even at this velocity, it would take me no more than 161 days to reach the surface of the moon." Pfaall expected his balloon to travel at a much greater speed because, as it rose, the force of the Earth's gravity would be constantly diminishing.

Pfaall believed that his body would become accustomed to the absence of any atmospheric pressure at high altitudes. He also believed that some air, however little, *must exist* at every altitude, and that he would be able to condense and breath it. "This," he declared, "would remove the chief obstacle in a journey to the moon."

At 6:40, his balloon entered some dense clouds which damaged his equipment and wet him to the skin. To escape, Pfaall threw out ten pounds of ballast. His balloon immediately began to climb more rapidly, and he soon rose above the difficulty. "In a few seconds after my leaving the cloud," Pfaall said, "a flash of vivid lightning shot from one end of it to the other, and caused it to kindle up, throughout its vast extent, like a mass of ignited charcoal." It was indeed a narrow escape. Had his balloon remained within the cloud, the lightning would have destroyed it.

The balloon was rising rapidly, and by seven o'clock, reached an altitude of more than 9½ miles. "I began to find great difficulty in drawing my breath," Pfaall said. His head, too, was excessively painful, apparently from the lack of atmospheric pressure. Blood was oozing from his ears, and his eyes seemed to be protruding from their sockets. Without thinking, Pfaall threw out another fifteen pounds of ballast — and nearly died. The balloon began to rise even more rapidly, and Pfaall was seized with a spasm which lasted for more than five minutes. He gasped for breath, bleeding all the while from his nose and ears, and even slightly from his eyes.

Lying down on the bottom of the basket, Pfaall decided to try an experiment that might save his life. Using the blade of his penknife, he cut open a vein in his left arm. "The blood had hardly commenced flowing," Pfaall said, "when I experienced a sensible relief, and by the time I had lost about half a moderate basin-full, most of the worst symptoms had abandoned me entirely." He lay still for about a quarter of an hour, then arose, almost free of pain of any kind.

By eight o'clock the balloon had risen seventeen miles above the surface of the Earth, and breathing became more difficult. At 8:15, he proceeded to adjust his "condenser." Pfaall had prepared a strong airtight bag and now pulled it over the entire basket and fastened it shut. In the sides he had inserted three panes of thick glass so he could see in every direction. His apparatus drew in the atmosphere surrounding the balloon, condensed it, and added it to the air already in the bag. By repeating the process several times, Pfaall was able to fill the bag with enough air to breath. So once again, he breathed with perfect freedom. Also, problems caused by the decreasing atmospheric pressure had actually *worn off,* as he had expected.

By ten o'clock, Pfaall had very little to do. Feeling sleepy, he laid down to rest.

April 3-5. Pfaall found his balloon drifting northward at an immense height. Overhead, the sky was a jetty black, and the stars brilliantly visible. His apparatus continued in good order, and nothing of importance occurred. He spent some time reading, "having taken care to supply myself with books."

April 7. Pfaall arose early, and, to his great joy, found the North Pole immediately beneath his feet. His altitude was *"not less,* certainly, than 7,254 miles from the surface of the sea."

April 10. Pfaall was suddenly aroused from his slumber, at about five o'clock this morning, "by a loud, crackling, and terrific sound, for which I could in no manner account." Pfaall wrote that, "It was of very brief duration, but, while it lasted, resembled nothing in the world of which I had any previous experience." At first, he feared that the balloon had burst. "I examined all my apparatus, however, and could discover nothing out of order."

April 13. Pfaall was again very much alarmed by a repetition of the loud crackling noise which had terrified him three days earlier. He thought long upon the subject but was unable to determine its cause.

April 15. Pfaall exclaimed: "About 12 o'clock I became aware, for the third time, of that appalling sound which had so astonished me before. It now, however, continued for some moments, and gathered intensity as it continued. At length, while, stupefied and terror-stricken, I stood in expectation of I knew not what hideous destruction, the car vibrated with excessive violence, and a gigantic and flaming mass of some material which I could not distinguish, came . . . roaring and booming by the balloon." It seemed to be a meteorite, or perhaps a huge fragment thrown into the air by a volcano on the moon.

April 17. On awakening from a brief slumber, Pfaall was thunderstruck! The surface beneath him had suddenly grown larger in size. "No words," he said, "can give any adequate idea of the extreme, the absolute horror and astonishment, with which I was seized, possessed, and altogether overwhelmed. My knees tottered beneath me—my teeth chattered—my hair started up on end." At first, Pfaall thought that his balloon had burst and that he was falling back to Earth. He feared that, in ten minutes, he would be dead.

Then Pfaall paused to reconsider and realized that he could not have fallen back to Earth so rapidly. Besides, the surface below him was vastly different, in appearance, than the surface of the Earth. Suddenly, Pfaall realized that the gravitation of the moon was now more powerful than the gravitation of the Earth. His balloon had swung around, and the Earth was now over his head, "while the moon—the moon itself in all its glory—lay beneath me, and at my feet."

Pfaall could see that the moon had no ocean or sea, lake, or river, or any body of water whatsoever. Instead, it seemed covered with volcanoes, and most were in a state of eruption — hurling debris up toward the balloon with an appalling frequency.

April 18. The balloon was descending more rapidly now, filling Pfaall with alarm. If the moon did not have an atmosphere, he would be unable to land safely. He would be dashed into atoms against its rugged surface.

April 19. To Pfaall's great joy, he detected a change in the moon's atmosphere. By ten o'clock, he had reason to believe that its density had considerably increased. His approach, however, was still alarmingly rapid. The moon's atmosphere was not dense enough to support the balloon, and Pfaall said: "I lost not a moment, accordingly, in throwing overboard first my ballast, then my water-kegs, then my condensing apparatus . . . and finally every article within the basket. But it was all to no purpose. I still fell with horrible rapidity, and was now not more than half a mile from the surface. As a last resource, therefore, having got rid of my coat, hat, and boots, I cut loose from the balloon *the basket itself. . . .* "

Without the wicker basket to hold him, Pfaall clung to some ropes around the balloon, and had barely time to observe that the whole country, as far as the eye could see, was thickly populated with tiny homes. He tumbled headlong into the very heart of a fantastic-looking city, and into the middle of a vast crowd of ugly little people. None uttered a single syllable, or tried to assist him. Instead, Pfaall said, they "stood like a parcel of idiots, grinning in a ludicrous manner, and eying me and my balloon askant, with their arms set a-kimbo."

Pfaall's letter, dropped in Rotterdam five years later, continued: "Thus may it please your Excellencies, after a series of great anxieties, unheard-of dangers, and unparalleled escapes, I had, at length, on the 19th day of my departure from Rotterdam, arrived in safety at the conclusion of a voyage undoubtedly the most extraordinary, and most momentous, ever accomplished, undertaken, or conceived by any denizen of Earth."

After living upon the moon for five years, Pfaall said, he had gained information of even more importance than the details of his mere voyage. He had much to say about the climate of the moon; of a zone of running water; of the people themselves; of their manners, customs, and political institutions; of their ugliness; of their lack of ears; and of their inability to speak. But above all, he had also gained information about those dark and hideous mysteries in the outer regions of the moon — regions which were never turned toward Earth.

Pfaall promised to describe all this, and more, but only in return for a reward. He wanted to return to his family and home. As the price for his information, Pfaall wanted a pardon for the murder of his three creditors. Pfaall added that the man in the balloon was an inhabitant of the moon, properly instructed to be his messenger to the Earth. The messenger would "await your Excellencies' pleasure, and return to me with the pardon in question if it can, in any manner, be obtained."

The mayor and Professor Rubadub had no doubt about the matter—the pardon should be granted. But Pfaall's messenger had disappeared—"no doubt, frightened to death by the savage appearance of the residents of Rotterdam." Thus, the pardon would be of little use. No man on Earth could be expected to travel to the moon to deliver it. The matter seemed, at least temporarily, to end there.

The most interesting part of Poe's story, Pfaall's description of the moon, was supposed to appear in a later installment—yet Poe never wrote it. While Poe was writing his story about Hans Pfaall, a New York paper published a similar hoax written by a reporter named Richard Locke. Moreover, Locke used the very idea that Poe had abandoned: the idea of an astronomer who described the moon after inventing a telescope powerful enough to observe all the objects on its surface.

After Locke's astronomer described the moon, Poe saw no reason to finish his own story. Poe explained that Hans Pfaall could add very little to the astronomer's account. "I did not think it advisable even to bring my voyager back to his parent Earth," Poe said. "He remains where I left him, and is still, I believe, 'the man in the moon.' "[4]

At first, Poe suspected that Locke copied him. Poe complained that he had spoken freely about his ideas, and "from many little incidents and apparently trivial remarks . . . I am convinced that the idea was stolen from myself."[5] Yet Locke denied that he saw the first installment of Poe's story, and Poe later accepted his denials.[6]

Poe remained jealous of Locke's success, however. Poe's own story failed to interest the public, perhaps because it included too many minor details. In addition, readers were more skeptical of Poe's premise. Readers seemed willing to believe that an astronomer had seen the moon, but not that an aviator had flown there. Also, a few readers noticed that Pfaall's journey began on April Fools' Day.

Poe published a second balloon hoax nine years later, and it became his greatest success. He seemed to write the hoax out of desperation, because he needed the money. His second hoax involved another exciting adventure, but without any of the bloody details that disgusted so many readers.

Poe moved to New York with his sick wife and mother in the spring of 1844, and they found some rooms on Greenwich Street. "The house is old and looks buggy," he complained, but it was all he could afford. He arrived in New York with only $4.50 in his pockets.

The *Sun* seemed to be the liveliest newspaper in New York and, to earn some money, Poe gave its editor a story about a fictitious balloon flight across the Atlantic Ocean.[7] The story reported that eight people sailed aboard the balloon. In fact, two of the men Poe mentioned, Monck Mason and Robert Holland, had already sailed from England to Germany. A third, Harrison Ainsworth, was a popular English novelist.

Poe's story appeared on April 13, 1844, and the *Sun's* clever handling of it added to the public's excitement. The *Sun* inserted a bulletin in its regular Saturday edition. It reported that a special pony express had just delivered the latest dispatches from the South. They revealed that a balloon had crossed the Atlantic Ocean in the incredibly brief period of three days. The *Sun* added that, by 10 that morning, it hoped to publish an "Extra" with a more detailed account of the voyage.

The *Sun's* "Extra" was not ready until almost noon. Nevertheless, it delighted Poe. The headlines announced:

ASTOUNDING NEWS
BY EXPRESS VIA NORFOLK!
THE ATLANTIC CROSSED IN THREE DAYS!
SIGNAL TRIUMPH OF MR. MONCK MASON'S FLYING
MACHINE!!!

The details were supposedly copied directly from the diaries of Monck Mason and Harrison Ainsworth. They explained that Mason had conceived the idea of using a powerful spring and propeller to move a balloon through the air and decided to construct a balloon large enough to cross the British Channel; the project, however, was kept secret from the public. The balloon was made of silk and contained more than forty thousand cubic feet of coal gas. Fully inflated, it could lift an estimated twenty-five hundred pounds, and the weight of the eight passengers totalled only twelve hundred pounds. That left a surplus of thirteen hundred pounds for ballast and supplies.

The aviators planned to cross the English Channel and to land near Paris. Their balloon's inflation was started very quietly at daybreak in North Wales on Saturday, April 6. Shortly after 11 a.m., "everything being ready for departure, the balloon was set free. . . . "

Saturday, April 6. Cut loose, and in high spirits, they rose gently but steadily. The weather was remarkably fine, and a light breeze carried them toward the British Channel. The first entry in Mr. Mason's diary stated: "The balloon was unusually steady, and looked beautifully. In about 10 minutes after starting, the barometer indicated an altitude of 15,000 feet." They were rapidly approaching some mountains to the south but soared over them in fine style. Soon the coast appeared immediately beneath them.

The aviators were anxious to test the rudder and propeller to determine whether the instruments were able to steer the balloon more to the east, toward Paris. Using the rudder, they instantly changed direction. Next, they set in motion the spring of the propeller and rejoiced to find that it propelled them, as desired. Hardly had they finished celebrating, however, when an accident occurred.

A steel rod connecting the spring to the propeller was suddenly jerked out of place. While the aviators tried to repair it, a strong wind from the east blew them toward the Atlantic Ocean. They were being blown out to sea at a rate of fifty or sixty miles an hour. Then Mr. Ainsworth made an extraordinary proposal—that they should take advantage of the strong gale and try to reach the coast of North America.

As the gale worsened, their speed increased, and they soon lost sight of the British coast. They passed over vessels of all kinds, and passengers aboard all the ships saluted them with loud cheers which they heard with a surprising distinctness. As night approached, they made a rough estimate of the distance traversed. "It could not have been less than five hundred miles, and was probably much more," Mr. Mason said. "The propeller was kept in constant operation, and, no doubt, aided our progress materially." As the sun went down, the gale turned into an absolute hurricane, and the wind continued from the east all night. They suffered a little from the cold. The dampness of the atmosphere was most unpleasant, but there was enough space in the basket so they could all lie down, covering themselves with blankets.

An entry in Mr. Ainsworth's diary added that the last nine hours had been the most exciting of his life. He prayed for success, and speculated that the gale might continue for four or five days, so they might easily complete their voyage in that time.

Sunday, April 7. Mr. Mason's diary reported that the gale had sub-sided and carried them along at perhaps thirty miles per hour, or more — but had veered to the north. They used the propeller and rudder to steer more to the west. Mr. Mason declared that he considered their experi-ment — the easy navigation through the air in any direction — as thor-oughly successful.

Mr. Ainsworth's diary added little about the day's journey, except the surprising fact that, at a high elevation, he experienced "neither very intense cold, nor headache, nor difficulty of breathing." Only Mr. Os-borne complained of a constriction of his chest, and it soon wore off. Mr. Ainsworth concluded: "We have flown at a great rate during the day, and we must be more than half way across the Atlantic. We have passed over some 20 or 30 vessels of various kinds, and all seem to be delight-fully astonished. Crossing the ocean in a balloon is not so difficult a feat after all. . . . "

Monday, April 8. Just before dawn, they were all alarmed by some odd noises. Particles of ice had formed on the balloon during the night, and now the ice was breaking off as heat in the atmosphere warmed the balloon and expanded the gas inside it. Mr. Ainsworth added that it was very difficult to determine their speed, since they moved *with* the wind. Nevertheless, he suspected that they must be near the American coast.

Tuesday, April 9. Mr. Ainsworth's diary contained a single brief entry: *"One p.m. We are in full view of the low coast of South Carolina.* The great problem is accomplished. We have crossed the Atlantic — fairly and *easily* crossed it in a balloon! God be praised!"

The aviators' diaries ended at this point. However, Mr. Ainsworth informed the *Sun* that it was nearly dead calm when they first saw the coast. The balloon was brought over the beach, "the tide being out and the sand hard, smooth, and admirably adapted for a descent." People living in the vicinity thronged out, of course, to see the balloon. But at first, few seemed willing to believe that the balloon had crossed the entire Atlantic.

The whole voyage, from shore to shore, had been completed in seventy-five hours. The *Sun* concluded that it was "unquestionably the most stupendous, the most interesting, and the most important under-taking, ever accomplished or even attempted by man."

Other writers insist that the hoax caused "excitement of the kind not known again until Orson Welles's "War of the Worlds" was broadcast nearly a century later."[8] New Yorkers were completely fooled, partly because the aviators' names were so well known, and because their journey was really possible.[9] Aviators in Europe had been considering a trip across the Atlantic, and Poe may have written his story after reading about their plans.

Poe claimed that people waiting for the *Sun*'s "Extra" filled the entire square around the newspaper's office, blocking its doors so that no one was able to enter or leave the building from sunrise until about 2 p.m. Poe said he "never witnessed more intense excitement to get possession of a paper," and that one reader paid fifty cents for a copy of the penny paper. During the whole day, Poe added, he tried to buy a copy for himself but was unable to do so.[10]

On Monday, the *Sun* admitted that its story was probably false. It explained that mails from the South had failed to bring "confirmation of the balloon from England."

Poe's third hoax, "Von Kempelen and His Discovery," described a man who transformed lead into gold. Typically, the story involved a mystery—and a scientific discovery. Poe apparently wrote it to poke fun at the California gold rush.[11] On January 24, 1848, workers discovered gold at Sutter's Mill near Sacramento. Poe published his hoax in 1849 and hoped that it would make Americans more skeptical of the tales being told about the gold in California—more hesitant to quit their jobs and join the migration there.

Poe's story explained that Von Kempelen was a short and stout man, with large, fat, blue eyes; sandy hair; a wide but pleasing mouth; fine teeth; and "some defect in one of his feet." He had vacationed at a hotel in Providence, Rhode Island, then traveled to the German city of Bremen. His great discovery was revealed there.

Von Kempelen never had much money while living in Bremen. When a great crime occurred there—a forgery—the police suspected him because he had just purchased a large property on Gasperitch Lane and refused, when questioned, to explain where he obtained the money to purchase it. The police arrested Von Kempelen but set him free because there was no evidence against him. "The police, however, kept a strict watch upon his movements, and thus discovered that he left home frequently, taking always the same road, and invariably giving his watchers the slip." Each time Von Kempelen was followed, he disappeared in an area of narrow and crooked passages. The police finally tracked Von Kempelen to an old house. Surprising him there, the police thought they had caught him in the midst of a counterfeiting operation.

The officers found a closet measuring eight by ten feet, fitted up with some chemical apparatus. In one corner was a very small furnace with a glowing fire in it, and on the fire were two containers connected by a tube. One of these containers was nearly full of lead. The other held some liquid that seemed to be furiously boiling away. Von Kempelen was wearing asbestos gloves and instantly seized these containers with both hands, throwing their contents onto the floor.

The police handcuffed and searched Von Kempelen, but found nothing unusual, excepting a paper parcel containing some *unknown substance*. All attempts to analyze this substance failed. The police also searched under a bed and discovered a large trunk. "Upon attempting to draw this trunk out from under the bed, they found that, with their united strength (there were three of them, all powerful men), they 'could not stir it one inch.' " Much astonished at this, one of the policemen crawled under the bed, and looking into the trunk, said:

"No wonder we couldn't move it—why it's full to the brim of old bits of brass!"

With much difficulty, the officers finally slid the trunk out into the room and examined its contents. They noticed that the brass "was all in small, smooth pieces, varying from the size of a pea to that of a dollar. . . . " The pieces were irregular in shape, although more or less flat, and looked much as molten lead looks after it is thrown upon the ground and left there to cool. None of the officers suspected that this metal was anything *but* brass. The idea of its being *gold* never entered their brains.

They were astonished when, the next day, it became known all over Bremen that the trunkful of brass which they had carted so contemptuously to the police station (without taking even the smallest scrap for themselves) was gold; "in fact, absolutely pure, virgin, without the slightest appreciable alloy!"

Von Kempelen was released from jail—and no sane person can doubt his great discovery. However, no one knows the identity of all its ingredients. "The simple truth is, that up to this period, *all* analysis has failed. . . . " Until Von Kempelen decides to reveal his secret, the matter is likely to remain a mystery.

Until then, the story concluded, many people hesitated to emigrate to California. They feared that gold would become less valuable because it was so plentiful there. Now, people would become even more hesitant to emigrate to California, for gold would become no more valuable than the lead that Von Kempelen used to manufacture it.

A fourth hoax concerned hypnosis (or "Mesmerism"). People knew little about hypnotic trances, and Poe wondered what would happen if a man died while in a trance. His story, "The Facts in the Case of M. Valdemar," appeared in a magazine, *The American Review,* in 1845. It is one of Poe's most gruesome stories, and readers were particularly disturbed by its ending.[12]

About nine months earlier, the story began, its author realized that no person had ever been mesmerized while dying. So no one knew whether a patient who was dying could be hypnotized, nor whether the hypnosis might delay or even prevent the patient's death.

The author thought of his friend, M. Ernest Valdemar. On two or three occasions, he had hypnotized M. Valdemar with little difficulty, and now his friend was dying of tuberculosis. M. Valdemar seemed a natural subject for the experiment. The author spoke to him frankly and found "to my surprise, his interest seemed vividly excited." Because of the unusual nature of his disease, M. Valdemar's physicians were able to predict the exact moment of his death, and he agreed to send for the author about twenty-four hours in advance.

On a Saturday, seven months ago, the author received, from M. Valdemar himself, a letter stating that he could not hold out much longer. In fifteen minutes, the author was in the dying man's chamber and was appalled by his appearance. It was then seven o'clock on Saturday evening, and both physicians agreed that M. Valdemar would die at about midnight Sunday. The doctors bid him a final farewell. They had not intended to return but, at the author's request, agreed to look in upon the patient at about ten that Sunday night.

M. Valdemar was still quite willing and even anxious to participate in the experiment. But in case of a sudden accident, the author wanted a reliable witness and therefore postponed his operations until about 8 p.m. Sunday. A medical student arrived at that hour, and the author commenced the motions necessary to mesmerize M. Valdemar.

Some minutes after ten o'clock the two doctors called. By this time the patient's pulse was imperceptible, and he was snoring heavily at half-minute intervals. After fifteen minutes, a deep sigh arose from his bosom, and the snoring ceased. At midnight, the author asked the gentlemen present to examine M. Valdemar's condition. After a few experiments, "they admitted him to be in an unusually perfect state of mesmeric trance."

They left M. Valdemar entirely undisturbed until about three o'clock in the morning, and then found him in precisely the same condition; "that is to say, he lay in the same position; the pulse was imperceptible; the breathing was gentle . . . ; the eyes were closed naturally; and the limbs were as rigid and as cold as marble. Still, the general appearance was certainly not that of death."

"M. Valdemar," the author asked, "are you asleep?" He made no answer, but they perceived a tremor about his lips. When the author repeated the question for a second and then a third time, the patient's entire body quivered, his eyelids opened slightly, his lips moved sluggishly, and in a barely audible whisper, he said:

"Yes — asleep now. Do not wake me! — let me die so!"

The author questioned the patient again:

"Do you still feel pain in the breast, M. Valdemar?"

The answer now was immediate, but even less audible than before:

"No pain — I am dying!"

One of the doctors returned a little before sunrise and expressed astonishment at finding the patient still alive. After feeling the patient's pulse, he asked the author to speak to him again. The author did so, asking:

"M. Valdemar, do you still sleep?"

Some minutes elapsed before he replied, and during the interval the dying man seemed to be collecting his energies to speak. After the question was repeated for a fourth time, he said very faintly, almost inaudibly:

"Yes; still asleep — dying."

The physicians wanted M. Valdemar left undisturbed, and expected him to die within a few minutes. The author insisted, however, on speaking to him once more, and merely repeated his previous questions. However, there was no longer the faintest sign of life in M. Valdemar, and they decided that he was dead. As they started to leave "a strong vibratory motion was observable in the tongue." This continued for perhaps a minute. At the end of this period, a voice arose from M. Valdemar's motionless jaws. The voice sounded broken, harsh, and hollow — as though it came "from a vast distance, or from some deep cavern within the Earth." M. Valdemar was replying to the question he had been asked a few minutes before—whether he still slept. He now said:

"Yes!—no; I *have been* sleeping—and now—now—*I am dead.*"

The medical student fainted, and two nurses fled. For nearly an hour, silently—without the utterance of a word—the others struggled to revive the student. When he regained consciousness, they again investigated M. Valdemar's condition. There was no longer any evidence of respiration, and an attempt to draw blood from his arm failed. The author stated, "The only real indication, indeed, of the mesmeric influence was now found in the vibratory movement of the tongue, whenever I addressed M. Valdemar with a question." The patient seemed to be making an effort to reply, but no longer was able to do so.

At ten o'clock, the author left the house with the two physicians. In the afternoon they called again to see the patient. His condition remained precisely the same, and they now agreed that no good purpose would be served by trying to awaken him. It was evident that, so far, death (or what is usually termed death) had been halted by the mesmeric process.

For *nearly seven months* they continued to make daily calls at M. Valdemar's house, accompanied, now and then, by medical and other friends. All this time the patient remained *exactly* as the author had last described him. Finally, last Friday, they decided to awaken him. For a time their efforts were unsuccessful. The first indication of revival was a movement of his eyes, accompanied by the profuse outflowing of a yellowish liquid, of a highly offensive odor, from beneath the lids.

At this point one of the doctors wanted the author to ask M. Valdemar another question, and he did so, as follows:

"M. Valdemar, can you explain to us what are your feelings or wishes now?"

The patient's jaws and lips remained rigid as before. His tongue rolled violently in his mouth, and at length the same hideous voice broke forth:

"For God's sake!—quick!—quick!—put me to sleep!—or, quick!—wake me!—quick—*I say to you that I am dead!*"

For an instant, the author was undecided about what he should do, but then struggled to awaken M. Valdemar. It was quite impossible for any human to be prepared for what followed. Horrified, the author watched: "His whole frame at once—within the space of a single minute, or even less, shrunk—crumbled, absolutely *rotted* away beneath my hands. Upon the bed, before the whole company, there lay a nearly liquid mass of loathsome — of detestable putridity."

The story seemed genuine and created "an intense excitement," especially in England, where it was reprinted in a pamphlet. Poe added to the public's excitement — and confusion — by refusing to discuss the matter. When asked whether the story about M. Valdemar was fact or fiction, Poe "carefully avoided giving the public a definite answer."[13]

Poe's other two hoaxes were long adventure stories. Both described journeys to unexplored lands. Some readers consider the longer, "The Narrative of Arthur Gordon Pym," one of the finest adventure stories ever written. Poe filled the story with one exciting adventure after another; nevertheless, it failed. The story may have contained too many minor (and boring) details. Or readers may have been disgusted by Poe's description of cannibalism and other acts of terror.[14] Yet the story fooled some reviewers. They thought that the narrative was a genuine account of an actual voyage.

Poe's second long hoax, "The Journal of Julius Rodman," described the first attempt to cross the Rocky Mountains. Monthly installments appeared in a magazine, beginning in January 1840. At the time, Americans were fascinated by the West, and Poe hoped that his story would be a popular one. But it ended abruptly, abandoning the explorers before they even reached the Rocky Mountains. Poe may have stopped writing the story because it failed to become as popular (and profitable) as he had hoped. Or he may have stopped after becoming ill, or after leaving his job at the magazine.

In 1846, newspapers reported that Poe and his wife, Virginia, were dangerously ill, "without money, and without friends."[15] Virginia died the following January, Poe two years later, on October 7, 1849. He was forty and, according to some accounts, drinking heavily.

American Humor: Mark Twain and Dan De Quille

FTER the gold rush in California, prospectors found the world's richest silver mines in Nevada. Fortune hunters from all over the world rushed to Nevada, hoping to find more of the valuable ore. After failing as miners, two of the fortune hunters—Mark Twain and Dan De Quille—turned to journalism. Together during those exciting days, Twain and De Quille became the territory's most famous writers. They also created its most successful hoaxes.

Their hoaxes were uniquely American, influenced by their life in the West—not by England's eighteenth-century satirists. Humor in the West was more exaggerated and absurd. It also reflected reality—the fakes, frauds, swindles, and violence that were a part of life in Nevada during the nineteenth century.

Several of the hoaxes that Twain and De Quille wrote also resemble the West's tall tales—preposterous stories intended only to amuse, not fool, their audiences. Even Twain seemed to be surprised when readers believed all his stories. He thought that some were obviously fictitious: that no one would be foolish enough to believe the stories, especially not his readers in Nevada.

Journalists in Nevada also became involved in the region's horseplay. Thus, other stories describe their rough and sometimes dangerous practical jokes.

De Quille was six years older than Twain and emigrated to California in 1857, hoping to become rich as a miner. In the spring of 1862, De Quille joined the *Enterprise,* becoming the region's first great writer. He was paid $60 a week to report the discoveries that made other men millionaires.

As a youth, Twain was apprenticed to a printer, then moved around the country, setting type for newspapers in at least five states. He changed professions in 1857, becoming a pilot on the Mississippi River. After Abraham Lincoln's nomination and election as president, Twain saw preparations for war everywhere. Traffic on the Mississippi was blocked, and Twain returned to Hannibal. He found the young men there joining military companies, some to fight for the North, and some for the South. Twain joined a group of Confederate Rangers and was elected a lieutenant. His service in the Confederate Army was brief, however, and the details are hazy. Twain includes a witty — but vague — explanation in his autobiography. "In June," he wrote, "I joined the Confederates in Ralls County, Mo., as a second lieutenant under Gen. Tom Harris and came near having the distinction of being captured by Col. Ulysses S. Grant. I resigned after two weeks' service in the field, explaining that I was 'incapacitated by fatigue' through persistent retreating."[1] Experts suspect that Twain disliked the harsh, uncomfortable life of a solider and simply walked away from his unit.

Twain left for Nevada on July 26, 1861. He lived with a brother in Carson City, then tried to strike it rich as a miner. Twain failed to find any silver or gold, but submitted several stories to the *Enterprise,* and its editors offered him a job on their staff.

The *Enterprise* was Virginia City's leading paper, and perhaps the most influential in the West.[2] Its editor-in-chief, Joseph T. Goodman, encouraged his reporters to write human-interest stories (including hoaxes), and they helped make the *Enterprise* famous. The reporters might summarize a murder in a paragraph or two, then devote an entire column to a humorous sketch. The more absurd, the more fantastic, and the more ridiculous their stories became, the more their readers seemed to like them.[3]

Twain and De Quille became friends and roommates, often writing at the same table and helping one another with their stories. Yet the two men were quite different. As a former prospector, De Quille was familiar with every stage of the mining process. He was also careful, honest, and hard-working, reporting every detail as accurately as possible. Moreover,

Nevadans genuinely liked De Quille. He was a solemn man, tall and thin, quiet and shy—known for his dignity and gentle manners.

Twain was more ambitious, but also more careless and carefree. Even an editor at the *Enterprise* expected De Quille—not Twain—to become the newspaper's most famous writer.[4]

Nevadans complained that Twain was a braggart—cold, mean, cheap, and selfish. A colleague at the *Enterprise* added that Twain was abnormally lazy.[5] A printer called him a dirty man, with a foul mind and vocabulary. Other Nevadans said Twain was unsocial, that he had a terrible temper and refused to join in all their fun. Moreover, he seemed to enjoy playing jokes upon other people but hated the jokes they played upon him.

A colleague responded that Twain's more intelligent friends—those who knew him well—learned that he sent much of his salary back to his family in Missouri instead of squandering it in Virginia City. The journalist added that Twain enjoyed the rough and carefree life in Virginia City, but never was carried away by it. He never took it too seriously, nor let it dominate his life.[6]

Dozens of friends and acquaintances have written about Twain and De Quille and their work at the *Enterprise,* but their stories are filled with inconsistencies and errors.[7] Twain's accounts of his life in Nevada are even less reliable. While writing about his life in the West, he often exaggerated and tried to make himself the hero of every story. After becoming a famous lecturer, he also found that his audiences wanted to hear something new, not the stories he had already published. To satisfy them, Twain invented more humorous details, anything likely to make his audiences laugh. After repeating the details dozens of times, he seemed to forget what was real, or he may not have cared.

Unfortunately, historians cannot read the stories that Twain and De Quille published in the *Enterprise*. Almost all of Twain's work, and much of De Quille's, was destroyed. On October 26, 1875, a fire started in a rooming house near Virginia City's business district. The flames destroyed two thousand buildings, spreading so rapidly that "few people were able to save any of their goods or valuables."[8] Eighteen years later, the *Enterprise* ceased publication, and only a few stray copies and clippings remain.

Partly to help forget the danger and drudgery in their lives, people in the West told tall tales. Miners told Twain and De Quille about the fossils—snails and toads—that came to life after being blasted from their ore. Other Nevadans described a miner who became rich after finding silver. The miner became ill, but recovered after going to a Turkish bath and sweating out all the silver absorbed by his pores. The silver recovered from his bathwater was valued at $417.92.

Other Westerners created more serious (and illegal) fakes and frauds that Twain and De Quille also observed. To swindle the public, some mine owners "cooked" their dividends. Their companies borrowed money and used it to pay their original owners huge dividends, so their profits seemed enormous. When the price of their stock rose, the owners quickly sold it for a good profit.

Speculators also sought the highest possible assessments for their ore, then sold their stock before anyone discovered that it was worthless. Twain reported that one assayer provided such good results every time he was asked to examine a piece of ore "that in time he acquired almost a monopoly of the business." To expose the fraud, other assayers supposedly broke a fragment off a carpenter's grindstone and asked a stranger to bring it in to be assayed. In an hour, the assayer announced that a ton of the rock "would yield $1,284.40 in silver and $366.36 in gold."[9] The assayer fled after newspapers reported the story.

Other swindlers "salted" their mines. While working as a reporter, Twain went out to look at an unusual discovery at a mine called the North Orphir. Its owners reported finding solid lumps of pure silver. Once there, Twain got out a pan and washed some of the ore in a puddle. He found a half-dozen black, bullet-looking pellets of pure silver. No one had ever heard of that happening before, and the price of the mine's stock soared. Then someone noticed the letters "ted States of" stamped on one of the pellets. The mine's owners had melted silver coins, blackened them until they looked like silver ore, and mixed them with rocks in the mine.[10]

Everyone in Nevada, including the state's journalists, also engaged in an unusual amount of horseplay, and it affected the stories they wrote. Typically, several of Twain's and De Quille's stories described nonexistent feuds. After moving to Nevada, Twain covered the legislature in Carson City, and a rival—Clement Rice—criticized several errors in his stories. In retaliation, Twain nicknamed Rice "the Unreliable." Rice realized that the feud was good publicity and continued to insult Twain, yet the two men remained good friends, often eating and drinking together.[11]

When Twain became ill, he asked Rice to publish the *Enterprise* for him. The next morning, the *Enterprise* published an article that apologized for all of Twain's errors. Twain seemed to confess that he acted "as mean as a man could be," and begged for everyone's forgiveness. After returning to work, Twain wrote an article denying everything that Rice had written. Twain added that Rice was a reptile, with no more intelligence than a rabbit.[12]

Twain played a similar joke on an editor. The editor had left for a vacation. Overwhelmed by work, Twain begged him to return. The editor refused and, a few days later, received a copy of the *Enterprise* in his mail. The stories on one page libeled twenty prominent Nevadans and questioned the virtue of the town's most prominent women. Fearing that the *Enterprise* would be ruined and its owners lynched, the editor galloped back to Virginia City and found Twain relaxing in a bar. Twain had printed only one copy of the paper and mailed it to the editor. As intended, it ended his vacation.[13]

Following some rough horseplay, other stories ridiculed Twain's nose. Twain often visited a gymnasium in Virginia City and put on some boxing gloves one day. He seemed to challenge an editor from the *Enterprise,* and the editor—an expert boxer—punched Twain as hard as he could. The blow landed squarely on Twain's nose, causing it to swell horribly. Twain also suffered a black eye, and was so embarrassed by his appearance that he volunteered to leave town, to visit and write about some mines at Silver Mountain near Markleeville, California.

While Twain was gone, De Quille wrote several stories about his nose. One story reported that Twain's nose was smashed "till it covered nearly the whole of his face." Twain supposedly rushed away for surgical advice, leaving a bloody trail for a half mile through the city. After dark, he ventured forth with his swollen nose—a vast, inflamed, and pulpy old snoot—to get advice about having it amputated. None of Twain's friends recognized him, and none could comfort him, for his nose would never be a nose again. "It always was somewhat lopsided," De Quille wrote. "Now it is a perfect lump of blubber."[14]

Another of De Quille's stories reported that other passengers had already boarded a stage, and that the driver was reaching for his whip when a huge, blood-red nose tried to climb inside. Two of the lady passengers screamed with fright, and other people came running from all directions. For awhile, it looked as though there was going to be a riot.

However, an agent for the stage company assured everyone that the nose was perfectly harmless. The dreadful monster was finally allowed inside, and the stage rolled away.[15]

A third story described the stage as it entered Silver Mountain. People there saw Twain's nose at the window "and raised a cry that a 'freak' show was coming." People dropped everything and surrounded the stage, trying to peer inside. The bystanders gave three cheers as the nose stepped out. Then, as the freak walked to a hotel, an old lady asked for permission to touch its nose. She said that it was the happiest moment of her life.[16]

Twain soon got revenge. After returning to Virginia City, he reported on De Quille's "frightful accident." Twain informed his readers that De Quille was returning home on a vicious horse, coming down the road at the rate of a hundred miles an hour. While turning a sharp corner, De Quille saw a horse standing square across the road. He tried to avoid the horse, but it was too late. According to Twain's account, De Quille was wrenched from the saddle and thrown some three hundred yards. He landed upon solid ground, "bursting himself open from the chin to the pit of the stomach; his head was also caved in out of sight, and his hat was afterward extracted in a bloody and damaged condition from between his lungs . . . one leg was jammed up in his body nearly to his throat, and the other was so torn and mutilated that it pulled out when they attempted to lift him into the hearse. . . . " De Quille's arms were also broken, and his back was considerably fractured.

"Aside from these injuries," Twain wrote, "he sustained no other damage."[17]

De Quille was confined to his room for a day or two. He had been thrown from a horse, he admitted, and sprained a knee.

Twain and De Quille rented two rooms on the second floor of a brick building in Virginia City. Yet, in print, they continued to attack one another as often as possible. They charged one another with drunkenness, theft, and other minor crimes.

Other reporters reprinted their stories — but also added to them. One of their stories reported that Twain and De Quille stole food from their neighbors' pantry. Other reporters also reported that Twain and De Quille hanged the neighbors' cat. The cat had disappeared, and a sensational story claimed that Twain and De Quille had tied a cord around the cat's neck and suspended it from a second-floor window.[18]

After returning home another night, Twain and De Quille found a giant standing just inside their doorway, threatening them with a sword. It was a huge dummy, barely visible in the dim light. Pranksters apparently hoped that Twain and De Quille would be frightened by the giant—and perhaps empty their pistols into it.

Other stories that Twain and De Quille wrote for the *Enterprise* were more obviously hoaxes—but continued to reflect their life in the West. De Quille specialized in hoaxes about the region's scientific and geological discoveries. They were gentler than Twain's, never bloody, crude, or vindictive.

De Quille's most famous hoax involved Mr. Jonathan Newhouse, "a man of considerable inventive genius." De Quille reported that Newhouse had constructed an apparatus called "solar armor" to protect travelers from the fierce heat while crossing the area's deserts. De Quille explained that "[t]he armor consisted of a long, close-fitting jacket made of common sponge, and a cap or hood of the same material." The armor was about an inch thick and, before starting across a desert, travelers saturated it with water. Travelers then suspended a sack under their right arm. It was filled with water, and a small tube led from the sack to the top of the hood. To keep the armor moist as they progressed over the burning sands, travelers pressed the sack occasionally, forcing a little water upward to the hood and jacket. As the moisture evaporated, it cooled the travelers to any temperature they desired.

De Quille added that Newhouse went to Death Valley, determined to try crossing that terrible place in his armor. He started out one morning from a nearby camp, telling the other men there that he would return in two days. The next day, an Indian who spoke only a few words of English came to the camp in a great state of excitement, indicating that he wanted the men to follow him. About 20 miles out into the desert, the Indian pointed to a human figure seated against a rock. It was Newhouse, still in his armor.

"He was dead and frozen stiff," De Quille wrote. "His beard was covered with frost, and—though the noonday sun poured down its fiercest rays—an icicle over a foot in length hung from his nose." Newhouse had died because his armor worked too well.

Other newspapers reprinted De Quille's story, and a European who believed it supposedly wrote to the London *Times,* suggesting that British soldiers in India should be equipped with similar armor.

Other readers were more skeptical. To answer their questions, De Quille published a second story, "A Mystery Explained." It seemed to quote a coroner's report and explained that the justice of the peace and coroner at Salt Wells at the north end of Death Valley had held an inquest on the body, and that the verdict was as follows: "We find that the name of the deceased was Jonathan Newhouse, a native of Knox County, Ohio, aged forty-seven years; and we further find that deceased came to his death in Death Valley . . . by being frozen to death in a sort of sponge called a 'solar armor,' of which he was the inventor and in which he was tightly laced at his own request. . . . "

Newhouse had left a carpet-sack in the camp at the edge of Death Valley, and the coroner added: "In this was found . . . several bottles and small glass jars, containing liquids and powders or salts of various kinds. . . . One of the largest bottles was labeled 'Ether,' known to them to be a very volatile liquid and capable of producing an intense degree of cold by evaporation."

Until then, it had been assumed that Newhouse used only water to moisten the armor. A witness, Mr. Robert Purcell, testified that he "observed Mr. Newhouse at a spring about fifty yards from camp, half an hour previous to his donning the armor, and recollects distinctly to have seen him handling one or two of the bottles and jars found in the carpet-sack; though at the time he thought nothing of it, and did not approach very near to the deceased, as he did not wish to be thought inquisitive."

The coroner was firmly convinced that these chemicals, either alone or diluted with water, produced the degree of cold which caused the man's death. After becoming painfully cold, Newhouse apparently attempted to reach the fastenings on his back. His movements compressed the rubber pouch under his right arm and thus injected more and more of the freezing fluid into his armor.

The men who went out with the Indian to find Newhouse said that moisture still oozing out of the spongy armor wet their hands, causing an intense pain. The men were forced to cut the armor's fastenings, then peeled the armor off Newhouse's body and left it lying in the desert "where it probably still remains."

Another of De Quille's hoaxes, "The Mystery of the Savage Sump," reported that a river flowed underground for nearly thirty miles, from Lake Tahoe to the Comstock. De Quille wrote the story in the form of a serious scientific report, and it fooled its readers for the next hundred years. The story explained that C Street in Virginia City was at exactly the same altitude as the surface of Lake Tahoe, and that water flowing underground from the lake saturated the area. If Lake Tahoe's surface was any higher, De Quille warned, the water would overflow, completely flooding the Comstock.

Water actually flooded several mines, and, to drain it, engineers wanted to dig a tunnel through some mountains. De Quille's story proposed another solution. It suggested that miners should dig new shafts until they found the underground river. Then, if engineers plugged up the river, the Comstock would remain dry forever.

A similar hoax proposed the construction of a pump that would run forever, an example of perpetual motion. De Quille reported that the pump would be powered by a windmill. On breezy days, the windmill would hoist both sand and water to the surface. When the wind died down, engineers would allow the sand to fall back into the hole, and the falling sand would operate turbine wheels that pumped more water.

A fourth hoax described "The Traveling Stones of Pahranagat Valley." De Quille reported that the Pahranagat Valley was located in the wildest and most sterile portion of southeastern Nevada. A prospector returning from the area brought back a number of the stones. They were heavy, almost perfectly round, and about the size of a walnut. When scattered within two or three feet of each other on any level surface, some mysterious force seemed to draw the stones together, to scatter them apart, and then to draw them back together in a never-ending movement. If a single stone was placed up to a yard away, it at once started off to rejoin the others. But if the stone was placed four or five feet away, it remained motionless.[19]

Other newspapers reprinted the story, and showman P. T. Barnum supposedly offered De Quille $10,000 for the stones—if he could make them perform in a circus tent. German scientists who had been studying electromagnetic currents also wrote to De Quille, asking for more information about the discovery. De Quille responded, truthfully, that the story was a hoax. His reply infuriated the Germans. The Germans thought that De Quille was lying, and they considered his conduct unprofessional. He seemed to be hiding—from fellow scientists—discoveries about the laws of nature.[20]

Another of De Quille's stories, more of a tall tale, described a poor man found wandering about the world without a dime. The little old man told De Quille that, three days earlier, he had been rich. He owned a bowling alley and was doing a terrific business.

His first customers had just come in that morning. One of the men picked up an especially large ball, took a short run, and threw it toward the pins. When the ball struck the alley, there was a terrible explosion that shook the entire building, tearing up the planks and shattering the glass in every window. More explosions followed as the ball bounced down the alley. When it reached the pins, the ball knocked down all ten, but caused an explosion so powerful that it shook the entire town.

What caused the explosion?

The old man explained that someone had slipped into his place the previous night and greased all his alleys, balls, and pins with nitroglycerine.[21]

Twain wrote his first hoax, "A Petrified Man," only a few weeks after joining the *Enterprise.* Twain reported that a petrified man, about 100 years old, had been found in the mountains south of Gravelly Ford. Every limb and feature of the stone mummy was perfect, Twain wrote, even its left leg, which had evidently been a wooden one. Twain added that a Justice "Sewell" or "Sowell" of Humboldt City immediately proceeded to the spot to hold an inquest, and that a jury ruled that the man died from protracted exposure.

Twain continued: "The people of the neighborhood volunteered to bury the poor unfortunate, and were even anxious to do so; but it was discovered, when they attempted to remove him, that the water which had dripped upon him for ages from the crag above, had coursed down his back and deposited a limestone sediment under him which had glued him to the bed rock upon which he sat . . . and Judge S. refused to allow the charitable citizens to blast him from his position."[22] Twain added that the judge's opinion was just and proper. Blasting the mummy from his perch would be little less than sacrilege.

Twain created the hoax for revenge. "I had a temporary falling out with . . . the new coroner and justice of the peace of Humboldt," he explained, "and thought I might as well touch him up a little . . . and make him ridiculous, and thus combine pleasure with business." The hoax portrayed Judge Sewall as a fool who rushed to the scene to determine what caused the death of a man who had been dead (and turned to stone) for 100 years. While writing the hoax, Twain even misspelled Sewall's name.

Twain also wanted to ridicule a literary fad—a mania for reporting petrifications. Twain explained that, "[o]ne could scarcely pick up a paper without finding in it one or two glorified discoveries of this kind. The mania was becoming a little ridiculous. I was a brand-new local editor in Virginia City, and I felt called upon to destroy this growing evil. . . . I chose to kill the petrification mania with a delicate, a very delicate satire."

Twain insisted that he never intended to deceive anyone. Rather, he considered the story "a string of roaring absurdities." Twain may have expected other editors to see the joke and help him ridicule Sewall. The fact that other editors believed the story surprised him.[23]

At first, Twain said, he became angry and disliked even thinking about the story. Then, as more and more newspapers reprinted it, he began to feel a secret satisfaction. Twain adds that he sent Sewall "about half a bushel" of the newspapers every day, and that he was arranging things so that Sewall would "soon begin to receive letters from all parts of the country, purporting to come from scientific men, asking for further information concerning the wonderful stone man."

"I did it for spite, not for fun," Twain concluded. "If I had plenty of time, I would worry the life out of the poor cuss."

Two murders inspired another of Twain's hoaxes. While writing to his mother one night, Twain heard five pistol shots. He set aside her letter, saying: "As such things are in my line, I will go and see about it." Twain returned several hours later and explained that a man from Missouri had killed two police officers. The men had been in a bar, and all three may have been drunk. The police officers apparently accused the man of singing "Dixie." For revenge, he shot them through the heart.

Twain's hoax began: "For a day or two, a rumor has been floating around that five Indians had been smothered to death in a tunnel back of Gold Hill, but no one seemed to regard it in any other light than as a sensational hoax. . . . " Twain said he asked a Gold Hill man about the rumor and learned that it was a terrible reality. The community's residents had been electrified by the news that a desperado had fled toward Gold Hill after murdering two policemen. Shortly afterward, someone arrived with the news that a man "had been seen to run and hide in a tunnel a mile or a mile-and-a-half west of Gold Hill." A party of citizens went to the spot, but each one of them seemed reluctant to approach an armed and desperate man, especially inside the dark tunnel. Instead, they decided to stop up the mouth of the tunnel, hoping to detain their prisoner until they could find someone obliged to enter and bring him out.

"The next day," Twain wrote, "a strong posse went up, rolled away the stones from the mouth of the cave, went in, and found five dead Indians! — three men, one squaw, and one child, who had gone in there to sleep, perhaps, and been smothered by the foul atmosphere after the tunnel had been closed up."

Twain insisted that the story was true, and concluded that, "The intention of the citizens was good, but the result was most unfortunate."[24]

Twain's most famous (and gruesome) hoax appeared in the *Enterprise* on Oct. 28, 1863. Titled the "Empire City Massacre," it fooled most readers — even those familiar with the region.

For the past six months, Twain wrote, a man named "P. Hopkins" or "Philip Hopkins" had been living with his family in an old log house. The family included nine children — four boys and five girls — and their house was located "at the edge of the great pine forest which lies between Empire City and Dutch Nick's." Twice in the past two months, Mrs. Hopkins had expressed fears concerning her husband's sanity, remarking that he had been subject to fits of violence and threatened to take her life. Because Mrs. Hopkins often exaggerated, no one paid much attention to her.

"About 10 o'clock on Monday evening," Twain continued, "Hopkins dashed into Carson on horseback, with his throat cut from ear to ear, and bearing in his hand a reeking scalp from which the blood was still dripping, and fell in a dying condition in front of the Magnolia saloon. Hopkins expired in the course of five minutes, without speaking. . . . A number of citizens, headed by Sheriff Gasherie, mounted at once and rode down to Hopkins's house where a ghastly scene met their gaze. The scalpless corpse of Mrs. Hopkins lay across the threshold, with her head split open, and her right hand almost severed from the wrist. Near her lay the ax with which the murderous deed had been committed. In one of the bedrooms six of the children were found, one in bed and the others scattered about the floor. They were all dead. Their brains had evidently been dashed out with a club, and every mark about them seemed to have been made with a blunt instrument. The children must have struggled hard for their lives, as articles of clothing and broken furniture were strewn about the room in the utmost confusion."[25]

The posse found two girls in the kitchen, bruised and insensible. In a day, they recovered sufficiently to be able to talk. The girls said their father knocked them down with a piece of firewood and stomped on them.

Twain added that Hopkins was about forty-two years old and, until very recently, never mistreated his family. Hopkins had invested in the region's best mines but, when the San Francisco papers reported that some mines cooked their dividends, he grew afraid and sold out. He had an immense amount of money, and invested it in the Spring Valley Water Company of San Francisco. He was advised to do so by a relative of his, an editor at the San Francisco *Bulletin*. Then the Spring Valley Water Company cooked its dividends, the company's water totally dried up, and the value of its stock went down to nothing. "It is presumed," Twain wrote, "that this misfortune drove him mad and resulted in his killing himself and the greater portion of his family."

Twain added that the San Francisco papers had permitted the water company to go on borrowing money and cooking its dividends while its cunning financiers crept out of the tottering concern, leaving the crash to fall upon its poor and unsuspecting stockholders.[26]

Once again, Twain had created a hoax for revenge. The San Francisco papers had reported that a Nevada mining company cooked its dividends. The papers then urged investors to sell all their stock in Comstock mines "and invest in sound and safe San Francisco stocks, such as the Spring Valley Water Company." After the story's publication, Spring Valley cooked its dividends, yet the newspapers in San Francisco failed to criticize it.

Twain realized that the San Francisco papers were likely to reprint his hoax. Thus, by creating the hoax, Twain was able to trick them into publishing some criticisms of the water company. In addition, Twain used the hoax to ridicule a saloon he disliked: the Magnolia saloon in Carson City. A man named Philip Hopkins owned the saloon, and Twain reported that the murderer, a man named "Hopkins," died on its front steps.

For Nevadans familiar with the area, the story should have obviously been a hoax. Many readers knew Hopkins, and knew that he was a bachelor—not a man with a wife and nine children. There may not have been a single red-haired woman in all of Washoe, nor any family with nine children. Moreover, Empire City and Dutch Nick's were two names for the same place, and only sagebrush grew in the area. The nearest pine forest was at Lake Tahoe, fifteen miles away.

Twain said his readers should have also realized that the murderer's wound would kill an elephant. "I make the man ride nearly four miles after he has cut his throat from ear to ear," Twain said, "when any fool must see that he would fall dead in a moment."[27]

Twain's story may have fooled some readers because it mentioned real people and places. In addition, Twain made the details so vivid, and the story so exciting, that readers failed to think about — or even notice — its inconsistencies. Instead, they rushed to the newspaper office to obtain more details.

The morning after the story's publication, Twain published a retraction titled "I take it all back." "The story published in the *Enterprise* reciting the slaughter of a family near Empire," Twain admitted, "was all a fiction."

Other editors, including some who had reprinted the story, attacked Twain for weeks. Typically, the Gold Hill *Daily News* called the story a lie, "utterly baseless, and without a shadow of foundation." Other editors called the story "cruel and idiotic," and in "shockingly bad taste." Still others complained that its publication disgraced Nevada. The editors feared that readers in other parts of the United States would believe the story, thus reinforcing the territory's reputation for blood and violence.

At first, Twain seemed to think that he was a failure. People everywhere were attacking him. He may have offered to resign, and was so upset that he could not sleep. De Quille said Twain tossed and tumbled, groaning aloud.

"Mark," De Quille advised him, "never mind this bit of a gale. It will soon blow itself out. This item of yours will be remembered and talked about when all your other work is forgotten."[28] De Quille was right. In a few years, Nevadans remembered only one of the stories that Twain wrote for the *Enterprise,* the "Empire City Massacre."

As the years passed, Twain began to brag about it. "Well, in all my life," he said, "I never saw anything like the sensation that little satire created. It was the talk of the town, it was the talk of the territory." Twain claimed that people who tried to read the story while eating their breakfast were unable to finish their meal. Twain added that he and De Quille took their customary table at a restaurant and observed, at the next table, a man reading the morning paper, "skipping with all his might, in order to get to the bloody details as quickly as possible. . . . "

The man's eyes spread open, his jaw swung asunder, his face turned red, "and the whole man was on fire with excitement." Unable to eat, he laid down his food and utensils and left.

"He never got down to where the satire part of it began," Twain said. "Nobody ever did. They found the thrilling particulars sufficient."[29] It was a lesson that Twain said he never forgot. People never read explanations, he concluded. They skip all that, hurrying on to enjoy the bloody details.

In 1864, Twain was left in charge of the *Enterprise.* He promptly insulted several women and challenged another editor to a duel. Dozens of people have written about the duel, and their stories are crazily inconsistent. Perhaps because the incident embarrassed him, Twain failed to mention it in *Roughing It,* a book he wrote about his life in Nevada. Forty years later, he described the duel in his *Autobiography.*[30] His description of the duel, however, seems to be another of his tall tales.

During the Civil War, the leading women in Carson City sponsored a masquerade ball and raised more than $3,000 to aid sick and wounded soldiers. After collecting the money, the women considered spending it on something else. As a joke, Twain wrote a satirical sketch about women who were unable to make up their minds. Twain added that the women decided to send the money to a Miscegenation Society in the East. The Miscegenation Society recommended that Americans restore peace by eliminating the cause of the Civil War: differences between the black and white races. The society explained that men who opposed slavery had a duty to mix the races so that, in a few years, mankind would be neither black nor white, but brown. (Ironically, Twain seems to have been fooled by a political hoax. The Miscegenation Society was a fraud.[31] President Abraham Lincoln was a Republican, and Democrats apparently invented the Miscegenation Society, then used it to imply that Lincoln's administration favored miscegenation—the blending of the black and white races.)

The women of Carson City were not amused. Twain's article accused them of diverting money from sick and wounded soldiers, a charge they considered libelous. Twain's reference to the Miscegenation Society was even more offensive. W. K. Cutler, whose wife presided over the masquerade ball, challenged Twain to a duel, and other husbands threatened to horsewhip him for questioning their wives' honesty.

Twain was already squabbling with James L. Laird, the editor of another newspaper in Virginia City, and Laird published an angry letter written by the women. After its publication, Laird and Twain exchanged a series of increasingly heated notes. Laird called Twain a liar. Twain responded by calling Laird a coward and fool, with "a groveling disregard for truth, decency, and courtesy." The *Enterprise* printed all their notes, and other newspapers reprinted them.

Twain's friends encouraged him to challenge Laird to a duel. They insisted that he had an obligation to uphold the *Enterprise*'s honor. They also promised Twain that, if he were killed, they would write a fine obituary for him. Twain hated firearms and was a poor shot, but Laird insulted him. If he failed to act, he would be disgraced forever.

A colleague at the *Enterprise* may have written the initial challenge for him. Because Laird failed to respond, the colleague continued to write one more insulting challenge after another. Laird finally accepted. Like Twain, he had no alternative, since he also faced disgrace.

According to most accounts, Twain did not sleep a wink that night. Instead, he wrote his will. Just before dawn, Twain and his second, Steve Gillis, went to a ravine on the outskirts of town. On their way, they borrowed a barn door for target practice. Twain was unable to hit a target on the door — or even to nick the door. Gillis was an expert marksman and, while testing Twain's revolver, supposedly shot the head off a bird. At just that moment, Laird's seconds arrived to make the final arrangements.

Most accounts add that Gillis slapped the smoking revolver into Twain's hand and congratulated him for shooting a bird in the air at thirty yards. Frightened by Twain's marksmanship, Laird's seconds rushed back and warned him to leave. Twain's autobiography adds that "Laird sent back a note in his own hand declining to fight a duel with me on any terms whatsoever."

Another account explains that Gillis secretly loaded the revolvers with powder but no bullets. At the word "Fire," Twain and Laird took one step forward and fired almost simultaneously. Laird fell to the ground, and everyone gathered around him, fearing that Gillis had rammed a bullet instead of a paper wad into Twain's revolver. A doctor shoved everyone else aside, unbuttoned Laird's vest, and found a paper wad lodged directly over his heart.[32] Feeling its impact, Laird feared that he was dying.

A slightly different account claims that either Twain or Laird was tipped off about the blanks and, when the revolvers fired, fell forward, using chicken blood to add to the realism.

Experts insist that all the stories are nonsense.[33] Twain and Laird may have challenged one another to a duel, but never fought it. The feud may have been another of their hoaxes, contrived for the publicity (or the fun of it). If the feud was genuine, friends may have arranged a meeting and compromise.

Regardless of what happened, a law recently adopted by the Nevada legislature made it illegal to challenge another person to a duel, to accept a challenge, or to serve as a second. A judge apparently issued a warrant for the men's arrest, and the governor warned Twain to leave. If convicted, Twain and Gillis might have been sentenced to two years in prison. On the night of May 29, 1864, they boarded a stage for San Francisco, thus ending Twain's career in Nevada.[34]

Despite their editor's prediction, Twain—not De Quille—became the *Enterprise*'s most famous writer. After working as a printer, a riverboat pilot, and a prospector, Twain became a writer in Nevada. While working alongside other talented writers, Twain became an inventive storyteller, mastering the techniques that made him famous: the use of exaggeration, fantasy, humor, slapstick, and satire.

De Quille remained in Nevada, working for the *Enterprise* for thirty-one years, longer than any other employee. He witnessed the Comstock's great boom and subsequent decline, and described the exciting times in a book, *The Big Bonanza*. It may be the best book ever written about life in a mining camp, but was a financial failure. De Quille knew more about the Comstock than Twain, but lacked the skills needed to write a best-seller.[35]

As miners recovered the last of the region's silver, its big silver mills closed, and its boom towns began a rapid decline. Some towns disappeared, and only a few people remained in others. With most of its readers and advertisers gone, the *Enterprise* ceased publication on January 16, 1893.

De Quille wanted to remain on the Comstock until he died but was left without a job. He was old and sick but tried to eke out a living by writing for other publications. A Comstock millionaire learned about De Quille's plight and paid all his debts. The millionaire also hired a companion to accompany him back to his family in Iowa, and gave De Quille a weekly allowance for the rest of his life—the amount he had earned while writing for the *Enterprise*.

De Quille died in Iowa on March 16, 1898.[36] But each year since then, the stories that Twain and De Quille wrote in Nevada have continued to entertain, inform, and even fool thousands of new readers.

Journalism's Most
Successful Hoaxes

Seven of the media's hoaxes were extraordinarily successful. The hoaxes fooled thousands, even millions, of readers. Years after its creation, one of the hoaxes continues to fool some Americans, even respected scholars.

The hoaxes also demonstrate the media's power: their ability to frighten an entire city—and then to escape any responsibility for the harm they caused.

For years, the men who owned and edited the media seemed immune to criticism. They were too rich and powerful to punish. Moreover, most journalists insisted that they never intended to hurt anyone. Rather, they wanted to help the public. Some of their hoaxes exposed serious problems. They also included clues that revealed the details were fictitious. It was not their fault, journalists said, if some readers ignored the clues.

Why did the hoaxes fool so many people? Journalists were able to make the hoaxes more interesting than the truth. They selected familiar topics and filled their stories with hundreds of exciting details. People never imagined that all the details could be fictitious. Other journalists studied their topics and included details that, because they were accurate, made their entire stories seem accurate.

Most of the hoaxes continued for at least a day or two. A hundred years ago, newspapers were the only means of mass communication. There were no telephones, radio, or television. If a newspaper published a hoax, it was impossible for the authorities to immediately notify everyone in a city that the story was fictitious. Hoaxes that described the events occurring in distant countries continued even longer, for several weeks or even months.

Hoaxes published during the twentieth century reveal the public's continued gullibility. Some Americans seem to believe everything the media report. Some even verify the details. After seeing a hoax, people swear that they witnessed the events or possess evidence proving that the details are true. A few people continue to believe the hoaxes even after journalists admit that they are fictitious.

The nation's most successful hoax was published in 1835 and was typical of other successful hoaxes. The hoax described a scientific discovery in a distant country. Other editors denounced the hoax, but it seemed to help—not hurt—the newspaper that published it.

Another hoax started in London. It was a bloody tale that described six or seven deaths aboard a train in Georgia. Readers in London enjoyed the tale, perhaps because it portrayed Americans as their inferiors, as crude and violent savages. Several Englishmen said the story was obviously true. The Englishmen had traveled in the United States and explained that they were familiar with the manners, customs, and violence of the people living here.

Another hoax was more frightening. It was published in New York and reported that dozens of wild animals had escaped from the Central Park Zoo. The story described the animals fighting with one another and attacking residents of the city. The final paragraph admitted that the story was a hoax. But typically, some readers panicked before getting that far.

An editor in Chicago published America's

most horrifying hoax. His hoax also reflects the power of the press—its immunity to criticism. Wilbur Storey was a brilliant editor and transformed the *Chicago Times* into one of the most popular and powerful dailies in the Midwest. Unfortunately, Storey was also a sensationalist. Because of his wealth and power, no one was able to control or censor him. Thus Storey was free to do as he pleased, even to report that hundreds of people—his readers' friends and relatives—were dead, burned in a Chicago theater.

Four reporters created another hoax in Denver. But standards in the field of journalism were changing. The reporters never told their readers—or even their editors—that the story was a hoax. Instead, the reporters apparently discussed it among themselves and passed the details on to a few colleagues. While retelling the story, their colleagues embellished the hoax, so it improved with age. Forty years later, another writer exposed the hoax, then added that it caused a war in China.

The nation's most persistent hoax described the White House bathtub. A Baltimore journalist, H. L. Mencken, created the hoax in 1917 and became alarmed when other people reprinted it. Mencken confessed, at least three times, that it was a hoax, but Americans remember the hoax, not Mencken's retractions.

The media's last great hoax appeared in 1924. It reflects, even more clearly, changes occurring in the field of journalism. A young reporter created the hoax, and his own editors exposed it. The reporter was fired, and his editors published both a retraction and an apology.

Fooling the Masses: Astronomer Sees the Moon's "Bat-men"

N 1835, the *New York Sun* published the most famous — and most successful — hoax in the history of American journalism. The *Sun* reported that an astronomer, using a powerful new telescope, saw creatures living on the moon. The creatures had wings, and some looked like angels.

Readers considered it one of the most remarkable discoveries ever made. From dawn until midnight that entire week, thousands of people gathered outside the *Sun*'s office. Some wanted the *Sun* to publish more information about the "bat-men." Others wanted copies of the *Sun*'s earlier editions. Still others wanted to see illustrations that the *Sun* had mentioned but never published.

Why was the hoax so successful? It involved the right topic (an exotic one), and was published at the right time and place, in the nation's new "penny press" for the masses.

Until the 1830s, newspapers served the elite — the wealthy and well educated. Most newspapers cost six cents a copy and emphasized serious articles about business, politics, and foreign affairs. Because the newspapers were so expensive (and dull), they attracted only a few thousand readers.

A young printer named Benjamin Day came from a poor family and sensed the need for a newspaper that would serve the masses. When Day discussed the idea with friends, they laughed at him.

To appeal to the masses, newspapers would have to lower their prices and change their definitions of news. The papers would have to provide more entertaining stories for men who worked twelve to fourteen hours a day as clerks, laborers, and factory hands. Thus, editors began to publish stories about crime, sex, and sports. They also looked for humorous stories, anything likely to make their readers laugh. For the first time, editors began to emphasize local news, stories about the events occurring in their own communities. Gradually, over the next ten or twenty years, they also began to look for stories of interest to women.

Day started the revolution by publishing the first edition of the *New York Sun* on September 3, 1833. He charged a penny a copy and limited each edition to four pages. The pages measured only eight by eleven inches and contained two columns of type. The stories were short and often copied from other publications. In addition, Day reported the minor cases heard in a local court: cases of theft, assault, prostitution, and drunkenness.

Within four months the *Sun*'s circulation rose to five thousand, making it the largest newspaper in New York. In 1834 the paper's circulation doubled to ten thousand and in 1835 it tripled to fifteen thousand. Other editors noted its success and copied Day's techniques. In cities throughout the East, they established other "penny" or "popular" papers for the masses.

A reporter named Richard Adams Locke created the *Sun*'s "Moon Story." Locke was a bright, pleasant young man who was born in England and studied at Cambridge.[1] In 1832 he sailed to New York with his wife and infant daughter, and there he started work as a reporter for the *Courier and Enquirer.* Benjamin Day met Locke a short time later and offered him $12 a week to write for the *Sun.*

Locke was interested in astronomy and knew that some European astronomers believed that the moon was inhabited. One astronomer said he discovered great artificial works constructed on the moon. Another astronomer reported discovering fortifications—defenses against artillery and assaults—similar to those on Earth. A third astronomer said he found great roads, as direct and regular as the railroads on Earth.

While reading an old journal, Locke noticed an article written by a

Scots astronomer who wanted to communicate with the moon. The astronomer, Dr. Thomas Dick, wanted to erect huge geometric symbols on the plains of Siberia, symbols that would be visible to the moon's inhabitants. Dick suggested that the governments of Europe might use the resources wasted on warfare to erect a triangle several miles in length.

Dick also believed that the sins of man (not the forces of nature) caused earthquakes, volcanoes, hurricanes, and other violent disruptions on Earth. He had written several books about his ideas; thus, the public was already familiar with them.[2]

Locke thought the idea of communicating with the moon was nonsense. Yet many of the *Sun*'s readers apparently believed Dick and also believed that an astronomer might be able to see the moon and the men living on it.

Sometime that summer, Locke began writing a series of stories about the moon. To make it more believable, Locke attributed his "discoveries" to Sir John Herschel, an English astronomer who may have been as famous in 1835 as Albert Einstein is today. Sir John was the son of Sir William Herschel, the astronomer who discovered the planet Uranus.

Until 1833, all the world's leading astronomers and observatories were located north of the equator. Late that year, Sir John Herschel sailed to Cape Town in South Africa to establish an observatory and to study the Southern Hemisphere. The public was interested in Herschel's work, and news stories reported his arrival in Cape Town on January 15, 1834.

Locke's series about Herschel began with a brief paragraph, published on August 21, 1835, which announced that Herschel had made some amazing discoveries while using an immense new telescope at the Cape of Good Hope.[3]

The actual hoax appeared in six installments, and the *Sun* published the first installment four days later. On Tuesday, August 25, it filled three columns on the *Sun*'s front page. The first installment explained that Herschel had observed distinct objects on the moon, proving that it was inhabited. Herschel had sent a complete report to the Royal Society in England. His assistant, Dr. Andrew Grant, had written a separate report for the *Edinburgh Journal of Science*. The Edinburgh journal immediately published Dr. Grant's report in a special supplement, and a gentleman returning from Scotland gave a copy to the *Sun*.

The *Sun*'s first installment started slowly, even dully, with a description of Herschel's telescope, explaining that it was quoting the special supplement just delivered from Scotland:

GREAT ASTRONOMICAL DISCOVERIES
LATELY MADE
BY SIR JOHN HERSCHEL, L.L., D.F.R.S., & c.,
AT THE
CAPE OF GOOD HOPE

Herschel's father, Sir William, had used a telescope four feet in diameter and 40 feet in length, but the objects he observed became dimmer when they were highly magnified. Because of that problem, Sir William was able to magnify the moon and the planets in our solar system only 220 to 900 times. He tinkered with the telescope and managed to improve its ability to magnify distant objects but died before testing it. His son, Sir John, tested the telescope with nearly perfect success. Using the new system, Sir John was able to magnify the moon six thousand times and to see objects on its surface only twenty-two yards in diameter. However, smaller objects on the moon still appeared "as mere feeble, shapeless points." Sir John observed the general geography of the moon: its continents, mountains, and oceans. The best maps were based on his observations, and no one hoped for any great improvements. Astronomers, reported the *Sun,* had exhausted every law of vision.

Then Sir John proposed a wonderful new idea, the use of artificial light to help magnify distant objects. Money was the only problem. The construction of a new telescope was expected to cost £70,000. Herschel appealed to the Royal Society and to His Royal Highness the Duke of Sussex. Their response was immediate and favorable. The chairman of the Royal Society contributed £10,000 and appealed to the king for more. The king, a sailor, asked only one question: Would Herschel's new telescope improve navigation? Told that it would, the king gave Herschel all the money he wanted.

Herschel designed a new telescope twenty-four feet in diameter, six times the size of his father's. Using new materials, workmen cast the lens on January 3, 1833, then let it cool for eight days. When they opened the mold, the lens was flawed. Proceeding more carefully, the workmen cast a new lens on January 27, and it was almost perfect. The lens weighed 14,826 pounds and was capable of magnifying objects forty-two thousand times. Using the new lens and artificial light, Herschel could see objects only eighteen inches in diameter on the moon's surface. Other refinements added to the telescope's power. Thus, Herschel would be able to study even insects on the moon.

The *Sun*'s first installment ended here. Its second installment, published August 26, filled nearly four columns and described the first objects Herschel discovered on the moon.

Three countries—England, France, and Austria—wanted to improve the astronomical observations in the Southern Hemisphere, it began, and paid for Herschel's expedition to the Cape of Good Hope. Accompanied by Dr. Grant and a party of English workmen, Herschel reached the Cape in 1834 and used two teams of oxen to transport his equipment about thirty-five miles to the northeast.

His telescope was fully completed that December, and operations began during the first week in January of 1835. At the request of the British government, everything about the telescope's manufacture, destination, and success was kept a secret. So for months, the world heard nothing about Herschel and his expedition.

On the night of January 10, the *Sun* reported, the astronomers focused the whole immense power of the telescope upon the moon. They observed a greenish-brown rock and discovered that it was covered with a red flower similar to Earth's rose-poppy. It was the first evidence of life in a foreign world. Continuing their exploration, the astronomers found a forest with trees unlike any on Earth. They also observed a flat green plain, another forest, and a beach with brilliant white sand, and rocks of green marble.

Later that night, the astronomers discovered a valley about eighteen or twenty miles wide and thirty miles long. On one side, they observed "herds of brown quadrupeds" (four-legged animals) that resembled buffalo, but were smaller than those on Earth. The moon's quadrupeds had horns, a hump on their shoulders, and shaggy hair. Another of their features was more unusual: a hairy flap or veil that covered their eyes. Herschel speculated that the flap protected the quadrupeds' eyes from the great extremes of light and darkness on the moon.

The next animal they observed "would be classed on Earth as a monster." It was a bluish color, with a head and beard like a goat, and a single horn. The female of the species had no horn or beard, but a much longer tail. The valley also contained a large river with lovely islands and numerous kinds of birds.

Clouds on the lunar surface forced the astronomers to abandon their exploration of the area. They named it "the Valley of the Unicorn."

The *Sun*'s second installment ended here. It promised, however, that the next installments would contain even more interesting details about the moon.

Four more installments followed, each under the same headline: "GREAT ASTRONOMICAL DISCOVERIES." They reported that the nights of January 11 and 12 were cloudy, but on January 13 the astronomers discovered lunar animals likely to excite every human on Earth. While inspecting a mountainous region, the astronomers applied their "hydro-oxygen magnifier to the focal image of the great lens." Using the new equipment, they detected old volcanoes, including some that continued to spew heated gases into the moon's atmosphere. The surrounding countryside seemed fertile, and they counted twelve beautiful forests, separated by open plains: probably prairies like those of North America. They also found more buffalo "but of much larger size."

Dr. Herschel classified fourteen new species of animals, including "a small kind of rein-deer, the elk, the moose, the horned bear, and the biped beaver." The beaver was most unusual. It had no tail and walked upright on two feet. "It carries its young in its arms like a human being," Dr. Grant said, "and moves with an easy gliding motion. Its huts are constructed better and higher than those of many tribes of human savages, and from the appearance of smoke in nearly all of them, there is no doubt of its being acquainted with the use of fire."

Later that night, the astronomers discovered small volcanic islands. Two were still erupting, creating clouds of smoke and ash. On another island, fifty-five miles long, the astronomers saw a melon-tree loaded with fruit, and a palm-tree with crimson flowers. They also observed a striped animal, about three feet high (like a miniature zebra), and "two or three kinds of long-tailed birds, which we judged to be golden and blue pheasants."

Continuing their exploration, the astronomers observed a valley containing a narrow lake, seventy miles long. Magnifying the valley, they saw "long lines of some yellow metal hanging from the crevices" and concluded, of course, that it was gold. The astronomers also discovered more animals. The first had a head like a sheep, a body like a deer, an amazingly long neck, and two spiral horns as white as polished ivory. Moments later, Dr. Grant reported, "[t]hree specimens of another animal appeared, so well known to us all that we fairly laughed at the recognition of so familiar an acquaintance in so distant a land." The animals were sheep, as fine and large as any in England.

"We were thrilled with astonishment," Dr. Grant continued, "to perceive four successive flocks of large winged creatures, wholly unlike any kind of birds, descend with a slow even motion from the cliffs on the western side, and alight upon the plain." The creatures walked on two feet, were about four feet tall, and covered — except on their faces — with a copper-colored hair. Their faces appeared yellowish, and a thick beard covered their lower jaw. They seemed to be talking and gesturing with one another, and the astronomers concluded that they were intelligent beings, a species of bat-men.

More of the strange creatures appeared near a small lake. Their wings were semi-transparent and extended from their shoulders to their legs. While bathing in the lake, some spread their wings out to their full width, "waved them as ducks do theirs to shake off the water," then closed them again. The astronomers observed both males and females of the species and decided "they are doubtless innocent and happy creatures." But on Earth, their behavior would be considered highly improper.

The astronomers censored some of their observations about the bat-men. Dr. Grant explained that the creatures' behavior "led to results so very remarkable that I prefer they should first be laid before the public in Dr. Herschel's own words. . . . "

The *Sun* interrupted Dr. Grant's narrative at this point to report that it had obeyed his private request to omit certain details about the bat-men's behavior. Clearly, the astronomers were referring to the bat-men's sexual behavior. They never used the word "sex," but their frequent references to it seemed obvious — and certain to add to the public's interest in the story.

On January 14, the astronomers discovered three huge oceans, seven large seas, and so many lakes that no one could count them. The astronomers also discovered a volcano powerful enough to throw fragments beyond the moon's atmosphere. The volcano's presence on the moon seemed to explain the great number of huge meteors that fell to the Earth's surface.

Applying full power to another valley, the astronomers discovered a magnificent work of art: a temple built of polished sapphire. The temple was about three hundred feet in diameter and one hundred feet tall, with a roof that seemed to be made of gold. Yet the temple had no walls, seats, altars, or offerings. Later that night, the astronomers discovered two similar temples, but again failed to observe anyone using them. The temples were a mystery: beautiful but empty, perhaps evidence of some past calamity on the moon.

The astronomers also observed a species of bat-men larger than the earlier specimens, and lighter in color. Most were eating a large yellow fruit. The bat-men ate the fruit rather crudely, with their fingers, and threw away the rind. They appeared to nibble at the ends of a smaller red fruit, shaped like a cucumber, sucking its juices. Dr. Grant said the bat-men "seemed eminently happy, and even polite." Those sitting nearest the piles of fruit selected the largest and brightest pieces and threw them to their friends.

The astronomers never observed the bat-men engaged in any kind of work. "So far as we could judge," Dr. Grant said, "they spent their happy hours in collecting various fruits in the woods, in eating, flying, bathing, and loitering about. . . . " (At this point, the *Sun* deleted some additional observations about the bat-men's "improper"—or sexual—behavior.)

Several animals lived near the bat-men. "The most attractive of these was a tall white stag with lofty spreading antlers, black as ebony." The stag trotted up to the bat-men, and grazed close beside them, without the least sign of fear. That seemed to be common. All the creatures on the moon seemed to be at peace with one another. None were carnivorous or ferocious.

An accident the following day ended the astronomers' observations for nearly a week. The astronomers normally lowered Herschel's great lens each day, so it lay almost flat along the ground. The lens was left in an upright position and, shortly after sunrise the next morning, Herschel and his assistants were awakened by the shouts of Dutch farmers. Dr. Grant reported that, "Dr. Herschel leaped out of bed from his brief slumbers and, sure enough, saw his observatory enveloped in a cloud of smoke." The sun had burnt a hole 15 feet in circumference completely through the reflecting chamber. Workmen from Cape Town repaired the telescope in about a week, but the moon no longer was visible then.

The weather improved, and new lunar observations became possible during March. Dr. Herschel was busy with other matters, but his assistants continued their exploration of the moon. They discovered a very superior species of bat-men, about the same height, "but of infinitely greater personal beauty." Dr. Grant said the bat-men appeared to be almost as lovely as angels. However, he reported nothing else about them, insisting that Herschel himself should publish the first detailed description of the new species.

The *Sun* ended its series at this point: "This concludes the Supplement, with the exception of 40 pages of illustrative and mathematical notes. . . . "

The *Sun* published its first installment on August 25. Anticipating a huge demand, Day printed more newspapers than usual and sold every one — so "not a copy could be found at any price." The demand increased as the *Sun* published the following installments. The *Sun's* presses ran at full capacity, ten hours a day, but never were able to print enough copies.

Day published the most sensational installment on August 28, the one describing the bat-men. By then the *Sun* had become the largest newspaper in the world, with a circulation of 19,360. Its closest rival, the London *Times,* had a circulation of 17,000.

Because of the demand for copies, Locke found a printer able to republish the entire series, including several illustrations, in a pamphlet. Locke ordered sixty thousand copies and sold them all in a month. The demand continued, and new editions of *The Moon Hoax* appeared for more than twenty years.

Two of the people waiting outside the *Sun's* office confirmed the story's authenticity. An elderly but respectable gentleman said he owned a business in London and had seen the telescope's fourteen-thousand-pound lens being loaded aboard a ship. Another man, also "of perfectly respectable appearance," said he had obtained a copy of the astronomers' original report.[4]

The story's rich detail and scientific terminology also fooled other editors in New York. Several praised Herschel's discoveries and reprinted the entire series. The *Sun* responded that it was generally pleased with its rivals' comments, and it quoted the most complimentary of them.[5]

The series embarrassed New York's older six-cent newspapers, which were reluctant to admit that a smaller penny paper had beaten them to such an important story. Some six-cent papers copied the "Moon Story" without giving any credit to the *Sun*. Others attributed the story to a "cheap paper" or to "a small morning paper" — anything to avoid mentioning the *Sun*.[6] A few rivals claimed that they obtained their own copy of the supplement to the *Edinburgh Journal of Science,* and that they reprinted their stories directly from it.

The editor of another New York daily, the *Herald,* immediately realized that the "Moon Story" was a hoax. Its editor also guessed that Locke had written it. He remembered that Locke had talked to him about optics and other unusual ideas mentioned in the story. Thus, the *Herald* immediately accused the *Sun* of publishing a hoax and of swindling the public. Without actually denying the charges, Locke responded that it was silly to imagine that two editors would meet to discuss optics.

Some readers thought the *Sun*'s rivals were simply jealous of its success. Moreover, those rivals were unable to prove that the series was fictitious. They pointed out some minor errors and inconsistencies, but none could sail to South Africa and question Herschel. In 1835, the round trip would have taken months.

Interest in the "Moon Story" spread around the world. Herschel had not observed any starvation on the moon, or any riots, poverty, or strikes. Nevertheless, philanthropists in England appointed a committee to determine whether the bat-men needed help. Similarly, a women's club in Springfield, Massachusetts, wanted to raise money to send missionaries to the moon.[7]

Even scientists at Yale University were fooled by the story. A delegation from Yale went to the *Sun*'s office in New York and asked Locke for permission to see the original supplement from the *Journal of Science,* including its mathematical formulas and footnotes. Locke responded that a printing office across the street was setting the original in type for a pamphlet. When the scientists went there, they were referred to another printing office, one much farther away. When the scientists went there, they found that its foreman had disappeared. By then, it was time for the scientists to board a train returning to Yale.

Other scientists apparently realized that the "Moon Story" was nonsense. They knew that no telescope built in 1835 could see small objects on the moon. They also knew that the moon had no water or air. Without them, there could be no life. Moreover, Herschel's discoveries seemed preposterous. Many fulfilled man's fantasies on Earth, especially the discovery of gold, angels, and unicorns.

Routinely, a few copies of the *Sun* were mailed to subscribers in Europe. In addition, the *Sun* reprinted the "Moon Story" in a pamphlet and sent copies to all the leading newspapers in Europe—without identifying its source.[8] A few weeks later, readers in the United States began to receive copies of the European papers. Instead of exposing Herschel's discoveries, the European papers seemed to confirm them. The European papers reprinted the story as fact, without even mentioning the *Sun.*

After being published in England and France, the details spread through Italy, Germany, Switzerland, Spain, and Portugal. Years later, some Europeans continued to insist that the details were true. Thus, the *Sun's* "Moon Story" amused, delighted, and deceived "almost the whole reading world."[9]

Few readers noticed an error that Locke made while writing the story. He said the story appeared in a supplement to the *Edinburgh Journal of Science,* yet that journal had ceased publication years earlier. It was replaced by the *Edinburgh New Philosophical Journal,* and Locke probably meant to quote it.[10] The "Moon Story" also contained several other minor errors and inconsistencies, perhaps because Locke was forced to write it too quickly. The *Sun* began to publish the first installments before Locke finished writing the last installments. As a result, he was forced to finish the series quickly, amid all the other work—the distractions and interruptions—that arise in newsrooms everywhere.

To help a friend, Locke confessed that the story was a hoax. A reporter named "Finn" had worked for the *Sun,* then joined the staff of another New York daily, the *Journal of Commerce.* Because of the public's interest in the "Moon Story," Finn's editors at the *Journal of Commerce* decided to reprint the entire series, and they asked him to obtain copies of it. Finn happened to meet Locke and told him that the *Journal of Commerce* was setting the story in type and might reprint it the next day.

"Don't print it right away," Locke warned him. "I wrote it myself."[11] Instead of thanking Locke, Finn exposed him. The next day, the *Journal of Commerce* denounced the hoax.

In mid-September, even the *Sun* admitted that its story was a hoax. But instead of apologizing for it, the *Sun* boasted that its story had amused the public and fooled the experts.

Most readers seemed to accept the hoax in good nature.[12] They were amused, not angry. But some refused to believe that Locke had written it. They suspected a French astronomer, Jean Nicolas Nicollet.[13] Nicollet's observations of the moon were famous, and he had come to America in 1830. Thus, some readers were certain that Nicollet had written the "Moon Story," or that he had at least helped Locke write it. In fact, Locke did not need any help. He had already written some science fiction and "devoted very many years of his life to mathematical and astronomical studies. . . . "[14]

Other readers suspected Edgar Allan Poe.[15] By coincidence, Poe was writing a similar story, his "Unparalleled Adventures Of One Hans Pfaall." A magazine had just published the first installment of Poe's story and, because the stories were so similar, some readers assumed that Poe had written both of them.

Poe realized that Locke's story was a hoax, but was unable to convince anyone else that it was. He complained that not one person in ten questioned Locke's story. Instead, people seemed eager to be deceived by it. Even a professor of mathematics at a Virginia college assured Poe that the story was almost certainly true. Poe then pointed out the story's most obvious errors—errors that he felt an alert reader should notice:

The bat-men could not fly on the moon because the moon had no air.

The moon could not have any oceans, seas, rivers, or lakes because the temperature on the moon was higher than the boiling point of water.

Herschel described the bat-men's bodies. But from Earth, he would be able to see only the top of their heads.

The "Moon Story" stated that the Earth is thirteen times larger than the moon. In fact, it is forty-nine times larger, and no competent astronomer would make that error.

Herschel's telescope supposedly magnified objects 42,000 times. Yet even a telescope that powerful could not reveal small objects on the moon.

The "Moon Story" claimed that Herschel used artificial light to improve his telescope's magnifying power. The idea was nonsense. It could not possibly work.

Herschel described the moon's geographical features, but his description was inconsistent. Moreover, it contradicted existing charts of the moon.

Herschel's description of the bat-men was copied from another article.[16]

Locke left his job at the *New York Sun* in the fall of 1836. On October 6, he helped establish another penny paper, the *New Era*. To increase its circulation, Locke wrote a new hoax, "The Lost Manuscript of Mungo Park." The hoax described the adventures of a Scottish explorer in Africa, but failed. By 1836, readers knew that Locke had written the moon hoax. They also knew that he edited the *New Era*, and immediately suspected that "The Lost Manuscript of Mungo Park" was another of his hoaxes. As a result, Locke never finished it.

In 1837, Benjamin Day sold the *Sun* to his wife's brother. Some time later, Day admitted that it was the "silliest thing I ever did." The *Sun* had stopped earning a profit because of a financial panic in 1837. In addition, Day had lost a libel suit, and other penny papers were failing. Fearing that the *Sun* might also fail, Day sold it for $40,000. Despite Day's pessimism, it prospered. It eventually merged with two other papers, becoming part of the *World-Telegram and Sun*. The new paper continued publication until 1967 — 134 years after Day published the first edition of his new penny paper for the masses.

In South Africa, Sir John Herschel continued his observations of the Southern Hemisphere, unaware of the series and the commotion it caused. Months later, an American named Caleb Weeks informed him about the hoax. Weeks, a resident of Long Island, traveled to Cape Town to obtain some giraffes and other rare animals for a zoo. He met Herschel at a Cape Town hotel and handed him copies of the New York papers. After reading the papers, Herschel reportedly laughed, then asked for more information about the story. Herschel seemed astonished and amused—but feared that his real discoveries in the Southern Hemisphere would be less interesting to the public than the discoveries that Locke attributed to him.[17]

Why did Day publish the hoax? Clearly, he expected it to increase the *Sun*'s circulation. The hoax also must have seemed like fun—and helped him outwit the city's older six-cent papers. After they copied the story, Day was able to expose and embarrass them.

Why did the hoax fool so many readers? Because it was the nation's first great hoax, readers were unprepared for it. Until then, they believed the stories published by New York's new penny papers. It was also a clever story and involved a topic—life on the moon—that interested most readers. Famous astronomers had already speculated about life on the moon, thus preparing the readers for the news of Herschel's discovery. Locke's references to Herschel and inclusion of other facts that were accurate also helped make his entire story—even his most fantastic details—more believable.[18]

The story's source, a respected scientific journal, added to its credibility. Wisely, Locke reported that the series appeared in a special supplement to the *Journal of Science*. As a supplement, it would be more difficult to find and expose as a fake. Locke also used an academic-sounding language appropriate for a scientific journal and started slowly, with a detailed description of Herschel's telescope. Most readers, perhaps even most scientists, were unable to understand all the technical malarkey. It was too complicated and boring. Nevertheless, it impressed them.

Finally, the workingmen who bought the *New York Sun* were especially gullible. Most were poorly educated, recent immigrants with a limited knowledge of English. They lived during an era of exploration and invention, and they depended upon newspapers to inform them about all the new discoveries, including discoveries in the field of astronomy. And when fantasy supplanted fact, they swallowed it whole.

Reinforcing a Stereotype: Railways and Revolvers in Georgia

EWSPAPERS in Europe often published stories critical of the United States, stories that portrayed Americans as uneducated and uncivilized ruffians. After reading the stories, Europeans began to think of Americans as barbarians (half horse and half alligator), who shot and killed their enemies, cooked them for dinner, and used bowie knives to pick the bones from their teeth.

In 1856, for example, the London *Times* reported that twenty-five passengers boarded a train in Macon, Georgia. During a 10½-hour trip to Augusta, the passengers supposedly fought five duels. Two passengers arranged a sixth duel, but one was killed before they were able to fight it. Two other passengers may have fought a seventh duel, but the train moved on before the results became known. There was also a murder. A child was killed because he cried too loudly.

Why did the *Times* publish the hoax? It was submitted by an apparently trustworthy source: an English gentleman. The gentleman had no motive for lying, and his story was well written, colorful, and dramatic. In addition, it would appeal to the paper's readers, confirming their sense of superiority.

If, by chance, the gentleman was mistaken, the *Times* was unlikely to suffer any harm. Readers in England would be inclined to believe the gentleman, not Americans' angry denials. Moreover, it would be difficult for anyone to prove that the deaths had never occurred in a country as large and distant as the United States. Even if someone was able to prove that the story was a lie, the only people likely to be upset by it were Americans, not the paper's regular readers or advertisers.

The *Times* was England's most respected paper, and editors throughout the United States depended upon it. They subscribed to it and reprinted its most newsworthy stories. Editors throughout the United States also noticed and reprinted its story about the Georgia railroad. Thus people everywhere began to read and talk about it.

The *Times* titled its story "Railways and Revolvers in Georgia." The story was submitted by a reader who wished to remain anonymous and who told the paper that he had boarded a train in Macon at 5 p.m. on August 28 of that year. The train was bound for Augusta, he said, and there were two cars. The first car carried the mail and luggage, with a few seats for smokers. The second car was for passengers—about twenty-five people, including three women. One of the women was elderly and traveling alone; during the entire trip, she never stirred or spoke. The other women were well dressed and respectable looking. One appeared to be about twenty, and the other about thirty. They came in together, accompanied by a well-dressed man whom the narrator called "A." The women sat immediately behind the narrator, and "A" sat alongside him. Because they were so close, the narrator overheard everything they said.

A second man, whom the narrator called "B," entered the car a few minutes later and said a few words to the women. "B" then took a seat two benches ahead of the narrator, but turned the seat around so that he sat facing the women and their companion. A tall, muscular man, about fifty, sat between them. The narrator called this man "C."

Even before the train left Macon, the women's conversation revealed that they expected trouble. Nothing occurred, however, until after their departure. When the conductor came into their car to collect the tickets, "B" said in a loud voice, so everyone in the car heard him, "Tell those two ladies that I have their tickets in my pocket."

The muscular man called "C" asked "B" about the matter and learned that he was a Frenchman, a barber and hairdresser with a shop in Macon. Both "A" and "B" had been seeing the youngest woman, and she flirted with both of them. The woman encouraged "A," but later turned to "B," who seemed to be richer and more generous with his money. "A" had proposed this pleasure trip, but the woman decided to go with "B" instead. Now "A" was determined to ruin the trip.

After "B" explained the situation, "C" asked whether he intended to fight. If so, he ought to send "A" a challenge. "B" responded that he had already done so, but "A" failed to respond. "C" then questioned "A" and learned that he refused the challenge because "B" wanted to fight with swords, and he was wholly unacquainted with the weapon. "A" was willing to fight with some other weapon and agreed to let "C" help them select it. "C" quickly arranged the affair so both "A" and "B" agreed to fight with pistols. Having also learned that other passengers in the car were carrying several weapons, "C" proposed that "A" and "B" should fight it out at once. He would ask the conductor to stop the train at a convenient place. Neither of the men, however, would listen. They wanted to fight after their arrival in Augusta the next morning.

Other passengers began to talk about duels. One of the passengers, a white-haired gentleman past sixty, accused another of being ignorant about the matter. The white-haired gentleman insisted that his opponent had never seen a duel and would be afraid to fight one. The other passenger, a respectable-looking man about forty-five, rose up and challenged the old man to follow him out of the car. The old man told his son—a fine little boy, about six—to wait until he returned. He followed the middle-aged man into the smoking car. After the preliminaries were arranged, the train was stopped. The men descended and the cars moved on, leaving them behind. The other passengers learned on the way—by telegraph—that the old man had been killed.

The conversations and debates among the other passengers continued as loudly as ever. Another man issued a challenge, but his opponent seemed reluctant to accept it. He demanded proof that the man who challenged him was a respectable gentleman. The challenger responded that, if his opponent refused to fight, he would whip him whenever he got off the train. Sometime afterward, his opponent left the car, and the challenger went after him. Other passengers heard their loud voices, their oaths and curses, but no firearms. No one ever learned the outcome of this encounter.

"C" continued to insist that "A" and "B" should settle their differences at once. They again refused, and "C" treated "B" so contemptuously that "B" began to quarrel with him, then challenged him.

By then, "C" had been joined in the car by a friend, a man much younger, taller, and stouter than himself. Due to the challenge, the train was stopped. "B" and his second, and "C" and his friend, got out. This time the conductor waited the result. "B" was killed.

When "C" returned to the passenger car, he offered "B's" father a chance to avenge his son's death, but the old man declined. "C" then addressed all the other passengers. He insisted that his actions were justified, and he praised the honorable institution of dueling. "C" ended his speech by blaming the young woman for the bloodshed. "C" said that he had never seen her before, did not know her, and did not want to know her. Her conduct showed that she was no better than a common prostitute. He offered to fight anyone who cared to defend her, then stepped into the smoking car.

Even before "C" left, the woman said she wanted him killed. She turned to "B's" father for help, and he responded that it would be certain death. Nevertheless, he agreed to defend her. "C" refused the father's challenge, saying that he was a coward since he refused to fight for a better cause—the death of his own son.

The young woman then appealed to all the other passengers. Her companion, the woman about thirty, begged her to stop. Because she would not, her companion got out at the next stop and returned to her home in Savannah.

Shortly after this, the train arrived at a station and nearly all the passengers got out for refreshments. Before the train started again, a young man who had been seated in the smoking car entered the passenger car and recognized the young woman. She told the young man of "C's" insults, and he at once offered to defend her. After the train was underway, the young man stepped into the smoking car and speedily arranged his duel with "C." Because the train was already behind schedule, the conductor refused to stop. The two men therefore agreed to fight in the smoking car. They used noiseless pistols, so the other passengers heard nothing but the young man's death cry.

At about this time, the little boy awoke. He was the son of the first man to be killed, and the young woman informed him of his father's death. She then pointed out "C" as the man who shot his father. The little boy burst into tears. In the midst of them, he began to call "C" a murderer. Angered by the boy's cries, "C" sent his friend to quiet him. The friend explained that "C" had nothing to do with his father's death, and that the woman was responsible for it. The child either did not understand or did not believe him, for he began to cry even more loudly than before. "C's" friend carried the boy outside to the car's platform and threatened to throw him off. Other passengers thought that "C's" friend was simply trying to frighten the boy, but the woman could see that he was serious, for the boy would not stop crying.

A tall, middle-aged gentleman, who until that moment had remained silent, rose up. Throwing off his cloak, the gentleman stepped out to the platform and persuaded "C's" friend to give him the boy. He then brought the boy back into the car and returned him to the woman. For a short time, the boy remained silent. When his cries resumed, "C's" friend threw him off the train.

Stunned by the boy's sudden death and the sound of his body falling from the train, the narrator lost consciousness for perhaps ten minutes. When his head cleared, he found that the train had stopped. Other passengers explained that "B's" father and the tall, middle-aged gentleman had gone out to fight "C" and his friend. The conductor stopped the train and was waiting the result. "C" and his companion came back. The others were killed.

As soon as "C" stepped back inside, the conductor started the train. "C's" friend was a little ways behind, and the train went off so rapidly that he was unable to catch up with it. However, he was so near that the narrator was able to hear his footsteps. The conductor paid no attention to the man's cries, but "C" rushed forward to stop the engine. To prevent further bloodshed, the conductor and his men stopped "C" and locked him up. About half an hour later, the train reached Augusta. The narrator never learned any of the men's names, nor those of the other passengers. "This is not surprising," he said, "for family names are seldom used when traveling in that country." The narrator added that he never learned what happened to "C" and his friend because the newspapers in Georgia never published any stories about the violence. However, he doubted that the men were brought to justice. The narrator explained that such incidents were common in Georgia. Scarcely a week passed without some fatal incident on the Georgia railroad.[1]

The *Times* admitted that its readers would be horrified by the story, for it seemed to be true.[2] The paper explained that it had investigated the narrator's background and published his letter only after learning that he was a respectable gentleman.

The *Times* calculated that, of the twenty-five passengers aboard the train, fifteen became involved in the drama. Twelve participated in the duels, and six were killed. Three others were left on the way. The train stopped so four of the duels could be fought at convenient spots along the way. Another duel was fought in the luggage car while the train was in motion. Of the six victims, two were fathers, and two were their sons. One father was killed while avenging his son's death, and one child was killed while mourning his father's death. Thus, twenty-five percent of the passengers were killed in 10½ hours. If the trip had continued for forty-eight hours, only one of the passengers would have reached Augusta alive.

The *Times* thought the slaughter reflected badly on the United States. Nobody was brought to justice. Indeed, there seemed to be no thought of law or investigation. Rather, the slaughter seemed typical of the way people in Georgia lived and died.

If the duels continued, the *Times* said, railroads in America would have to make suitable arrangements for their passengers. The railroads might provide pistol stands at all their stations. In case some wounds were not immediately fatal, they might also provide surgeons at every station, or the railroads might mark every second or third stop on their schedules as a "Shooting Station." They might also provide shooting cars, with facilities to carry the corpses. Because some passengers would die before presenting their tickets, conductors would have to change their methods for collecting them. The *Times* suggested that conductors might search all the passengers who were slain, or the victors might be held responsible for the tickets of rivals they shot.

The *Times* also contemplated the political issue of whether any government should attempt to limit this drain on its population. The paper feared that the violence would be impossible to control, just as it was impossible to control drinking, swearing, and other manly amusements. But for obvious reasons, the evil would eventually have to end. If everyone in America killed a man, or—like "C"—killed three men, the population would soon be depleted.

The story infuriated Americans living in Europe. A Southerner who signed only his initials, H.C.W., called the story "a miserable hoax."[3] In a letter published on October 18, the Southerner said he expected a newspaper as good as the *Times* to immediately expose so monstrous a fabrication. He was astonished, therefore, to find that the paper said the story must be true because it came from a respectable gentleman.

H.C.W. added that his feelings had often been hurt since his arrival in England. People there seemed to believe every lie invented about the

South. In this case, the narrator presented a tale so full of improbability and monstrous atrocities, all occurring in rapid succession, that it became ludicrous, an outrageous falsity.

H.C.W. feared that casual readers might fail to notice the story's numerous flaws and discrepancies. The narrator claimed that six men and a young child were murdered, yet it was absurd to think that anyone would ride a train if such events were allowed to occur. Few passengers would reach their destinations alive.

H.C.W. added that the conductor in charge of a train possessed the same power as the captain of a ship. Besides the conductor, the train must have also had a fireman, several brakemen, and a mail or luggage agent. Before matters got out of hand, it would have been easy for the conductor to obtain their help and eject the young woman and the men fighting over her, or the conductor might have taken the mail, quietly disengaged the engine, and left the passenger cars at the next station.

H.C.W. also questioned the story's other details, especially

The number of guns — all primed and ready for their bloody work — found among such a small number of people.

The narrator's claim that the events had occurred on the night of August 28. Almanacs showed that the moon that night must have been old, faint, and late. Thus the duelists must have been splendid marksmen to shoot so accurately in the dark.

The narrator's failure to use any names, as if people living in the South did not use or even need any names.

The fact that no one sought justice or cried out for revenge. Even the victims' relatives remained silent.

If the story were true, H.C.W. wondered, why had the narrator withheld it for so long? Also, why had he given it to a newspaper so far from the scene of the crime? H.C.W. speculated that the narrator might be a Northerner who invented the tale to influence that year's presidential elections, or he might have invented the tale to fool the English, to satisfy their taste for blood.

H.C.W. said he might have believed the story if the violence had occurred in Kansas. Ruffians from all parts of the United States had gathered in Kansas, and lawlessness had become common there. H.C.W. did not believe that such violence could occur in Georgia. Therefore, he wanted the narrator to substantiate his claims and to explain why he and the other witnesses failed to notify the proper authorities.

A similar letter, signed "A New-Englander," insisted that the narrator had an obligation to identify himself while denouncing a series of such disgraceful crimes.

It was difficult, the New-Englander admitted, to prove a negative, to prove that an event had not occurred. But a gentleman in London at that moment had spent September 1 in Macon and arrived in Augusta on the evening of September 2. Thus he had passed over the very scene of these horrors only four days after they supposedly occurred. The survivors and witnesses were bound for Augusta, and the gentleman now in London remained there until September 6. Yet he never heard the faintest rumor of any such slaughter. It was impossible to believe that the residents of Augusta would fail to talk about a series of such exciting events, especially since they occurred in front of so many witnesses.

The New-Englander added that Georgia was not a new state, but one of the original thirteen. It was always conservative, with higher social, political, and moral standards than its neighbors. Besides all this, several of its chief towns (Augusta, in particular) were largely inhabited by emigrants from the North. Thus, criminals were likely to be brought to justice in Georgia, and especially in Augusta.

The New-Englander also revealed that railroad timetables failed to show any trains leaving Macon at 5 p.m. Moreover, the narrator said that a woman had left his train to return to Savannah. Yet the narrator's train was already on the main line to Savannah. To get to Savannah, the woman should have remained in her seat. The passengers traveling to Augusta left the main line at Millen, a substation on the route.

The New-Englander added that the train's crew was unlikely to permit a duel in the smoking car. If the doors between the two cars were left open, a stray bullet might strike another passenger. Yet if the doors were closed, passengers in the second car could not have heard the young man's death cry.

It also seemed absurd to think that anyone could fire a pistol with deadly aim while a train was in motion. Moreover, one of the participants in every duel was killed and his opponent uninjured. There were no wounds. It was all "as clean and complete as in a play or a tale of fiction." Similarly, the entire story occurred within two railroad cars, yet the participants' fathers and friends appeared as suddenly and mysteriously as if through trapdoors.[4]

On October 24, the narrator identified himself as John Arrowsmith of Liverpool. In a second letter to the *Times*, Arrowsmith revealed that he was an Englishman and had traveled to Louisiana in 1828, when he was still a youth. He had lived in Louisiana since then, but never became a U.S. citizen or voted in any election. He had married a native of Louisiana, however, and she dearly loved her country. So while writing the narrative, he was not motivated by any political considerations, especially not by any that favored the North. He had no motive for harming the reputation of the United States, the South, or Georgia.

Arrowsmith said his motives were pure. He wrote the narrative to expose the crimes. Acquaintances in Liverpool insisted that he had a duty to do so. The delay in his narrative's publication was "one of necessity." Similarly, he had not revealed his identity while writing the narrative because he feared he might be in some danger.

Arrowsmith then answered his critics. He said the New-Englander's railroad guides might fail to show any trains leaving Macon at 5 p.m. because train schedules throughout the United States had recently changed. Arrowsmith added that a woman had left his railroad car to return to Savannah. She lived in Savannah and could not get there in his car. But how she got to Savannah seemed unimportant. Other discrepancies may have arisen because he was unable to mention every detail. If he had, his narrative would have become too long.[5]

Even another newspaper in London questioned Arrowsmith's story. The *Examiner* noticed that Arrowsmith called himself "An Eye-witness" but seemed unable to answer every question that his critics asked. The *Examiner* insisted that it was not challenging Arrowsmith's honesty; rather, it suspected that, as a young and inexperienced foreigner in America, Arrowsmith may have been the victim of a hoax. Whenever two passengers left his railway car, someone may have told him that it was to fight a duel. If only one returned, he may have believed that the other was killed.

The *Examiner* added that, if Arrowsmith had witnessed the duels as he said, they must have taken place at night, in the dark, or by candle or torchlight. The paper also wondered how Arrowsmith had managed to hear a child's body falling off a moving train.[6]

The *New York Times* reprinted Arrowsmith's story, then commented that any sane reader would realize at once that it was a hoax.[7] A few days later, it denounced Arrowsmith's second letter. At first, the paper had suspected that there was no such person as Arrowsmith. The whole affair might be a hoax invented by some American, or perhaps some Englishman might have been fooled while riding a train in the South. But now Arrowsmith had identified himself, and his second letter revealed that he had lived in Louisiana for twenty years. In twenty years, the paper said, he must have become familiar with the region, with its humor and railroads, so that he could not be fooled "by such a bundle of cock-and-bull stories."

The paper had also uncovered some details about Arrowsmith's life in New Orleans. "There was such a gentleman in that city some 10 or 12 years ago," it said, "working in the cotton trade, as the broker or agent or speculator for certain English and Scotch concerns. . . . " The gentleman had made a costly error, speculating that the price of cotton would rise. The *New York Times* feared that, if Arrowsmith was not crazy at the time, "he has since qualified himself for the Lunatic Asylum."[8]

A newspaper in New Orleans, the *Daily Picayune,* found that Arrowsmith had lived there so quietly for twenty-eight years that scarcely a soul seemed to know him, except for those in the cotton trade. But now, in a day, he had become famous throughout Europe and America.[9]

The *Picayune* said Arrowsmith did not seem to be guilty of creating a deliberate hoax, of inventing gross falsehoods for malicious purposes. Instead, he seemed to be the victim of some hallucination. The paper speculated that Arrowsmith may have suffered a fit of delirium tremens. Men often experienced the delirium after drinking too much. When the men recovered, they thought their drunken fantasies were sober facts.

In London, the New-Englander agreed that Arrowsmith's second letter to the *Times* was weak. Arrowsmith said he was trying to prove his story's truthfulness, but seemed to present "a very lukewarm bit of argument in support of some very minor items of his original statement."

The New-Englander had obtained railroad schedules for the months of both August and September and said that neither schedule showed any trains leaving Macon at 5 p.m. Besides that, a single line of rails served as a main artery for the entire South. If one train traveling over that line failed to reach a station at the proper time, it would cause a serious danger of collision and delay all the other trains, moving in both directions, throughout the district.

The New-Englander also questioned Arrowsmith's total ignorance of the participants' names. Arrowsmith said people in the South did not use their last names while traveling. But did that make sense? Would men engage in long, angry debates without ever using one another's names? Would they engage in duels without ever asking whom they were fighting? Could anyone announce the results without identifying the victims by name?

The New-Englander wanted Arrowsmith to explain why he kept the story a secret for so long and why his secrecy was "a matter of necessity." If Arrowsmith wanted to accomplish some good, the New-Englander said, he should have published his story in Augusta, or, he should have given his story to the newspapers or authorities in New York. Surely, he would not have been in any danger there.[10]

The president of the Georgia railroad, John P. King, called Arrowsmith's story an insulting fabrication.[11] In an angry letter to the *Times,* King insisted that the laws against it were so severe that no one in Georgia had fought a duel in twenty years. King added that not a single traveler had ever been killed, or even seriously injured, while riding a passenger train in Georgia, not by a duel or any other cause.

Despite the story's obvious falsity, King feared that the ignorant and down-trodden masses in Europe might believe it. He was also upset by the story's portrayal of women in Georgia. King said he had spent some time in London and could say, truthfully, that the women in Georgia were more modest and refined than any in Europe.

Finally, King wondered whether the *Times* expected England to benefit from its frequent publication of stories likely to cause ill will between the two nations. Or was the paper trying to encourage the United States to split into two separate nations? If not, King asked, why did it seize every opportunity to encourage such a catastrophe?

The *Times* responded that Arrowsmith's letter was more credible than King's. It admitted that Georgia's laws against dueling might be severe. It doubted, however, that Georgia enforced its laws.

Much of the track between Macon and Augusta was controlled by a second company, the Central Railroad of Georgia. Its president, R. R. Cuyler, also denied every detail in Arrowsmith's story.[12] Moreover, Cuyler's letter to the *Times* was transmitted by the British consul for the state of Georgia. The British consul lived in Savannah, had known Cuyler for nearly thirty years, and swore that he was "a gentleman of undoubted veracity."[13]

Other newspapers, including the *New York Times,* reprinted Cuyler's letter.[14] The *New York Times* praised the letter but also explained why Arrowsmith's story had fooled the London *Times.* Soon after Arrowsmith's story reached New York, three representatives from the London paper also arrived there: Mr. Delane, its editor; Mr. Fillmore, its special American correspondent; and Mr. Davis, its regular New York correspondent. The *New York Times* reported that all three men considered Arrowsmith's story a stupendous hoax. Thus the story would never have been published if Delane had remained in London, or if the editor left in charge of the London *Times* had been a clear-headed man of common sense.[15]

The *New York Times* added that the London paper might be excused for its original error, gross as it was, but that there was no excuse for its actions since then. Arrowsmith's story had been exposed as a hoax, and the *Times* was making itself utterly ridiculous by continuing to insist that it was true.

On December 11, the London *Times* admitted that it was mistaken. The letters from R. R. Cuyler and the English consul in Georgia had convinced it that Arrowsmith's story was a hoax. The paper concluded that, unless Arrowsmith could provide some fresh and overpowering evidence, "his case has broken down."[16]

Arrowsmith's motives, however, remained a mystery. The *Times* could not believe that Arrowsmith had deliberately invented such a parcel of falsehoods. It seemed too obvious that they would be exposed. Moreover, Arrowsmith had nothing to gain from them. It was difficult to imagine that he hated the state of Georgia, or that he wanted revenge against a railroad. "His only hope," the *Times* said, "could be to raise a foolish laugh for a month." Then, for the rest of his life, he would be branded as a liar or fool.

There was also the hypothesis of insanity. The *Times*, however, was inclined to be charitable. It concluded that Arrowsmith had been the victim of a hoax. But now, whatever the truth, Arrowsmith should respond. For his own sake, he should explain how he had been fooled, or he should confess that he had lied.

The *Times* also revealed more about its own role in the matter. Its editors had read Arrowsmith's first letter with amazement. It was a wild story, but filled with such specific details that they decided to communicate at once with Liverpool to learn more about the man who wrote it. To their surprise, men of the highest standing in Liverpool responded that Arrowsmith was a truthful and honorable man. Under these circumstances, the *Times* decided to publish his letter. The paper insisted that its own reputation was not at stake. If Arrowsmith's story were true, it ought to be made public. If it were false, it would be exposed as a hoax.

In that case, Arrowsmith—not the *Times*—would be the target of ridicule.

That seemed unlikely, however. Here was a gentleman who had come forward deliberately. He was under no pressure to do so. He had put together the narrative at his leisure and sent it to a newspaper for publication. Inquiries had shown that he was a man of good character. There was no reason to believe he had concocted a parcel of ridiculous falsehoods.

On December 13, the London *Times* published a third letter from Arrowsmith. Arrowsmith said he had tried to ignore the numerous contradictions and criticisms of his story, but friends thought his silence was an admission of guilt. Therefore, he wanted to again insist that the whole of his narrative was substantially true.[17]

The *Times* responded that Arrowsmith had "come forward handsomely," boldly adhering to his story. The paper still doubted his story, but was utterly unable to explain whether he was the victim of a hoax or the victim of a hallucination. It was no longer enough for Arrowsmith to merely reaffirm his story, it said. If he wanted people to believe it, he would have to provide more concrete evidence of its truthfulness.[18]

In the United States, the *New York Times* noted that Arrowsmith had reiterated his story, but seemed to do so reluctantly, and in a subdued tone—perhaps because he realized that few people still believed him. The paper then offered to pay all of Arrowsmith's expenses if he would return to the United States and prove that his story was true.[19]

Many readers in England continued to believe Arrowsmith's story, especially readers who had traveled in the United States. A letter mailed from Liverpool explained that Arrowsmith's "circumstantial and affirmative evidence outweighs the negative."[20] The letter was signed "Fairplay," and its author said that he had read the letter written by the president of an American railroad and noticed that he was not aboard the train. Fairplay suggested that the railroad's president would not hear about the duels, even if they did occur, because his employees would want to keep them a secret.

A second Englishman agreed, without hesitation, that Arrowsmith's story was probably true. The Englishman explained that he had lived in the United States for several years and was familiar with the character and manners of the people there. Moreover, he doubted that a person of Arrowsmith's character would invent such a tissue of falsehoods. Thus, the burden of proof lay not with Arrowsmith, but with the railroad. Its managers could easily obtain the statements of its conductors and engineers. They could also find many of the passengers, since most lived in the small towns along its route.[21]

A third correspondent, "T.S.," said that if the Americans simply questioned Arrowsmith's story he might not argue with them. But to say that Arrowsmith's story was impossible — that several duels could never occur aboard a railway car — was too much for someone who had visited the United States to believe.

T.S. added that a gentleman of Arrowsmith's character had no motive for lying. Also, it would not be surprising — even in England — to hear of a series of fights, all arising out of one quarrel in which a loose woman was mixed up. The only difference was that, in England, the fights were settled with fists or clubs. In the United States, they were settled with revolvers.[22]

On February 18, R. R. Cuyler, president of the Central Railroad of Georgia, submitted the proof that readers in England demanded.[23] Cuyler said he had received copies of the *Times* and realized that many of its readers — especially Arrowsmith's colleagues in Liverpool — required further proof that his story was wholly untrue. To satisfy them, Cuyler obtained depositions from seven men who had been aboard the train. All seven absolutely denied Arrowsmith's narrative.

Gasper J. Fulton, the conductor in charge of the train, said he had read Arrowsmith's narrative, and swore that it was wholly false. Fulton said the train started from Macon at its regularly scheduled time: 7:15 p.m. on August 28, 1856. It was a Thursday evening, Fulton stated, and the train passed through all the stations between Macon and Augusta on schedule, arriving in Augusta at 3:30 on Friday morning. The entire run "was performed without any irregularity, difficulty, disturbance, or accident of any kind whatever." The other depositions were signed by John H. Hadley, a clerk in charge of the mail; Henry A. Felker, the engineer from Macon to Millon; Francis Doyle, the engineer from Millon to Augusta; John Brown and Robert Gray, the firemen from Macon to Millon; and Patrick Fleury, the fireman from Millon to Augusta.

Cuyler then speculated about Arrowsmith's motives. Arrowsmith's first letter to the *Times* said he was submitting his story reluctantly, on the advice of friends. Arrowsmith's last letter to the *Times* again indicated that he was influenced by someone else. Thus Arrowsmith may have written both letters at the request (or under the control) of some friend. While investigating Arrowsmith's character, Cuyler also learned that he was the nephew of a respected businessman in Liverpool. Cuyler speculated that Arrowsmith's uncle may have heard his story about the Georgia railroad and insisted that Arrowsmith should publish it "as a duty to civilization and Christianity."

Two days later, Arrowsmith responded. In his fourth letter to the *Times,* Arrowsmith said he had read the Americans' depositions and noticed the date they mentioned, a Thursday. Arrowsmith said he now remembered that he left Macon on a Friday and arrived in Augusta on Saturday. He had kept a diary while living in America but failed to consult it while writing his narrative. He had just opened his diary for the first time since returning to England and found that it confirmed his suspicions. He left Macon on Friday, August 29th, not on Thursday the 28th.

Arrowsmith apologized for his error. If anyone was interested, he said, they could verify his story by looking at the registers of the Augusta Hotel in Augusta and at the Columbia Hotel in Macon. He had signed the registers at both hotels. Anyone looking at the hotel registers might also find the names of other passengers who were aboard the train with him.[24]

Arrowsmith's fourth letter may have seemed pathetic. By February, other people had proven that Arrowsmith's story was false, yet he continued to insist that it was true. Thus, instead of responding to his fourth letter, most editors ignored it.

Arrowsmith's motives remain a mystery. Some Americans were certain that Arrowsmith was sick, drunk, or mad, or that his story may have started as a prank. Arrowsmith may have heard (or invented) the story while living in America. After returning to Liverpool, he apparently told the story to his friends and relatives there, swearing that it was true. The story horrified everyone, and friends insisted that he had an obligation to publish it: to expose the crimes. Arrowsmith complied, not realizing the consequences.

Like Arrowsmith, the editor who published his letter was mistaken about its consequences. At first, the letter may have seemed too good to ignore, too exciting and well written. In his anxiety to print it, the editor left in charge of the *Times* apparently failed to notice its numerous discrepancies, and he also failed to realize how easy it would be for Americans to expose them.

Readers in America embarrassed everyone—Arrowsmith and the *Times*—by proving that the story was fictitious, an obvious lie. Thus England's greatest newspaper was forced to admit that it had been hoodwinked.

⑥ Helping the Public? Wild Animals Escape in New York

N a Monday morning 18 years later, another frightening hoax filled the *New York Herald*'s entire front page. It was November 9, 1874, and the *Herald* reported that dozens of wild animals had escaped from the Central Park Zoo. Some of the animals were fighting among themselves. Others were attacking residents of the city. Because of the danger, the mayor ordered every citizen, "except members of the National Guard," to remain in their homes.[1]

Rumors about the wild animals swept through the city, and there was no way to stop them or to calm the public. Some residents of the city were afraid to go outside. Parents feared that the animals might have attacked their children as they walked to school. Other readers armed themselves, then went hunting for the animals roaming the streets of New York.

The hoax is unusual because, years later, the two men who wrote and edited it revealed more about the story's origins and consequences. The men admitted that they wanted to deceive the public. Nevertheless, both men were surprised by the commotion they caused.

The men explained that they were trying to help the public, to warn people about a problem at the zoo. Moreover, the story's final paragraph admitted that it was a hoax. Thus the men expected their readers to be amused, not frightened. Some readers might be fooled, but only for a minute or two, until they reached the final paragraph. Typically, however, most readers panicked before getting that far.

The *New York Herald* used 11 headlines to summarize the story, beginning with

AWFUL CALAMITY

The Wild Animals Broken Loose
from Central Park

TERRIBLE SCENES OF MUTILATION

A Shocking Sabbath Carnival
of Death

SAVAGE BRUTES AT LARGE

Awful Combats Between The Beasts
and the Citizens

The *Herald*'s reporter never identified himself. He had been at the zoo on Sunday afternoon, he said, standing within a hundred yards of the spot where the calamity began. The afternoon had been calm and peaceful. People wandered through the zoo, pausing to admire a beautiful zebra and to laugh at the monkeys. The zoo's most dangerous animals were housed in a single building, and its doors were locked at 5 p.m. But hundreds of people—men, women, and children—lingered in the park.

Chris Anderson was one of the attendants and looked after a rhinoceros named "Pete." Another zoo keeper saw Anderson poking his cane through the bars at the great beast. The zoo keeper warned Anderson to stop, but Anderson continued to torment Pete and—by accident—apparently poked him in the eye. Infuriated by the abuse, the huge animal began to smash down the walls of his cage. Anderson rushed forward and tried to strike the rhinoceros once again but failed to stop it. The entire building began to shake, and the front of Pete's cage collapsed. Pete rushed out, his head lowered. Anderson tried to jump sideways, but Pete knocked him down and trampled him out of recognition. Pete backed away from the mangled body, then attacked again, plunging his horrid horn into the dead keeper, dashing the last possible spark of life.

People outside the building heard the noise, and it aroused their curiosity. Some peered in the windows and saw Pete smashing open the cages of other wild animals.

Another zoo keeper, a man named Hyland, advanced bravely toward Pete. Hyland was pale as marble but carried a Navy revolver in his hand. Pete attacked him in an instant. Hyland sprang aside and fired, hitting Pete on the left shoulder. Pete swerved, but the bullet scarcely hurt him. With a snort, Pete turned back toward Hyland, who retreated, but too late. "The horrid horn impaled him against the corner cage and killed him instantly, tearing the cage to pieces and releasing the panther. . . . "

By then, every animal in the building was excited by the smell of human blood and the sight and sound of the bloody struggles outside their bars. Another zoo keeper, a tall man about thirty-three years old, sprang into action. He found a rifle kept loaded for such emergencies but was horrified when he peered into the building. The panther was crouched over Hyland's body, gnawing horribly at his head. The rhinoceros was plunging blindly forward against cages holding the leopards, the hyena, the prairie wolf, the puma, and the jaguar. The bars on their cages snapped like kindling wood beneath its tremendous weight.

The rhinoceros also destroyed the cages of the wild swine, the American tapir, the two-toed sloth, and a pair of kangaroos. A lion named Lincoln was the next to escape. Zoo keepers had failed to properly fasten the door on Lincoln's cage, and it popped open in the midst of the turmoil.

Some animals began to fight among themselves. The wolf sprang up on the flanks of the Bengal tiger. Shaking off the wolf's feeble hold, the tiger turned and fell upon his less muscular foe. Other animals began rolling over and over, striking each other with their mighty paws. With a single blow, the lioness tore the skin off the puma's flank. As they fought, another beast tugged and crunched at the arms or legs of a corpse.

The lion was standing alone, roaring, pawing the ground, and lashing its tail. The *Herald's* reporter had remained behind to record every detail. Suddenly, like a flash, he realized that the lion was looking at him. To avoid being eaten, he turned and ran.

Other spectators had already fled. However, many ran only a short ways, then looked back and realized that they were not being pursued.

They lingered at a safe distance and became more confident when they saw a zoo keeper approaching with a rifle. Overcome by curiosity, some returned and were standing near a window when, "with a terrific roar, LINCOLN THE LION CAME CRASHING THROUGH THE GLASS."

A single blow knocked one young man to the ground. Another was crushed beneath the lion's weight. The lion planted his paw upon one of their bodies and filled the air with a fearful roar. As the lion stood almost facing him, the zoo keeper knelt down to take aim. Unfortunately, his shot failed to kill the beast.

Crowds of people began entering the zoo, attracted by the roaring of the beasts and the noise of the rifle. The *Herald*'s reporter also observed a number of park police armed with revolvers, and citizens with rifles. Lincoln the lion leaped into the midst of them. It landed in a circle of fear-stricken people: of fainting women, screaming children, and terrified men. Lincoln paused for perhaps a second, lashing his tail and glaring horribly around him. Two young men had tripped and fallen and lay on the ground before him. The men were struggling to rise, and had nearly succeeded, when Lincoln pounced upon the nearest. With one stroke of his fore paw, Lincoln tore the man's clothing and flesh to pieces.

By then, Colonel Conklin had formed a small army of zoo keepers, citizens, and police. They were reinforced by an entire platoon of police from the Nineteenth Precinct. When the rhinoceros emerged from the building, the men fired a tremendous volley which, of course, did little or no good against its thick, tough hide. But the volley confused the rhinoceros momentarily, and it turned and trotted back into the building. Misled by its retreat, the men cheered and rushed forward. Had the great brute deliberately planned an ambush, it could not have been much more successful. When the men were within a dozen feet of the door, the puma sprang into their midst. "Almost on the heels of the puma came the black and spotted leopard, followed by the jaguar, the African lioness, and tiger."

The tiger was the most dangerous and bloodthirsty animal in the whole collection; nevertheless, a zoo keeper named Archambeau tried to lasso it. Without warning, the tiger sprang fifteen feet in the air, catching Archambeau by the right shoulder. The two went down together, the tiger on top. Other men tried to save Archambeau, but the rhinoceros came lumbering out of the entrance at a half trot and drove everyone away. It planted one of its enormous feet on the prostrate Archambeau, squeezing the last breath from his body.

Armed men and curious spectators fled in every direction. Some people fell, "and a case is reported of a citizen stabbed at this moment by an Italian over a quarrel as to which should first ascend a tree."

Maddened by the bullets fired at it, the lion careened wildly out of the park and out onto Fifth Avenue, and it was followed by the Bengal tiger. The reporter who witnessed the calamity ran to the Windsor Hotel and telegraphed the *New York Herald* for reinforcements. Later, he talked to a number of witnesses. They described the events that followed and obviously believed everything they said. Nevertheless, many of their statements were inconsistent. Others contained details that could not possibly be true.

Based upon their accounts, the *Herald*'s story continued. Witnesses said the rhinoceros overturned a cage containing a brown bear that escaped with some bruises. Someone had forgotten to feed the jaguar that Sunday and, desperate with hunger, it jumped over a fence surrounding the tall and gentle giraffes. The jaguar slaughtered one of the helpless animals. A leopard in another part of the zoo killed a child and mutilated several women, then entered an enclosure containing the pelicans, the pea fowl, and ostrich — killing all of them.

Men fired more than a hundred shots at the rhinoceros, but its sides were so tough that they seemed to be covered with slabs of iron. "Shoot him in the eye," people shouted, but the men were too nervous and frightened to strike that particular organ. The rhinoceros continued to destroy more cages, freeing or killing all the animals inside them. An elephant joined the rhinoceros in attacking weaker animals, such as the camel, zebras, bull, and llama. The bull was killed instantly, and one of the zebras was crushed without pity. Another zebra ran toward Eighth Avenue and kicked several boys who tried stop it.

The elephant used its trunk to destroy the monkeys' cage. The monkeys screamed and laughed; the noise was perfectly indescribable. Several perched on the elephant's back for a very short time, and two entered a carriage standing outside the park on Fifth Avenue. The hyena killed one of the monkeys, and wolves wounded several others. But considering the risks, a surprising number escaped.

Late that evening, someone finally lassoed one of the elephant's hind legs, then tied a huge log to the other end of the rope. One by one, men lassoed the elephant's other legs "until they were able to throw him on his side and tie him so that he could not rise." The men were about to shoot the elephant, point blank, when his keeper appeared, tears streaming from his eyes. With his arms outstretched, the elephant's keeper placed himself between the helpless beast and the angry crowd. "The keeper would not move and, with many curses, the great brute's life was saved."

The rhinoceros left Central Park and attacked a party of young girls, killing one of them. Another girl, a frail creature subject to heart disease, received such a nervous shock "that her death may be looked for at any moment." At 90th Street, the rhinoceros gored a horse and overturned a wagon. A milkman driving the wagon suffered a dislocated shoulder. The rhinoceros also destroyed a shanty. The family inside had been eating supper; all escaped "except a child in the cradle, which was burned to a crisp."

Apparently unaware of the beast's ferocious nature, a crowd of men and boys followed behind it. A fortunate accident ended its life. It became very dark, and witnesses saw the rhinoceros fall into a sewer excavation fifteen feet deep.

Other animals continued to fight among themselves. A lion and tiger provided the day's greatest combat. With a single bite, the lion tore away half the tiger's flanks. With characteristic ferocity, the tiger "buried his teeth in the lion's neck until the King of Beasts howled with the keenest anguish. . . . Blood covered the avenue and, in the distance, awestruck spectators looked on in breathless fear." A bullet whistled between the animals' ears, ending their fight.

After saturating itself in the blood of eighteen victims, the African lioness lay down beneath a huge tree, and was killed by a party of Swedish hunters on their way to farms in Nebraska. Ten of the hunters, armed with rifles, crawled on their bellies until within a few paces of the lioness. Suspecting danger, the lioness suddenly arose with a roar. "It was at this moment that Jansen Bjornsen, the leader of the hunters, blew his shrill whistle." Five of the immigrants fired, and the lioness fell with a dull thud, evidently dead. The five immigrants whose guns remained loaded then rushed up and emptied their weapons into its body.

Gov. John A. Dix, a splendid shot, arrived in the city in the nick of time. The Bengal tiger had been responsible for at least twenty deaths, and Dix shot the beast as it rounded Madison Avenue and 34th Street.

Crowds filled Fifth Avenue every Sunday afternoon, and the animals caused a general stampede. People ran down side streets and into churches, filling them hours before their services were scheduled to begin. In ten minutes, not a soul could be seen in any direction.

A man named Schell walked toward Central Park, convinced that rumors he heard about the animals were a cruel hoax. As Schell neared Central Park, he heard a number of shots, then saw some men carrying a body. As Schell watched, the men heard a terrifying roar behind them, dropped the body, and fled. Schell hid in some shrubs and saw a tiger go straight up to the corpse and utter a series of horrible howls.

"I felt my blood run cold," Schell said. He kept perfectly still, however, afraid the beast might see and attack him.

While still hidden in the bushes, Schell saw several other men running toward him. They were fleeing another animal, possibly a lion, behind them. Two of the men drew revolvers and fired at the tiger. To Schell's relief and theirs, the tiger uttered a howl of anguish and ran. Someone must have left a door open, and the tiger entered the Church of St. Thomas, causing a deplorable panic. "Men and women rushed in all directions away from the beast, who sprang upon the shoulders of an aged lady, burying his fangs in her neck, and carrying her to the ground."

Someone ran to a nearby hotel for help, and one of its guests rushed to the church with a rifle. He found the beast in the middle aisle, crouched over his victim. "Without a moment's hesitation, he brought the weapon to his shoulder and fired. The beast stumbled over, and the rifleman ran up and struck him over the head, driving the hammer through the brute's skull."

Other people fired rifles and pistols from the windows of their homes, causing a terrible danger to pedestrians. "There is no instance reported of any of the animals having been hit," the *Herald* continued, "while it is believed many citizens were struck by the missiles. One policeman, Officer Lannigan of the Seventh Precinct, was wounded in the foot near Grand Street by a shot from a window during a chase after the striped hyena, which was mistaken by the crowd for a panther. This cowardly brute was finally killed by a bartender armed with a club."

The day's most awful tragedy occurred aboard a ferryboat. An attendant was closing a gate on the 23rd Street ferry and saw a fierce animal, possibly another tiger, bound onto the vessel. Horses harnessed to wagons were standing in the rear of the vessel. Terrified by the beast, the horses plunged forward into the river. The wagons, and all the people inside, fell in behind them. Some passengers remained aboard the boat but were badly mangled by the ferocious brute. The boat's pilot saw the horses and wagons tumbling overboard and immediately returned to shore. His fast action saved many lives, but the tide was running out to sea and carried the bodies with it.

Throughout the evening, the dead and injured were taken to Bellevue Hospital. The doctors were kept busy dressing the fearful wounds, and the cries of the unfortunate in the accident ward were most painful to hear. It was necessary to perform a number of amputations instantly. One young girl died under the knife.

The *Herald* published a partial list of the casualties: thirty-two people killed, eighteen people injured, and fifty-nine animals slaughtered. Other victims had not yet been identified. The *Herald* estimated that "[t]he list of mutilated, trampled, and injured in various ways must reach nearly 200 people of all ages, of which, so far as known, about 60 are very serious, and of these latter, three can hardly outlast the night." Many of the slightly injured were taken to their homes, so that the full extent of the calamity would not be known for at least another day.

The *Herald* also described the wild animals still at large. They included the cheetah, the Cape buffalo, the panther (a most ferocious beast, supposed to have killed two policemen), the opossum (not dangerous), the wild swine, and the puma lion (a very savage animal, said to have bitten a large piece out of a policeman's shoulder). Three snakes, a dozen monkeys, and the black leopard were also missing. In addition, the *Herald* warned, "There is a sharp lookout for the black wolf. He escaped into the city but looks so much like a Dutchman's dog he may evade detection until he has committed some lamentable tragedy."

The *Herald* added that the mayor had issued a proclamation: "All citizens, except members of the National Guard, are enjoined to keep within their houses or residences until the wild animals now at large are captured or killed." Citizens would be notified when it was safe to leave their homes by the firing of cannons in a dozen locations throughout the city.

The *Herald* praised a general for promptly calling out the Seventh, Eighth, Ninth, and Sixty-ninth regiments of the National Guard. It also praised the police for their success and courage. Regrettably, many of the policemen had been badly mauled or killed.

A smaller headline appeared above the story's final paragraph: THE MORAL OF THE WHOLE. "Of course," the paragraph admitted, "the entire story given above is a pure fabrication. Not one word of it is true. Not a single act or incident described has taken place. It is a huge hoax, a wild romance, or whatever other epithet of utter untrustworthiness our readers may choose to apply to it. It is simply a fancy picture which crowded upon the mind of the writer a few days ago while he was gazing through the iron bars of the cages of the wild animals in the menagerie at Central Park."

The *Herald* warned, however, that the zoo was so poorly maintained that a real disaster might occur at any moment.

Almost twenty years later, the *Herald*'s managing editor admitted that the hoax was his idea. The editor, Thomas B. Connery, insisted, however, that he never expected the hoax to cause any serious harm. "My object," he said, "was entirely good—to warn the public and the authorities of an impending danger."[2]

Connery walked through Central Park every morning and said he usually stopped to look at the animals. He found "great amusement in watching the habits of the animals, about whose cages there was always assembled a crowd of delighted little children and their nurses. One day," Connery added, "I reached the spot just as the attendants were about to transfer a leopard from an animal-carriage to a cage. Through carelessness, I suppose, the operation was bungled, and, to my horror, I saw the animal slip between the carriage and cage." Connery expected the leopard to flee. Hundreds of people were in the park, and the leopard might have attacked any one of them. Fortunately, the attendants quickly recaptured it.

Connery began to imagine what might happen if a more serious accident occurred. To prevent one, he considered writing a column scolding the zoo's attendants for their carelessness. However, he feared that the attendants would be more careful for only a short time. The public would forget the column, and nurses and children would continue to visit the zoo, despite the dangers still lurking there.

The idea came to him in bed that night. Connery decided to devise a harmless little hoax, just realistic enough to warn people about the dangers. "The idea grew fast and furious, especially the fun of it," Connery said. "I saw only the laugh which the publication of such a tremendous hoax would produce. To my shame be it confessed, I was utterly blind to the serious side of the hoax."

The *Herald* employed two brilliant young writers, Harry O'Connor and Joseph I. C. Clarke. O'Connor possessed a vivid imagination and often wrote humorous stories for the *Herald*. Connery asked him to write the hoax but disliked the results. He then turned to Clarke. He asked Clarke to go to Central Park and rewrite the story, making it more realistic.

Fortunately for both Connery and Clarke, no one suspected them of being involved in the hoax. Another journalist explained: "Connery was not the least bit of a fakir, but a most serious-minded, trustworthy man, with what seemed a rather timid personality."[3] Similarly, Clarke worked hard as the *Herald*'s night editor, and no one thought that he had enough time to write such an elaborate hoax. For months after its publication, other reporters and editors stood around Clarke's desk and speculated about who had written the story. Most suspected Stanley McKenna, the *Herald*'s police reporter.

Other readers suspected the *Herald*'s owner, James Gordon Bennett, Jr. Bennett had approved the hoax but never expected it to be so realistic. When copies of the *Herald* were brought up to his bed that Monday morning, Bennett reportedly laid back and groaned.[4] Some time later, Bennett told Connery: "The fun of it all is my friends won't believe such a serious man as you originated the hoax. They all blame me for it."[5]

Connery was also in bed when one of his children ran up to him, carrying a copy of the *Herald* and exclaiming, "Oh, papa, what a dreadful thing!" Connery went down to breakfast and discovered that his wife kept their children home from school. Their servants were afraid to go out, and "every face was unusually pale."

Connery started for a barber shop where three or four men were waiting to be shaved. One of the men began talking about the wild animals, and the customer being shaved at that moment was so frightened by the conversation that he jumped up and ran out without his coat or hat. Connery boarded a horse-car and heard another gentleman talking to his neighbor about the awful calamity. When told the beasts were still at large, the neighbor left without another word, "clutching his cane nervously, as if fearful of encountering one of the escaped animals." Connery began walking down Fifth Avenue and encountered *Herald* newsboys shouting "Extra!" "Escape of the Wild Beasts!" "Great loss of Life!" Connery jumped into a cab and, upon reaching his office, immediately stopped the paper's presses.[6]

Connery found a roomful of people waiting for him. The *Herald*'s police reporter told the funniest story. After reading the *Herald*'s headlines, other editors in the city had sent their reporters out to get the latest details. Similarly, the police superintendent rushed to his office and telegraphed instructions about handling the calamity to every precinct. Before the superintendent finished reading the story, a mob of excited reporters descended upon him. Some accused him of favoring the *Herald* and wanted to know why he withheld the story from them. The superintendent responded that he did not know anything about the dreadful affair and could not understand how it occurred without his knowledge.

The reporter who wrote the story, I.C. Clarke, described a similar panic among his neighbors.[7] "There was a public school in our street," Clarke said, "and one after another I saw mothers come round the corner, make a dash for the school, and presently come forth with one or more children and dash homeward, dragging the little ones after them. By George! It scared me. I went some half mile up to my mother's home through almost empty streets. I found the family around the lunch table in consternation. My cousin, Jennie, was reading my story in a broken voice, and my mother and sister were in tears. They rose up as I came in, 'Thank God, you are safe!' "

Clarke told his family that the story was a hoax and showed them the final paragraph. They promptly denounced the writer, saying, "He must be a terrible fellow." Clarke agreed, then hurried to the *Herald*'s office. Clarke found that the story had fooled even some of its employees. An old Civil War correspondent came in prepared for the worst, a huge Army revolver tucked in his belt.

Despite the commotion, Clarke said he felt "clear of blame." "It was a vivid bit of realistic writing that shocked a couple of million people, written under orders," he explained. "How to treat the result was not in my hands."

Other newspapers denounced the hoax. The *New York Daily Tribune* complained that many people read only the *Herald*'s headlines.[8] As a result, "fathers telegraphed home to prevent their children from going to school or their wives from venturing out of doors." People also called the police "and were much enraged when informed that the whole story was a hoax."

A letter from one of the *Tribune*'s readers complained: "I never suffered more intensely than I did this morning on glancing at the cruel hoax which the *Herald* circulated in an extra and which I purchased from a newsboy. . . . " The woman said she lived three blocks from

Central Park and had instructed her family's nurse to take her two babies to the park. She left home after breakfast and, after buying a copy of the paper, only glanced at its headlines.

"I, of course, had but one thought," she said. "I rushed for the nearest carriage; offered the driver all I had— $15—if he would get me home in the quickest possible time. He did nobly, and I was home in 25 minutes. . . . It seemed an hour. When I saw my children safe, I was completely overcome. But when I found that this was all a cruel hoax, my indignation was so great that I could not express it in fitting terms. I feel that I have been outraged, and every member of the community likewise."[9] Now, she wanted someone to punish, or at least rebuke, the editors of the *New York Herald*.

Another paper, the *New York Times* speculated that "a few harum-scarum young men" dreamed up the hoax while drinking too much wine at a poker party.[10] The *Times* complained that the *Herald* had tried to be funny and failed. It found no humor in the *Herald*'s description of a lion that "tugged and crunched at the arms and legs of a corpse," nor in its description of a child in a cradle "burned to a crisp."

The *Times* published a half dozen letters critical of the *Herald* and its hoax. Parents were most upset, and an indignant father asked, "Is there any law that will reach the perpetrators of such an infamous outrage on the public as the canard in this morning's *Herald?*"[11] The man explained: "My children had started for school about 10 minutes before we saw this monstrous joke. A carriage was sent for at once to go after them, my wife trembling lest they should be already killed. I had read aloud part of this long rigmarole when, glancing at the last paragraph, I saw the explanation. My wife says she will not have such a paper in the house again, and has ordered it stopped."

A woman complained that the hoax also frightened thousands of people outside the city. They feared that their friends and relatives in New York were dead. The woman added that gentlemen may have discovered the hoax sooner, but women did not know the customs of newspaper men. "Every face in the room was white when I reached the last paragraph," she said, "and all felt sick at heart at the appalling tale. To more than one family member will this bring horror and dread, perhaps actual illness, for women are not made to be the butts of such practical jokes."

Despite the criticisms, the hoax seemed to help, not hurt, the *Herald*. Connery said the *Herald*'s circulation "did not drop by so much as one subscriber."[12] Clarke said the excitement increased the newspaper's circulation.[13] Historians agree that the *Herald*'s critics "failed to make a dent in its prestige." Rather, the incident helped it.[14]

Both Connery and Clarke also responded to the criticisms published by the *New York Times*. They said the *Times*'s editor may have been indignant because he was fooled by the hoax. Connery heard that the *Times*'s editor left his home "with a brace of pistols, prepared to shoot the first animals that would cross his path." Clarke adds that the *Times*'s city editor, George F. Williams, was "a Civil War veteran of bright journalistic qualities, but a very excitable man. . . . " After glancing at the *Herald*'s story, Williams rushed to his office in a fury, collected every reporter he could find, stuffed them into a coach, and drove to the police headquarters. Entering alone, Williams attacked the officers there for hiding the story from his staff. After making a fool of himself, he returned to the *Times* in silence.

Why did the hoax frighten so many readers? The *Herald* was one of New York's most popular daily newspapers. After its publication that Monday morning, rumors about the animals swept through the city. Once started, there was no way to stop them. There was no other means of mass communication: no telephones, radio, or television — nothing to inform the public that the story was a hoax. Some newspapers were published that afternoon, but they reached fewer readers and came out much later in the day. As a result, many New Yorkers continued to believe the story until they received a new paper the next morning.

The two men responsible for the hoax expected it to fool their readers, but only for a moment or two, until they reached the story's final paragraph. If so, they were seriously mistaken. Readers frightened by the story's headlines and details never reached the final paragraph. They panicked before getting that far.

Since then, other journalists have made the same mistake. They created other hoaxes and included other clues intended to inform their readers that the stories were fictitious. But no matter how many clues the journalists provide, some readers always fail to notice them, for they are too busy enjoying the bloody details.

7   Is the Press Too Powerful? Chicago's Awful Theater Fire

 Chicago paper published the country's most horrifying hoax. After reading it, thousands of people feared that their friends and relatives were dead: "BURNED ALIVE" in a downtown theater.

Wilbur Storey was one of the country's most brilliant editors. But the hoax that Storey published about a Chicago theater also reflected his power: his ability to publish almost anything, and the city's inability to do anything about it.

During the nineteenth century, there were few limits on the press. The U.S. Constitution prohibited government censorship, and other institutions lacked the power to defend themselves, to effectively rebuke the editor of a large and profitable daily. The people horrified by a hoax might complain, or they might threaten to cancel their subscriptions. But their threats were a minor annoyance to a man like Wilbur Storey. Moreover, Storey felt that he was right, that his hoax helped the public by exposing a serious problem in the city.

Storey's hoax was also sadly prophetic. Twenty-eight years later, a fire occurred almost exactly as Storey predicted, killing 571 people and injuring 359.

Storey purchased the *Chicago Times* in 1861. He paid only $13,000 for the paper, but it was losing money and attracted fewer than a thousand subscribers. Within five years, Storey transformed it into one of the largest and most influential dailies in the Midwest.

As editor, Storey was skillful and bold. He did a better job of reporting the news than any of his rivals. He also developed a talented staff, established the region's first Sunday paper, and published a strong editorial page. An employee called Storey's editorial page "one of the most forceful things in American journalism." He explained that Storey's editorial page was fighting all the time, sometimes wrong, but usually right — and always interesting.[1]

Yet Storey made few friends in Chicago. A biographer claims that Storey "was generally hated by almost everyone who had occasion to deal with him."[2] Enemies called Storey conceited, stubborn, thoughtless, and vindictive. They complained that Storey never admitted making a mistake, never apologized, and never considered the feelings of other people — not even his own employees'. Moreover, Storey often criticized other people, and his attacks were savage, yet Storey never seemed to worry about the harm he inflicted.

In addition, Storey was a sensationalist. He filled the *Times* with stories about rapes, robberies, murders, and seductions. One of the newspaper's headlines may have been the most sensational in the history of American journalism. On November 27, 1875, the *Times* reported that four men were hanged for murder. One of the men had confessed, repented, and declared that Jesus was waiting to receive him. To summarize the story, the *Times* published these three words: "Jerked To Jesus."

As part of its sensationalism, the *Times* also published several hoaxes, but called them "supposititious" journalism. The most horrifying hoax appeared on a Saturday morning, February 13, 1875. It reported that a terrible fire roasted the audience in a local theater.[3] Eleven headlines appeared above the story, beginning with

BURNED ALIVE
———

The Angel of Death Brings
Terrible Mourning
to Chicago
———

Burning of a Theater Last
Night — Hundreds Perish
in the Flames
———

The eleventh headline added:

Description of a Supposititious Holo-
caust Likely to Occur Any Night

Thus the final headline revealed that the story was a hoax. Some readers, anxious to get to the more sensational details, skipped over it. Other readers failed to understand it. Still others believed the hoax because it seemed so detailed and realistic.

Perhaps to avoid a libel suit, Storey never identified the theater. His failure to do so added to the public's horror. Because no one knew where the fire occurred, everyone with friends or relatives who attended any of Chicago's theaters that Friday night may have feared that they died in the flames. By 10 a.m., newsstands were sold out, and people were peering into the theaters to see the ruins.

The *Times* reported that the theater was almost full, and that extra stools were placed in aisles on the main floor. The gallery was also overflowing, and theater employees locked a gate so that spectators who purchased cheap tickets in the gallery could not go down a stairway to higher-priced seats on the main floor. The top gallery contained a motley crowd of bootblacks, newsboys, the poor, the colored, "and a general conglomeration of hobble-dehoys and gutter snipes." The audience was large because the play offered something for everyone—love, blood, combat, and murder.

At about 10:30 p.m., perhaps a little later, the audience was await-ing the final act. Some men had already left, a custom in American theaters. They had stepped out early for a drink in nearby saloons. In this case, it saved their lives.

The theater's gas lights were turned down, and a bell warned specta-tors that the curtain was about to rise. The curtain rose two feet, then fell back to the stage. Spectators guessed that a rope had broken and that the damage would be repaired in a few minutes. A man seated near the stage thought he heard someone on it say "Fire." When he told a friend, several ladies jumped to their feet in great nervousness, but their male escorts quieted their fears.

Moments later, spectators noticed an unusual brilliancy on the stage. As the light intensified, they realized that it was indeed a fire. An actor swung back the curtain and screamed, "Hurry to the door, for your lives, the stage is afire!" Survivors said the scene became one of stupendous horror. "Timid females raised their hands to heaven, shrieked wild, despairing cries, and fell—trampled into eternity by the heavy heels of the maddened, rushing thong. Mothers pleaded piteously, in the turmoil and the roar, that their darling little daughters might be spared. . . . " Stout men, with muscles of iron, clasped their wives and sweethearts to their chests and cursed and blasphemed.

Flames spread across the theater, soared upward toward the ceiling, then swooped down upon the audience. The stage became a "roaring, seething, curling mass of flame, which lit up the interior of the theater with an awful glare and blistered and burned the unfortunate people who stood nearest to it."

Members of the orchestra perished first. The orchestra's leader had jumped onto the stage and ordered his men to remain calm. Even as he spoke, the curtain burst into flames and fell on him.

The fire continued its savage roar. Spectators in the gallery tried to jump to the main floor but were killed by the fall. Firemen were helpless. The swirling, seething flames burst out the theater's windows and threatened nearby buildings. The flames spread so rapidly, and the fire became so hot, that firemen could not get their hoses close enough to pour any water into the building. Some firemen aimed their hoses through the doorway, but people were still pouring out, sweeping away everything in their path.

Other firemen tried to smash through the theater's side walls. "Had someone undertaken this work before the fire broke out," the *Times* said, "no doubt, many valuable LIVES COULD HAVE BEEN SAVED. Or, had the building been constructed with side doors, of sufficient capacity to empty the house in a few minutes, the catastrophe would never have transpired. . . . "

People from downtown businesses, saloons, and hotels flocked to the scene, hindering the firemen. Soon a squad of policemen cleared the sidewalks.

Firemen extinguished the last flames early Saturday morning, but rescuers had to wait another half hour before they could enter the building. A policeman, followed by several firemen and one or two reporters, found the auditorium filled with smoke that blinded their eyes and impeded their progress. They encountered bodies everywhere—lying on the stairways, jammed between the seats, stretched out on the carpeting. "There were blackened corpses covered with the grime of the conflagration; and bloody corpses trampled to death and mutilated. There were corpses crisp and hideous, and hair burned off, the white teeth grinning, the hands fleshless. There were others that sat in their seats, who had evidently been seized with a fright and rendered incapable of moving."

By 1 a.m., rescuers had carried 157 bodies out of the theater. Other victims remained inside, buried beneath the debris. Rescue workers laid the corpses side by side on the sidewalk so they could be identified by friends and relatives. Police tried to keep the scene quiet and orderly, but it was horrifying. One by one, the dead were carried away, some to nearby hotels, others to the morgue. The crowds dispersed, but rescuers continued their search. "The bodies of the unfortunate musicians were among the last to be taken out of the debris. They were all so charred that recognition was almost impossible."

Reporters worked faithfully to obtain an accurate list of the dead. The *Times* published the names of 108. Twice that number had died, it said, but the others had not been identified. Many of the names that appeared in the *Times* were incomplete—only a last name, or an initial and a last name. Many of the names were also quite common in Chicago, and some were obviously misspelled. Because of this, thousands of readers thought that the victims were their friends, neighbors, or relatives—people with similar names.

The *Times* also listed the injured and described their injuries. It explained that almost all their injuries occurred when the spectators were trampled upon or fell from the balcony.

Typical entries included

Mrs. C.H. Bonta of Syracuse had her left leg broken just below the knee.

Mrs. R.P. Myer was taken out of the crowd with one eye completely destroyed.

Mary Johnson, No. 478 North Clark Street, was internally injured. The surgeons have given up hopes of her recovery.

Anne Jackson, a miss of 11 years of age, residing on Bangamon Street, who had the left leg broken and head bruised by being trampled upon.

Mrs. J.S. McCarthy, a charming young woman from Buffalo, had her left arm broken and several fingers dislocated.

What caused the fire? The *Times* reported that, after a long and tedious search, one of its reporters found the theater's stage manager,

Mr. George Myer, refreshing himself in a nearby restaurant. After persistent questioning, Myer told the story. Arrangements for the final act had almost been completed, and stage hands were ready to raise the curtain. A piece of scenery was being moved into position, and it fell against a gas burner used to light the theater.

Women shrieked and ran. Men tried to remain calm, to extinguish the flames and save the audience. They realized that an unusual commotion on the stage — the slightest hint of fire — would cause a panic. Workmen climbed above the fire and tried to throw pails of water upon it. Because of the excitement, they threw most of the water on the floor. A gentleman grabbed a fire extinguisher and was climbing the stairway, but a pail dropped by an excited water carrier rolled off an overhead platform, struck the gentleman's left shoulder, and threw him violently to the stage, completely stunning him. "But for this unfortunate accident, this gentleman might have saved the building."

After realizing that the flames were out of control, the stage manager finally sounded an alarm. The *Times* criticized his actions, saying, "Had he dispatched a man to the front when the scenery ignited, and quietly have told the people to get out, many lives might have been saved. . . . "

The paper hoped that the fire would have a beneficial effect — that it would warn people about the dangers in Chicago theaters and encourage the city to eliminate the dangers. "The time to move in this matter is at this critical juncture," it said, "even while the charred remains of the unfortunate victims are lying stark upon their biers. . . . "

After reporting all the details, the paper admitted that its story was fictitious. It warned, however, that the city's theaters were so poorly built, and so crammed with flammable materials, that a fire was likely to occur at any moment. It blamed greedy theater owners who cared nothing about the public's safety. It explained that land was expensive, and that theater owners were reluctant to do anything that would require more space or money. They had only one desire: to fill their theaters with spectators and their cash boxes with money.

The *Times* added that its own architect had inspected every theater in the city and found that none was safe. It listed eight of the theaters and, one by one, exposed their flaws. The architect warned that spectators seated in separate balconies were forced to use the same stairways, and that spectators leaving one balcony would slow the escape of others. The architect also warned that most stairways were too narrow, and that many failed to lead directly outside. He recommended that every theater should have numerous and spacious exits, and that the exits and stairways should be located at both the front and rear of every theater. In addition, every stairway should be at least four feet wide and should become wider as it descended. Doors should open outward, away from the audience.

The architect complained that builders used too many flammable materials, partly to lower their costs and partly to speed construction. "Almost all of the buildings in Chicago are erected too rapidly, and theaters especially so," he warned. "As a rule, buildings cannot be constructed in haste and made well at the same time." The architect predicted a terrible disaster: "Then, perhaps, the authorities will be forced to take action. It would be useless to hope for it sooner."

Who wrote the hoax? No one knows. Storey may have written it himself, or he may have suggested the idea to a reporter familiar with the city's theaters. The reporter may have consulted an architect, or he may have invented the architect along with all the other details.

Why did the *Times* publish the hoax? Storey often crusaded for the public's welfare and may have sincerely worried about people's safety in Chicago's theaters. In addition, Storey was a sensationalist who knew that the hoax would startle his readers, capturing their attention more effectively than a mere story or editorial. Moreover, it was an era of hoaxes. The *New York Sun* had published its famous moon hoax 40 years earlier, and the *New York Herald* had published its wild animal hoax only a few months earlier.

The next morning, the *Times* insisted that its hoax "served a very important purpose in directing public attention to this serious subject." The paper hoped that the public would demand an immediate and thorough reform. The public would have to act, it said, because the city's theater owners neglected their responsibilities. Their theaters were "mere tinder-boxes" and "human fire traps."[4] It estimated that, if a fire started when one of the city's most dangerous theaters was filled with spectators, "two-thirds, or certainly one-half, of its spectators would be burned, suffocated, or trampled to death."

Chicago's Common Council had already adopted a law making it illegal to block the theaters' narrow aisles with chairs and stools, yet several theaters continued to use them. The *Times* insisted that "[a]rrest and punishment is the simple remedy. . . . " The *Times* also insisted that the architect it quoted (but never identified) was not a myth "but one of the most competent practical architects in the city."

A letter from J. H. McVicker, the manager of McVicker's Theater, responded: "McVicker's Theater is perfect in construction and under no circumstances can harm happen to the audience. . . . There are 11 outlets from the auditorium — four leading to the rear alley, four to the side alleys, and three to the front street. They are all independent of each other; the doors open out; and, in addition, there are a number of windows, not 8 feet from the ground, from which even the *Times'* architect might jump and not hurt his delicate form."[5]

McVicker added that he never placed any chairs in his theater's aisles, and that two thousand spectators could leave the theater in three minutes.

After publishing McVicker's letter, the *Times* also published a response written by its architect. The architect agreed that McVicker's was one of the safest theaters in Chicago but warned that spectators seated in its upper galleries would be unable to escape out the sides of the theater. Some spectators might be pushed out the theater's windows, he admitted, but those who went first would be jumped upon by those following. "The windows of the galleries are much more than 8 feet from the ground," the architect continued. "Will Mr. McVicker please state the exact height that men, to say nothing of women, in an alarmed crowd, hemmed in front and pushed from behind, can jump with safety . . . ?"

Another letter, written by R. M. Hooley, defended Hooley's Theater. Hooley complained that some readers thought the fire occurred in his theater. It was invaded "by an awe-struck multitude eager to feast their vision on the wreck and ruin your article described." Hooley added that city officials had inspected his theater and declared it safe. Moreover, the *Times'* reporter made several errors in his story, and other types of buildings in Chicago — hotels, factories, and churches — were more dangerous than its theaters.

"Then why," Hooley asked, "should the theaters of the city be branded as unsafe . . . ?" He complained that the *Times*'s hoax "was not right." His property should not be attacked "to satisfy the morbid cravings of a reckless reporter in quest of sensation."[6]

Other editors seemed to enjoy Storey's predicament. Storey published the region's most popular newspaper and regularly scooped them on major stories. Now they had an chance for revenge.

Readers everywhere were attacking Storey, and newspapers as far away as Milwaukee published their letters, including a second letter written by J. H. McVicker, who insisted that his theater was "perfect in construction and safe in every particular." He suggested that the *Times*'s architect was a myth and challenged him to "materialize." McVicker wanted him to meet other respected architects at his theater "for the purpose of making a thorough investigation of the premises."[7]

McVicker also complained that innocent victims were unable to respond to the press's errors. He then proposed a comparable hoax that someone might play upon the *Times*. A member of the U.S. Supreme Court might write an article warning that the ink used by newspapers was poisonous. Copies of the article might be posted during the night at fifty thousand places in Chicago. The posters might add that the editor of the *Times* died because he read his own paper, that every printed page contained smallpox, and that attempts to fumigate the paper's office had failed.

A "responsible judge" and a "competent practical physician" (people similar to the *Times*'s architect) might swear that the story was true. McVicker predicted that many readers would believe the story and stop buying newspapers. Thus journalists would suffer the same harm they inflicted upon other innocent victims.

Another Chicago paper, the *Tribune,* called Storey's hoax "worse than murder."[8] It explained that a woman became a raving maniac after reading the hoax and seeing her husband's name listed among the victims. Her husband was a prominent businessman and commuted from their home in Evanston, Illinois. He had intended to return home Friday afternoon but decided to remain in Chicago to entertain a friend and customer. He sent a note to his wife, saying that he planned to take the friend to a theater.

His wife received a copy of the *Times* as her family sat down to breakfast on Saturday. She saw the words "BURNED ALIVE," then noticed her husband's name listed among the victims. One of his initials was wrong, and his name misspelled—but it was enough! She shrieked and fell to the floor. Her mother-in-law grabbed the paper from her hands, then collapsed alongside her, killed by the shock. "She was as really murdered as though the assassin had sent a bullet through her heart," the *Tribune* said.

The poor wife regained consciousness but arose from the floor a raving maniac. She recognized no one, and physicians said that if she lives (which is extremely doubtful), "her reason is gone forever, and that her remaining days, whether they be few or many, must be spent in a mad-house."

The final paragraphs admitted that the story was a hoax—purely "supposititious," just like the *Times*'s story about the fire. The *Tribune* explained: "Whether anything of the kind has resulted from the publication of the hoax, we do not know. If there has not, no thanks are due to the editor of the *Times,* for it was calculated to accomplish just such calamities as we have imagined, and no amount of subterfuge or specious argument can justify such violations of journalistic decency."

The *Tribune* also published several angry letters written by its readers. One of the readers asked, "Is Storey, of the *Times,* crazy or a fool?" The reader called his hoax a dreadful mistake and insisted that Storey should "be driven from the city."[9]

Another letter complained that the *Times* reeked with falsehood, overflowed with fraud, catered to vulgar tastes, and pandered to the lowest passions. The letter added that, after reading the hoax, a woman in another city "fainted away, and could not for some time be resuscitated." Her son was in Chicago and planned to attend a theater on Friday night. When the woman heard about the fire and learned that he was listed among the victims, she shrieked: "'My God! My God! O, my poor boy,' and fell senseless into the arms of her friends."[10]

Another writer said he had been in Vinton, Iowa, and received a letter saying that his wife and only child planned to attend a Chicago theater. While at a train depot in Vinton, he met a passenger with a copy of the *Times*. It was the only Chicago paper available there, and the other passenger left before he was able to obtain all the details. Fearing that his wife and child were dead, the man boarded the next train for Chicago. After describing his suffering, the man asked, "Well, am I to blame because I love my wife and child?"[11]

A special dispatch from South Bend, Indiana, revealed that residents there had heard rumors about the fire, but a train carrying copies of the Chicago papers failed to arrive on time. The rumors "spread with a great rapidity, and a number of parties who had friends and relatives visiting Chicago, and expecting them to be visiting McVicker's, rushed to the telegraph office. . . . " The operator wired Chicago and asked whether the story was true. The response revealed that it was a hoax.

Other residents of South Bend had rushed to the city's news depots and waited there for copies of the Chicago papers. When the papers arrived, only the *Times* contained a story about the fire, "yet so great was the excitement that it was some minutes before the cruel, heartless hoax was discovered. . . . One man, whose wife was to have been at McVicker's Friday night, was for a time nearly wild with excitement."[12]

A dispatch from Fort Wayne, Indiana, added that people there had rushed to buy copies of the morning papers "and, when the discovery was made that the whole report was simply a *Times'* hoax, indignation was freely expressed." The city's evening papers demanded "that its editor be legally punished for obtaining money under false pretense."[13]

Despite the hoax, the *Times* continued to prosper, making Storey a millionaire. Storey, however, never seemed to enjoy his wealth. His personal life was too unhappy. He later fell from a railroad car, injured an ankle, and walked with a limp for the rest of his life. He married three times but had no children. One of his wives refused to live with him, but also refused to grant him a divorce. Another, whom he loved, died.

Historians add that Storey drank too much, associated with prostitutes, and contacted syphilis. The syphilis "led to slow insanity and a total paralysis."[14] He died on October 27, 1884, sixty-four years old and "a blind imbecile."[15]

Without him, the *Times* and its excellent staff seemed to disintegrate. His successors were less controversial but also less talented. An employee called them "mediocre people without inspiration." Thus the *Chicago Times* "drifted and died."[16]

Nineteen years after Storey's death, a fire in a Chicago theater occurred almost exactly as his hoax predicted. The theater was crowded, the fire started on its stage, and the spectators panicked.

The Iroquois Theater had just opened on Market Street (later renamed Wacker Drive). On December 30, 1903, the theater offered an afternoon performance of "Mr. Bluebeard," starring Eddie Foy, Sr., and the Seven Little Foys. Because of the Christmas season, the audience was larger than usual, and many of the spectators were children.

The fire started during a song. Stage hands tried to extinguish it, and several seconds passed before the audience realized what was happening. Eddie Foy reacted heroically. As the flames spread around him, Foy strode onto the stage, faced the audience, and commanded: "Keep quiet. Quiet. Get out in order! Don't get excited!"[17]

The actors and stage hands were closest to the fire but escaped out back exits. Spectators said the opened stage doors created a draft that almost blew them off their feet. Air sucked in through the doors blew the flames out over the audience, upward into the galleries, and out the gallery doors. Spectators in the second balcony died quickly. Dozens were trapped in doorways, crushed against the doors by people pushing them from behind. Other spectators suffocated and fell in the narrow aisles. Children were trampled and pinned in the crowd until they choked. People who remained in their seats suffocated there. Others died while jumping from a crowded fire escape.

The next morning, the *Chicago Tribune* devoted its entire front page to a list of the dead: 571 people, most of them women and children. Another 350 were injured.

Why did so many people die? The Iroquois Theater contained 1,602 seats, but more than 1,800 people were crammed into the building. About 440 were admitted to an upper balcony, including 75 to 100 without seats. When the fire started, people standing in the back and in the aisles blocked the exits. Other spectators died because some doors opened inward: toward the audience. The pressure caused by people rushing toward the doors made it impossible for anyone to open them.

City officials discovered that the theater's asbestos curtain failed to fall all the way down to the stage.[18] The curtain was supposed to be fireproof but "no scrap more than a few inches in dimensions was found." Also, several exits were locked. The stage manager was not on the stage, and the man who was supposed to lower the asbestos curtain was not in the theater. Chicago required automatic sprinklers on every theater stage, but the Iroquois Theater did not have any. Chicago also required fire alarms connected directly to the city's alarm system, but the Iroquois Theater did not have any. Moreover, the theater never held a fire drill, and some ushers were only fifteen years old.[19]

In 1875, Storey's hoax had called the city's theaters "tinder-boxes" and "human fire traps." The hoax predicted a terrible disaster and warned: "Then, perhaps, the authorities will be forced to take action. It would be useless to hope for it sooner."

Storey was right. After the fire at the Iroquois, every theater in Chicago was closed. Their owners were ordered to widen the theaters' aisles and exits, to fireproof their scenery, and to install automatic sprinklers and steel (not asbestos) curtains. But for the victims—571 dead and 350 injured—it was too late.

So was Storey crazy? Or was he a bold (but eccentric) prophet?

The hoax clearly reflects Storey's brilliance and power, his ability to upset an entire community. It also reflects his failure. Storey wanted to startle his readers, to attract their attention. His sensationalism horrified them, and they responded by attacking the *Times*, not by eliminating the problems in Chicago theaters. Thus Storey succeeded in frightening the public and, typically, he escaped unpunished. But Storey failed to correct the problems or to prevent the 571 deaths.

8 Improved and Updated: The Hoax That Caused a War

 few hoaxes, like good wine, improved with age. Why? While reprinting the hoaxes, other reporters also embellished them. Most reporters added only a few minor details, often a "local angle" needed to satisfy their editors. The reporters claimed that a local citizen was involved in the story, or they quoted a local expert willing to confirm the details. Reporters unable to find a local expert were tempted to invent one. As the hoaxes spread from city to city, reporters also "updated" them, speculating about their outcome and other recent developments.

Reporters who created the original hoaxes also discussed them with friends, often while relaxing in a bar after work. Their friends passed the details on to other journalists. Thus newsroom tales about the hoaxes passed from one generation of journalists to the next. While repeating the stories, journalists continued to embellish them. Some of the details they added were more exciting than the original stories.

In 1899, for example, four reporters created a hoax while drinking beer in a Denver bar. At first, it seemed to be another light-hearted jest, something the reporters needed to fill their papers' Sunday editions. Reporters in other cities may have suspected that the story was a hoax, but felt compelled to go along with it, to confirm its authenticity.

A new and more exciting version, published forty years later, claimed that the hoax caused a war in China.

Two thousand years earlier, the Chinese had erected a wall that stretched for 1,500 miles, from the Yellow Sea to the Gobi Desert. More than a million laborers helped build China's Great Wall, and tens of thousands died. Granite blocks used in portions of the wall weighed more than two tons. Today, no one knows how — without any machinery — laborers hauled the stones up China's steep mountainsides. Chinese legends say that mountain goats dragged them up.

On June 25, 1899, a story on page 6 of Denver's *Sunday Post* reported that a Chicago engineer named Frank C. Lewis stopped in Denver while en route to China. The *Sunday Post* explained that Lewis was going to bid on the job of tearing down the Great Wall.

Lewis said the wall was twenty to thirty feet high and wide enough to accommodate six horsemen. It was astonishing, he admitted, that a country as old and decrepit as China would think of destroying the wall. "Nevertheless," he insisted, "it is so, and I am on my way to investigate and report." After razing the wall, Lewis continued, the Chinese wanted to construct on its site a remarkably fine roadway. They planned to use stones and other materials in the wall to lay the roadbed, and also to construct smaller roads that would branch out from the main one. The main road would be wide enough to accommodate a railroad.

"The country is exceedingly fertile and thickly populated," Lewis continued. "It will bring a vast commerce, I should think, to the port of Shanghai . . . and also give a great boom to Peking, which is only a few miles distant from the Great Wall."

Lewis represented a syndicate of Chicago's most prominent men, and the story identified several of them. It added that only one other American concern, a New York syndicate, was interested in the project. The Chinese, however, had used the proper diplomatic channels to seek bids from other groups in England, France, Germany, and Russia. Thus two British syndicates, a French syndicate, and three German ones were expected to compete for the job.

The *Sunday Post* added that Lewis planned to leave Denver at four o'clock that morning aboard a train to San Francisco. From there, he would sail straight to Peking.[1]

The *Post*'s story was long, rambling, and repetitious — but not exclusive. Two other newspapers, the *Denver Sunday Times* and the *Re-*

publican, published similar stories. Their details differed, but all three agreed on the main point: that American engineers wanted to tear down the Great Wall.

The *Times* published its story on page 5 and quoted the same source: Frank C. Lewis, "a well-known railroad builder of Chicago." The *Times* declared: "One of the greatest undertakings ever attempted by an American syndicate in foreign lands gives promise of blossoming into fruit." It explained that Lewis represented a syndicate of Chicago capitalists and was traveling to China to negotiate with the government there "with a view to tearing down a portion of the Chinese wall."

The *Times* revealed that Lewis had lived in China for four years. While there, he learned that the country's rulers were discussing the possibility of tearing down at least a portion of the Great Wall and using the ruins to build a road to Nankin. "The idea," Lewis said, "was to pulverize the rocks and make a roadway that would be level and smooth. . . ."[2]

Lewis seemed optimistic about his chances of winning the contract. His syndicate had raised $650,000 in cash, he said, and would be able to start the work almost immediately. The syndicate would buy most of its machinery in the United States. It would have to obtain the heaviest crushers that are made, "owing to the fact that many of the pieces of rock are unusually large."

"Of course," he continued, "we know that it would bankrupt the Chinese government if they concluded to tear down the entire wall, but when you take into consideration the fact that we can hire the laborers for a few cents a day, a large amount of work can be accomplished on a few millions of dollars." Lewis added that the Chinese government was also considering the construction of hundreds of miles of railroads, "and my instructions are to grab at everything in which there is a chance to make money."

A third Sunday paper, the *Republican,* placed its story about Lewis on page 20. It reported that Lewis had arrived in Denver at 6:30 that Saturday evening and registered at the Oxford Hotel. After eating dinner at the hotel, he immediately boarded a sleeping car on a Union Pacific train. It agreed that the train left for San Francisco early that Sunday morning.

Lewis told the *Republican* that he had started negotiating with the Chinese months earlier. He wanted to build a road "which will eventually become the highway between Nankin and the vast empire of Siberia." He had spent several years building railroads in China. When he heard about the notion of building a highway from Nankin to China's northern border, he saw an opportunity for American capital. Lewis added that the Chinese wall had become useless, and an Englishman had suggested using its massive stones to build the road. The idea had been taken up by the Chinese government, Lewis said, "and there is a fair chance that it will be carried out."[3]

From Denver, the story was telegraphed to the Midwest. On Monday, it appeared on the *Chicago Tribune*'s front page. The *Tribune* noted that Lewis was a Chicago engineer and represented a syndicate of Chicago capitalists who wanted to tear down a portion of the Chinese wall. The paper added that Lewis would not reveal the men's names; however, it was believed that Mayor Harrison "and numerous other prominent men are interested in the plan."

The *Tribune* sent its own reporters out to interview the men, and it printed their responses at the end of its story. An engineer named "Frank C. Lewis" actually lived in the Chicago area, but the reporters were unable to find him. Lewis's family explained that he was in Pittsburgh. The *Tribune* added that his relatives had heard of the Chinese wall project but insisted "that Mr. Lewis was not going to China." The paper also reported that Mayor Harrison "laughed when asked if he were interested." Harrison said he was too busy at home to bother about China's ancient wall.[4]

On Tuesday, the story reached the East Coast. The *New York Times* published a four-paragraph story on its front page. Its story emphasized the fact that a New York syndicate was expected to bid on the work.[5] Other newspapers also reprinted the story, and one quoted a Chinese official who was visiting New York and confirmed all the details.

Forty years passed before the story was exposed as a hoax. Ironically, the writer who exposed the hoax created an even greater hoax. He claimed that the story started in Denver caused China's Boxer Rebellion.

In 1939, writer Harry Lee Wilber published his story in a magazine, the *North American Review.* Wilber explained that four newspapers were published in Denver during the summer of 1899: the *Republican,* the *Denver Times,* the *Denver Post,* and the *Rocky Mountain News.* Each newspaper assigned a reporter to cover the hotels near a railroad depot, and the reporters interviewed prominent guests visiting the city. He said that four reporters — Al Stevens, Jack Tournay, John Lewis, and

Hal Wilshire—met at the depot one Saturday night and confessed to one another that they were unable to find any stories for their Sunday editions.

Stevens announced that he was not going to return to his office without a story, he was going to fake. Reluctant to be scooped (even by a fake), the others agreed to cooperate with him. They walked to the Oxford Hotel at about ten o'clock. While drinking some beer there, Lewis suggested that they create one big hoax instead of four little ones. The others agreed and considered several ideas. They might report that five men had come to Denver to acquire land for a new steel mill, or they might invent a kidnapping story. They might claim that detectives from Boston or New York were in Denver, following two people suspected of kidnapping a rich young woman. The reporters rejected both ideas. Their readers might become too suspicious of them. Besides, if anyone telegraphed the police in Boston or New York, the story about the kidnapping would be exposed as a hoax in an hour or two.

Tournay and Lewis suggested creating a foreign story, one that would be more difficult to expose as a hoax. They considered a story about Russia, but no one knew enough about that country to write it. Spain seemed to be a good country; they might write about one of its bull fights. Or they might write about Holland and its windmills. Then someone mentioned China and its Great Wall.

"Let's tear it down," Lewis suggested.

Wilber says the four reporters agreed upon the basic details. They would write that a party of engineers from a Wall Street firm had arrived in Denver, en route to China. The engineers planned to inspect the Great Wall and to consider its eventual demolition. The Chinese wanted to level the entire wall as a gesture of good will "and to show the world that China welcomed trade."

After drinking more beer, the reporters walked to the swanky Windsor Hotel and asked a clerk there for help. With his cooperation, each of the reporters signed the hotel's register. They used fictitious names, the names of their fictitious Wall Street engineers. The clerk promised that, if anyone asked about the engineers, he would say they never talked to him. They had talked to the press, however, paid their bills, and left early that Sunday morning. After drinking another beer, the reporters agreed "to maintain absolute secrecy" for as long as they lived.

Wilber's article in the *North American Review* adds that the *Post* printed its story in red ink. Wilshire's editor supposedly liked the story, but was unhappy because it was not an exclusive. Nevertheless, he published it on page 1.

Wilber adds that a Denver bishop returned to the United States several years later. The bishop, Henry W. Warren of the Methodist Episcopal Church, had just completed a long trip through China. He spoke at Trinity Church in Denver, and Wilshire was assigned to cover the story. The bishop talked about "the power of the printed word." As an example, he told the congregation that China's Boxer Rebellion had been caused by several reporters who created a wild tale. The tale claimed "that the huge sacred Chinese wall was to be razed by American engineers, and the country thrown wide open to hated foreigners."[6]

The Chinese were infuriated when they learned that American engineers intended to demolish their Great Wall. In retaliation, they massacred hundreds of the Westerners living in their country.

Unfortunately, the *North American Review* failed to identify Wilber, and Wilber failed to identify his source. Moreover, Wilber's story contained at least a dozen errors. None of the Denver papers published the story in red ink. None published the story on their front page. None mentioned four engineers. They mentioned only one (Lewis), and he represented a Chicago syndicate (not a firm on Wall Street). The Denver papers also reported that Lewis stopped at the Oxford Hotel (not the Windsor), and that the Chinese planned to tear down only a portion of their wall (not the entire wall).

Despite Wilber's errors, other publications reprinted his story. In 1956, his entire story was reprinted in a book, *Great Hoaxes of All Time*.[7] A second book, published in 1958, seems to have rewritten Wilber's story, but also reveals his source. It explains that "the last survivor, Hal Wilshire, let out the secret."[8]

In 1970, a Denver magazine reprinted Wilber's story. In addition, it confirmed the fact that a man named Henry White Warren served as bishop of the Methodist Episcopal Church in Denver around the time of the hoax. Moreover, Warren had traveled to the Orient, including China, and "doubtless lectured about the Orient in numerous churches, Denver's Trinity among them."[9]

Both the original hoax and Wilber's tale about its effects reappeared in 1982 and again in 1984. In 1982, *Reader's Digest* published an article about China's Great Wall. A paragraph on the final page repeats, as fact, Wilber's claim that the Denver hoax "triggered riots throughout China and helped to ignite the Boxer Rebellion in which thousands of lives were lost."[10]

In 1984, a columnist at Denver's *Rocky Mountain News* was asked about the tale and responded that, so far as she was able to trace it, "the story first appeared in print in the *North American Review* in 1939." The columnist then repeated most of Wilber's details, including several of his errors.[11]

Wilber may be at least partially correct. Bishop Warren may have said that reporters caused the Boxer Rebellion. As a missionary who served in China, Warren may have been reluctant to admit the truth: the fact that American missionaries contributed to the war. The missionaries, especially Catholics, demanded special favors and interfered with China's legal system. Missionaries also encouraged the Chinese to abandon their traditional culture and religions. Chinese leaders feared that the missionaries were weakening their citizens' morals and destroying their culture, especially their emphasis upon the family. Thus they viewed Christianity as a serious threat to their way of life, "much as a modern American might view communism."[12]

The reporters who created the hoax must have known that Warren was mistaken and that other factors, not their story, caused the Boxer Rebellion. The problems in China had started hundreds of years earlier and, at the time of the hoax, the newspapers in Denver published numerous stories about them.[13] Since the reporters worked for the papers, they must have read, perhaps even proofread, at least some of the stories. Also, experts on China and the Boxer Rebellion never heard of the hoax. Books about the Boxer Rebellion never mention it.

Why did Wilber make so many errors? Wilber obviously failed to check the facts, even those easily available in Denver libraries. Instead, he may have based his story entirely upon newsroom tales about the hoax—the exaggerated tales passed from one generation of journalists to the next. Or Wilber may have interviewed one of the reporters, perhaps Hal Wilshire. If Wilber waited several years before writing his story—until Wilshire's death—he may have forgotten some details. Then, to make the story more interesting, he may have guessed at (or exaggerated) others.

Why did other writers repeat Wilber's errors? The reporters in Denver created an interesting story, and Wilber obviously improved it. The task of checking Wilber's details (and correcting his errors) would have required days of hard work, including a trip to Denver to search for the stories published in 1899. If, after all that work, the other writers succeeded — if they exposed Wilber's errors — their stories about the hoax might become less interesting (and less valuable).

Thus they had no incentive to expose the hoax. It was easier and more profitable for them to repeat it, along with all of Wilber's embellishments.

An Enduring Hoax: H. L. Mencken's Fraudulent History of the White House Bathtub

 charming tale about the White House bathtub has become America's most enduring hoax. A Baltimore journalist created the hoax in 1917 and confessed, three times, that it was nonsense. Despite his confessions, the hoax continues to appear in respected publications. President Truman repeated the hoax, and all three television networks broadcast it. Even respected historians quote and reprint it.

The hoax persists because it is such a whimsical tale. Its author, H. L. Mencken, created the hoax for the fun of it, to distract Americans from the horrors of World War I.

Mencken's father owned a cigar factory in Baltimore and expected him to take it over. Instead, Mencken applied for a job with the Baltimore *Morning Herald*. Because he was young and inexperienced, its editor refused to hire him. He suggested, however, that Mencken might return now and then to see whether there were any stories for him to cover.

Other editors gave similar advice to the young men looking for newspaper jobs. Many of the young men never returned. Others returned once or twice, then became discouraged because they were never given anything to do. Mencken reappeared at 7:30 every night for a month. At the end of the month, the editor sent him to a neighboring suburb, and he returned with a story about a stolen buggy. After that, he was given more assignments, then hired at a salary of $7 a week.

By the age of twenty-five, Mencken was the newspaper's editor-in-chief.[1] In 1906, the newspaper was sold, and he became editor of the Baltimore *Sunday Sun*. He also began to write a column for the paper, and other newspapers reprinted it. Thus he became a national celebrity.

The *Sun* stopped publishing Mencken's column during the First World War, apparently because he favored the Germans (rather than the English or French). A friend at the *New York Evening Mail* asked Mencken to write a column for that paper, but warned him to avoid topics related to the war. The friend wanted Mencken to amuse, not offend, his readers.

One of Mencken's new columns insisted that New York should withdraw from the United States. Another column insisted that poetry was wicked and immoral. Mencken explained that all the columns — his verbal fireworks — were intended "to inject a little lighthearted fun into rather grim war days."

Mencken's most famous hoax appeared in the *Evening Mail* on December 28, 1917. His column, titled that day "A Neglected Anniversary," began: "On December 20, there flitted past us, absolutely without public notice, one of the most important profane anniversaries in American history — to wit: the 75th anniversary of the introduction of the bathtub into these states. Not a plumber fired a salute or hung out a flag. Not a governor proclaimed a day of prayer. Not a newspaper called attention to the day."[2]

The day had not been entirely forgotten, however. Eight or nine months earlier, a young surgeon connected with the Public Health Service in Washington had discovered the facts while looking into the early history of public hygiene. At his suggestion, a committee was formed to hold a banquet celebrating the bathtub's seventy-fifth anniversary. Before the plans were complete, Washington banned the sale of alcoholic beverages. Thus, the plans had to be abandoned, and the day passed wholly unmarked, even in the nation's capital.

Mencken added that the nation's first bathtub was installed on December 20, 1842, in Cincinnati, "then a squalid frontier town, and even today surely no leader in culture." Cincinnati contained many enterprising merchants, and one of them, a man named Adam Thompson, dealt in cotton and grain. Thompson often traveled to England and acquired the habit of bathing while visiting that country.

The English bathtub was a puny contrivance, little more than a glorified dishpan, and people needed a servant to help fill and empty it. Thompson conceived the notion of improving the English tub, of devising one large enough to hold the entire body of an adult male. Thompson also wanted to devise a new water supply: pipes from a central reservoir, so people would no longer need a servant to haul water to the scene.

In 1842, Thompson built the nation's first modern bathtub in his Cincinnati home. Thompson had a large well in his garden, and he installed a pump to lift water into his house. The pump, operated by six Negroes, worked much like an old-time fire engine. Pipes carried the water to a cypress storage tank in the attic. Two other pipes ran from the tank to the bathroom. One, carrying cold water, ran directly to the bathroom. "The other, designed to provide warm water, ran down the great chimney of the kitchen and was coiled inside it like a giant spring."

The tub itself was made of mahogany by Cincinnati's leading cabinet maker. "It was nearly 7 feet long and fully 4 feet wide. To make it water-tight, the interior was lined with sheet lead, carefully soldered at the joints. The whole contraption weighed about 1,750 pounds, and the floor of the room in which it was placed had to be reinforced to support it."

On December 20, 1842, Thompson took his first two baths in this luxurious tub, a cold bath at 8 a.m. and a warm bath some time during the afternoon. Heated by the kitchen fire, the warm water reached a temperature of 105 degrees. On Christmas Day, Thompson invited a party of gentlemen to dinner, showed them the tub, and gave an exhibition bath. Four guests, including a French visitor, risked plunges into it. The next day, all Cincinnati heard about it. Local newspapers described the tub and opened their columns to violent discussions about it.

The opposition was bitter. Critics said the tub was undemocratic and unhealthy, an "obnoxious toy from England, designed to corrupt the democratic simplicity." Doctors worried that bathing was dangerous, a possible cause of "phthisic, rheumatic fevers, inflammation of the lungs, and the whole category of zymotic diseases."

The controversy spread to other cities. In 1843, Baltimore considered an ordinance to prohibit bathing between November 1 and March 15. The ordinance failed by only two votes. Virginia placed a tax of $30 a year on all the bathtubs installed in that state. Four cities — Hartford, Providence, Charleston, and Wilmington — imposed special and very heavy water rates upon citizens who installed bathtubs in their homes. In 1845, Boston made bathing unlawful, except upon medical advice, but its ordinance was never enforced and was repealed in 1862.

Clearly, the Thompson tub was too expensive for most people. In 1845, the common price for installing one in New York was $500. A Brooklyn plumber devised a zinc tub and, after 1848, all the plumbers in New York were putting them in. Medical opposition soon collapsed. In 1859, the American Medical Association held its annual meeting in Boston, and a poll of its members showed that nearly 55 percent regarded bathing as harmless. Twenty percent regarded it as beneficial.

Millard Fillmore, the nation's thirteenth president, gave the bathtub recognition and respectability. While still vice president, Fillmore visited Cincinnati and inspected the original Thompson tub. Thompson had died, but the gentleman who bought his home preserved its bathroom. Fillmore was entertained in the home, and biographers say he took a bath in the tub. Experiencing no ill effects, he became an advocate of the new invention. After becoming president, he instructed his secretary of war to seek bids for the construction of a bathtub in the White House. For a moment, his instructions revived the old controversy. Opponents complained that other presidents had gotten along without any such luxuries. Disregarding the clamor, Fillmore's secretary of war called for bids, then awarded the contract to a firm of Philadelphia engineers "who proposed to furnish a tub of cast iron, capable of floating the largest man."

Fillmore's bathtub was installed in 1851 and remained in the White House until the Cleveland administration, when it was replaced by the present enameled tub. President Fillmore's example broke down all the remaining opposition. By 1860, newspaper advertisements showed that every hotel in New York had a bathtub, and some had two or three.

Mencken thought that his hoax was so obviously fraudulent that no one would believe it. To his amusement, then to his consternation and finally to his horror, he began to see the hoax reprinted, or its "facts" quoted, in other publications.[3] In 1926, Mencken decided that his joke had gone far enough; thus, he confessed that the entire story was fictitious. He published the confession in his syndicated column and claimed that it appeared in thirty newspapers with "a combined circulation of more than 250 million."[4] (That may have been a mistake or, more probably, another of Mencken's exaggerations. Today, all 1,650 of the nation's daily newspapers have a combined circulation of only sixty-four million, one-fourth the total Mencken attributed to the thirty newspapers that published his column.)

Mencken's confession, "Melancholy Reflections," appeared on May 23, 1926. It admitted that his story was "a tissue of absurdities, all of them deliberate and most of them obvious."[5] At first, he said, he had regarded the hoax with considerable satisfaction. Some of the nation's most respected publications reprinted it as fact, and some readers asked for more information about the topic. Other readers sent him additional details that helped prove his story was true.

"But the worst was to come," Mencken continued. "Pretty soon I began to encounter my preposterous 'facts' in the writings of other men. They began to be used by chiropractors and other such quacks as evidence of the stupidity of medical men. They began to be cited by medical men as proof of the progress of public hygiene. They got into learned journals. They were alluded to on the floor of Congress. They crossed the ocean and were discussed solemnly in England, and on the continent. Finally, I began to find them in standard works of reference. Today, I believe, they are accepted as gospel everywhere on Earth."

Mencken said he was reluctant to reveal the truth because he would be criticized for it. The residents of Cincinnati had begun to boast that the bathtub industry started in their community, and Mencken feared that they would charge him with "spreading lies against them." Furthermore, "[t]he chiropractors will damn me for blowing up their ammunition. The medical gents, having swallowed my quackery, will now denounce me as a quack for exposing them. And in the end, no doubt, the thing will simmer down to a general feeling that I have once more committed some vague and sinister crime against the United States, and there will be a renewal of the demand that I be deported to Russia."

Mencken concluded that people dislike the truth, and that the people who try to tell it become unpopular. Nevertheless, Mencken confessed: "All I care to do today is reiterate, in the most solemn and awful terms, that my history of the bathtub, printed on December 28, 1917, was pure buncombe. If there were any facts in it, they got there accidentally and against my design."

Despite Mencken's confession, other publications continued to reprint his hoax. So on July 25, 1926, he tried again. In an essay titled "Hymn to the Truth," he said that, initially, he liked the hoax. "It was artfully devised," he explained, "and it contained some buffooneries of considerable juiciness. I had confidence that the customers of the *Evening Mail* would like it." Unfortunately, they liked it too well. "That is to say," he continued, "they swallowed it as gospel, gravely and horribly. Worse, they began sending clippings of it to friends east, west, north, and south, and so it spread to other papers, and then to the magazines and weeklies of opinion, and then to the scientific press, and finally to the reference books."[6]

Mencken added that he had revealed the hoax's absurdities two months earlier, on May 23. "I confessed categorically that it was all buncombe," he said. Thirty great newspapers, including the Boston *Herald,* had published his confession. The *Herald* placed his confession under a four-column headline on its editorial page. Next to his confession, the *Herald* placed a cartoon labeled, "The American Public Will Swallow Anything." Mencken complained that three weeks later — and in the same section — the *Herald* reprinted his hoax "soberly, and as a piece of news."

Mencken's second confession continued: "What ails the truth is that it is mainly uncomfortable, and often dull. The human mind seeks something more amusing, and more caressing. What the actual history of the bathtub may be I don't know: digging it out would be a dreadful job, and the result, after all that labor, would probably be a string of banalities. The fiction I concocted back in 1917 was at least better than that. There were heroes in it, and villains. It revealed a conflict, with virtue winning. So it was embraced by mankind, precisely as the story of George Washington and the cherry tree was embraced. . . . "[7]

Finally, Mencken again concluded: "No normal human being wants to hear the truth. It is the passion of a small and aberrant minority of men, most of them pathological. They are hated for telling it while they live, and when they die they are swiftly forgotten. What remains in the world, in the field of wisdom, is a series of long tested and solidly agreeable lies."[8]

In 1927, Mencken rewrote portions of his second confession, "Hymn to the Truth," and reprinted it in a book. Thus, for a third time, Mencken admitted that his story was "a tissue of somewhat heavy absurdities, all of them deliberate and most of them obvious." Nevertheless, he estimated that at least nine-tenths of his readers believed it.[9]

In 1926, a distinguished magazine, *Scribner's,* published an article about the history of bathing. *Scribner's* explained that the nation's first presidents bathed in the Potomac River, sometimes in the nude. President John Quincy Adams plunged in whenever the weather was suitable, but it was a risky business. *Scribner's* explained that Adams left his clothes lying on the river bank. When someone stole them, the president was forced to send a boy to the White House for more. President Adams was also trapped in the Potomac by one of the nation's first female correspondents. Adams had refused to grant her an interview, apparently because he disliked the notion of female correspondents. *Scribner's* reported that the woman sat on President Adams's clothes and refused to let him wade ashore until he agreed to give her a story.

Scribner's added that other presidents continued to bath in the Potomac "up to Millard Fillmore, who when he came into office caused the first bathtub to be installed in the White House."[10] The magazine then repeated all Mencken's nonsense about the bathtub.

Even a newspaper in Mencken's home town repeated the hoax. In 1929, the *Baltimore News* published a front-page column that said white enameled bathtubs were about to become obsolete and would be replaced by up-to-date tubs that came in more vivid colors. The column explained, "There are delicate blues and pinks for blonde beauties, green for red-haired belles, and more inflammatory tints for brunettes."[11] After describing the new colors, the column added that a wealthy grain dealer in Cincinnati had installed the nation's first private bathtub but "was the subject of much ridicule and some bitter denunciation." Millard Fillmore saw the Cincinnati tub and had one installed in the White House, "bringing down upon his head the wrath of his political opponents."

Two years later, Arthur Train wrote *Puritan's Progress,* an informal account of the Puritans and their descendants, including "their manners & customs, their virtues & vices." On page 51, Train states that the first American bathtub "was, I am informed, made of mahogany and lined with sheet lead, and exhibited by its proud owner at a Christmas party in Cincinnati in 1842."[12]

Mencken's story also fooled the *New York Times.* On August 4, 1935, the *Times* reported that tenants on the city's East Side were demanding the installation of bathtubs in their apartments. The paper then summarized the history of the bathtub, and its summary included Mencken's "facts" about the Cincinnati tub.

The *Times* also discussed the history of New York's bathtubs, and may have been even more mistaken about it. It explained that an apartment building still standing on 42nd Street had been one of the first to install all-iron tubs with claw feet. The building had been constructed in about 1870, and workmen hoisting bathtubs into the building created a sensation. Not far away was a model tenement, constructed during the 1890s for the poor. The *Times* reported that every apartment in the tenement contained a bathtub, but that poor families taken into the building "stored their fuel in the bathtubs and bathed the baby in the coal scuttle."[13] The paper admitted that some readers might deny it; nevertheless, the practice was common throughout the United States.

Readers responded that the *Times* was obviously mistaken. They explained that most housing projects were centrally heated. Because the projects were also supplied with gas and electricity, their occupants did not need any coal.[14] But even if they had used coal, they were unlikely to store it in their bathtubs.

In 1917, Mencken said he was celebrating the bathtub's seventy-fifth anniversary. Other journalists apparently noted the date. Twenty-five years later, on December 20, 1942, they celebrated the bathtub's one-hundredth anniversary. Since then, the story has continued to reappear, usually in January. President Fillmore was born on January 7, 1800, and journalists mention the bathtub in stories about his accomplishments as president.

Even President Truman repeated the story. Workmen remodeled the White House during the early 1950s, and everyone involved in the remodeling seemed to believe that President Fillmore installed the building's first bathtub. When reporters criticized President Truman's plans to add a balcony to the White House, Truman responded that there had been considerable opposition to the first bathtub, too.[15]

"CBS Evening News" repeated the story in 1976. The *Baltimore Sun* immediately responded, "On the CBS Evening News last Wednesday, Roger Mudd reported on the graveside ceremonies for the anniversary of the birth of President Millard Fillmore 'best known for the compromise of 1850, the postage stamp, and the first bathtub in the White House.' " The *Sun* complained that Mencken's tale about the bathtub—"and the stuff about Cincinnati, too"—was nonsense.[16]

The ABC and NBC television networks apparently made the same mistake. Thus Mencken's hoax was passed on to another forty-five or fifty million Americans.[17]

A few publications, including the *Saturday Evening Post,* have tried to expose the hoax. On November 13, 1943, the *Post* reported that Adam Thompson may have invented the bathtub, but that H. L. Mencken invented Thompson.[18] It explained that Thompson and his tub were part of an unusually persistent hoax that Mencken perpetrated in 1917. It concluded: "Like some Frankensteinian monster, Adam Thompson has got completely out of his creator's control. Mencken has denied the truth of his yarn at least three times. Thompson continues to bob up in print just the same. He will undoubtedly keep right on doing so after this."

The *Washington Post* published another exposé on January 4, 1977, but realized that it would also fail to stop the hoax. The paper predicted that its exposé "will not even slow it up, any more than a single grape placed on the railroad tracks would slow up a freight train."[19]

The *Post* called Millard Fillmore a genuine patriot and an effective president, but "the victim of one of the most charming myths in the nation's history." It added that no one knew the true story of the first White House bathtub. Moreover, it agreed with Mencken, who said that digging out the true story would be a dreadful job, and probably less interesting than his hoax.

In fact, a magazine editor named Beverly Smith had dug out the true story twenty-five years earlier. In 1952, Smith reported: "Never in 26 years of reporting had I run into such a baffling comedy of errors, fakes, and legends."[20] The first evidence that Smith uncovered indicated that President Rutherford B. Hayes used the first White House bathtub sometime after 1877. Later evidence indicated that Andrew Jackson denounced the first White House bathtubs as undemocratic and removed them in 1829. Other evidence indicated that, by accident, H. L. Mencken was right: that President Fillmore installed the first White House bathtub.

After weeks of additional research, Smith concluded that the first presidents to occupy the White House—John Adams and Thomas Jefferson—may have had personal, portable tubs. Andrew Jackson spent $45,000 refurbishing the White House and clearly enjoyed "warm, cold, and shower baths." Thus, the most conclusive evidence indicated "that the first regular bath . . . was installed somewhere between 1829 and

1833 by the rough, tough, tobacco-chewing Tennessean, Andrew Jackson. . . . "[21]

Jackson never told the American public about his bathtub, probably because bathtubs were still a luxury and would have tarnished his image. One of his predecessors, Martin Van Buren, was defeated when he ran for re-election, in part because of his image as a dandy. Van Buren was "accused of turning the White House into a palace, drinking champagne and taking warm baths."[22]

Despite Smith's revelations, respected historians and scholars continue to quote Mencken's hoax. In 1973, Daniel J. Boorstin published *The Americans: The Democratic Experience*. Dr. Boorstin was director of the Smithsonian Institution, and his book was part of a three-volume study of U.S. history. Reviewers deemed his book "scholarly" and "generally excellent." But on page 353, Dr. Boorstin states, "In 1851, when President Millard Fillmore reputedly installed the first permanent bath and water closet in the White House, he was criticized for doing something that was 'both unsanitary and undemocratic.' "[23]

Another historian repeated the hoax in 1981, but with an unusual twist. Paul F. Boller, Jr., author of *Presidential Anecdotes,* wrote that Mrs. Fillmore, not her husband, "installed the first bathtub in the Executive Mansion."[24] Boller's publisher liked the story so much that he placed a picture of President Fillmore—seated in the tub—on the book's cover.

A paperback edition, published in 1982, corrected the error. It explained: "Even his chief claim to fame—installing the first bathtub in the White House—is without foundation.[25] Despite Boller's correction, his publisher kept Fillmore's picture on the book's cover.

Why has the hoax fooled so many readers? Mencken concluded that Americans like some lies more than the truth—that lies are often more interesting. Also, he wrote about obscure events that occurred seventy-five years earlier. Few readers knew anything about the topic, and none could easily check the details. Moreover, he wrote the hoax in a convincing manner, mixing fact with fiction and including details that impressed his readers. Thus his story was not a total fraud. He invented the Cincinnati merchant named Adam Thompson but also mentioned prominent Americans whom the public knew and trusted, including President Fillmore.

Attempts to expose the hoax failed because many of the people who read Mencken's first column failed to notice or read his retractions.

Millions of other Americans saw his hoax reprinted elsewhere. Many of the other publications failed to reprint Mencken's confessions. As a result, Americans continue to believe and repeat his hoax.

While paging through old newspapers and magazines, Americans will continue to find copies of Mencken's hoax reprinted in them. Because the hoax is so amusing, some readers—even respected scholars— will believe, quote, and reprint it, thus passing the hoax on to another generation of Americans.

10 The End of an Era: New York's Sin Ship

HE story was sensational! It reported that a seventeen-thousand-ton ship was anchored in the Atlantic Ocean, and that the ship was offering rich New Yorkers all the liquor they could drink. The ship was mysterious. But the story also involved crime, danger, adventure, and beautiful women.

Like most hoaxes, it fascinated the public. But after creating the hoax, a young reporter lost control of it. Other newspapers quoted his story. Sources from Washington to San Francisco were questioned about it. The Coast Guard searched for the ship, and the British government was embarrassed by it.

The story seemed to confuse other reporters and editors. None wanted to be scooped by a young rival. Some journalists may have suspected that the story was a hoax, but none could prove that it was a hoax. Thus none ignored the story. Instead, they searched for the ship and published dozens of other stories about it, stories that contained a mixture of fact, speculation, nonsense, and lies.

At first, facts uncovered by other reporters seemed to confirm the ship's presence in the Atlantic. As a result, news agencies transmitted the story to newspapers throughout the United States, and millions of Americans began to read about New York's "sin ship."

It was the third—and last—major hoax published by a New York paper. The first (and most successful) appeared in the New York Sun. On

August 21, 1835, the *Sun* began to publish its famous "Moon Story." New York's second major hoax appeared thirty-nine years later. On November 9, 1874, the *New York Herald* reported that wild animals had escaped from the Central Park Zoo.

Like the earlier hoaxes, the "sin ship" may have seemed like a harmless prank. Moreover, it succeeded for a week. Why? The details were realistic and excited the public. But ethical standards in the field of journalism were changing. At the end of the week, the young reporter was punished—not rewarded—for his work.

The 18th Amendment to the U.S. Constitution—prohibition—went into effect in 1920. The amendment banned the manufacture, transportation, and sale of alcoholic beverages, except for medicinal purposes.

On a Saturday morning, August 16, 1924, the *New York Herald Tribune* described an obvious violation of that amendment. A four-column headline on the newspaper's front page reported that New Yorkers were buying liquor aboard an ocean liner anchored 15 miles offshore. A smaller headline added:

> Wine, Women, Jazz and
> Revelry Turn Night to
> Day on Mystery Ship
> Flying the British Flag

The story was written by Sanford Jarrell, a young reporter for the *Herald Tribune*. Jarrell revealed that the ship was a playground for the rich, and that the ship had anchored "beyond the pale of the law." His story continued: "A Negro jazz orchestra furnishes the music to which millionaires, flappers, and chorus girls whirl on a waxed floor with the tang of salt air in their lungs. . . . Yachtsmen bent on gay parties go out there daily and anchor in the vicinity of the ship, which caters royally to their whims and fancies."[1]

There had been rumors about floating cabarets along the Atlantic Coast, but Jarrell insisted, "[t]his boat is neither rumor, nor is it fiction."

Jarrell said it had taken him two days to find the ship. Fire Island was a popular summer resort located off the southern shore of Long Island, and residents there had observed something "lit up like a chandelier." After hearing about the story, Jarrell went out in a fast boat but was unable to find anything. He returned that Thursday morning and questioned some boatmen. They had heard about the ship, they said, but none knew her exact location.

Later that Thursday, Jarrell found a rum runner suspected of making frequent trips to the ship. The rum runner agreed to take him out, but only after he proved that he was a newspaper reporter, not a government agent. Jarrell accompanied a party of pleasure seekers, three young women and four men. They left aboard a thirty-five-foot boat called a "sea sled," and Jarrell noted that the vessel seemed "ideal for smuggling rum and outdistancing revenue cutters." Half an hour later, the boat's motor backfired, and the tiny engine compartment burst into flames. The two-man crew extinguished the flames before they caused any serious damage, then continued out into the Atlantic.

About an hour later, they struck a submerged log, cutting a jagged hole in the boat's hull and breaking several blades off its propeller. A pump kept the boat from sinking, but it drifted helplessly for two hours. The crew managed to repair the boat before it drifted farther out into the Atlantic, then headed slowly back toward shore.

A fast power boat passed them, and Jarrell learned that it was carrying ten men and women to the ship. Jarrell and a young woman named "Irene" abandoned their crippled boat. After joining the party of ten, they reached the big ship.

Jarrell's description of the ship's ballroom fascinated his readers. "There and on the promenade deck were 60 people in all," he wrote. "The men were obviously wealthy, at least they had plenty of money to spend. They bought drinks with abandon. . . . The food was quite reasonable and very good. There were a dozen uniformed waiters who looked after the wants of the guests in a very efficient fashion. The drinks, on the other hand, were sold at exorbitant prices, much higher than in New York speak-easies. . . . "[2] The cheapest drink cost a dollar.

Other details in Jarrell's story were even more startling:

A copy of the Statue of Liberty had been constructed on one deck, and guests toasted it after midnight.

No one was given any free drinks. But now and then some gentleman would order drinks for everyone, at a cost of about $100.

The seamen were British and "almost the only sober people aboard."

After midnight, the party grew more and more hilarious, and the seamen carried drunken guests to bed.

The ship made no attempt to hide, but her identity was a mystery. Jarrell explained: "No doubt when it left its port in England, the name of the boat was plainly lettered on the bow and stern. Such lettering cannot be observed today. Even guests who had been aboard the ship before did not know its identity."

Rum runners called it "that German liner." But Jarrell reported that, "It is believed a syndicate of wealthy Englishmen bought her and decided to take a quiet flyer in the American bootlegging game."

Many of the ship's linens, towels, and lifebelts bore the inscription "Friedrich der Grosse." Other pieces of equipment were new and bore no inscriptions. The ship's rugged fittings indicated that she had been built in Germany, and Jarrell speculated that she had been used as a German liner, then operated in the South American trade. "In 1922," Jarrell continued, "a passenger vessel called the City of Honolulu was burned in the Pacific and, although records are confusing, it was said . . . that she was the former Friedrich der Grosse."

Other ships were also carrying liquor to the United States, but the other ships returned to Bermuda or the Bahamas to replenish their supplies. Jarrell estimated that the seventeen-thousand-ton liner would be able to carry enough liquor "to last for years, even at a rate of consumption which would dazzle the dourest statisticians." However, the ship would have to return to a port more often to refuel. Her profits were another puzzle. Jarrell estimated that about a hundred people boarded the ship on weekends, but that fewer than fifty boarded it on weekdays. To earn a profit, even at her exorbitant prices, the ship would need at least five hundred customers every night.

Jarrell added that he spent that Thursday night aboard the liner. He went to sleep at 4 a.m. "in a neat little stateroom which cost only $5." He was awakened at 6 a.m. and told that a launch was leaving in half an hour. Thus, his story concluded:

> A remote dream has become reality. The time may come when our 12-mile limit line will be dotted with her sisters. If Great Britain does not, at the instance of our government, put down its official foot on such practices, an industry may flourish out where waves are waves and belong to no man or country. Great hotels may spread like bread on the waters, with clientele recruited from the drinking aristocracy of the nation.

Other newspapers copied Jarrell's story. Typically, the *New York Evening Post* summarized Jarrell's description of the "sin ship," then

added that customs agents were investigating the matter. The *Post* speculated that the ship might have sailed directly from Scotland with a load
of whiskey, and that the ship was trying to increase her profits by operat-
ing as a floating cabaret while selling most of her whiskey to the area's
rum runners. The paper explained that a large ocean liner could not earn
a profit from a cabaret alone.[3]

The *Post* added that passengers arriving aboard another ocean liner
"said they had seen a craft resembling the 'floating cafe.' " It also reported that liquor dealers in Bermuda feared that smaller rum runners
carrying liquor to the United States might be captured by prohibition
agents or sunk by winter storms. To continue their sales in the United
States, the Scots had been expected to send large steamers, such as the
one Jarrell described, directly to the United States. Moreover, customs
officials "had suspected for some time that wealthy New Yorkers were
holding skylarking parties aboard ships in Rum Row."

Another New York daily, the *World,* added: "One verification of
Jarrell's story came last night from Capt. Charles Veltman, fisherman,
of Bay Shore, who has been taking out fishing parties since 1886. Capt.
Veltman said that early last evening two or three reputed rum runners,
'drunk,' had been boasting along the waterfront that they had just come
in from the floating jazz palace."[4]

Boatloads of New Yorkers—some curious, others thirsty—began to
crisscross the Atlantic Ocean off Fire Island, looking for the ship. Some
fishermen claimed that they could find the ship, and they apparently
earned hundreds of dollars by renting their boats to the curious: to
reporters, sightseers, and prohibition agents.

At 9 a.m. Sunday, five reporters and photographers from other
newspapers rented a sixty-five-foot boat "from a grumpy seafarer who
insisted that he knew where the mirage ship could be found."[5] The journalists were followed by a boat carrying six young men, probably prohibition agents also looking for the ship. The sea was rough, and the
journalists were thrown about violently. One was hurled against a railing
and "painfully hurt." They returned to shore, still followed by the six
young men.

Jarrell's second story appeared that Sunday. It was published on the
Herald Tribune's front page and reported that officials in Washington
had ordered the Coast Guard cutter Seneca "to hunt down and report on
the seventeen-thousand-ton steamship." Other Coast Guard cutters had
been ordered to watch for similar vessels that might be lying just outside

the territorial waters of the United States. The Coast Guard had also been ordered to "uncover the means by which such vessels receive coal and other supplies."[6]

The *New York Times* agreed that a Coast Guard cutter had been ordered to search for the ship, but added: "It is not believed she (the "sin ship") will hover long in the vicinity of the American shores, for Great Britain frowns upon the practice of flouting the local laws. . . . "

At first, no one seemed to know how U.S. laws could be applied to the "sin ship." The *New York Times* explained that rum runners obtaining liquor from larger vessels could be seized when they returned to the United States. However, government agents might not be able to seize launches that carried only visitors to and from such vessels. Continuing its speculation, the paper added: "It is thought likely in Washington, however, that pleasure seekers who visit the floating barroom would be much inclined to bring a bottle or two back with them, and if they did so, they and the launches would both be liable under the transportation clause of the Volstead Act."[7]

The *Times* also revealed that Coast Guard officers had been approached a year earlier by a man who wanted to sell stock "in just such an enterprise."[8] The man had not actually tried to sell any stock to the Coast Guard officers, but wanted to learn whether the venture could work.

"A veteran shipping man" quoted (but not identified) by the *Times* was more skeptical. He warned that the entire story "would turn out to be an adroit piece of moving-picture publicity to herald some feature picture soon to be released."

Even more skeptically, the *New York World* reported that the ship "has vanished like a mirage."[9] Moreover, the *World* immediately challenged portions of Jarrell's story. Jarrell's first story had claimed that, "[o]n Monday night, the vessel could be very plainly seen from Fire Island." When questioned by reporters, Coast Guardsmen on Fire Island insisted that they never saw the ship. Yet any ship anchored only fifteen miles off the island would be visible from their watch tower.

A smaller paper, the *Bay Shore Journal,* revealed that one of its reporters had accompanied Jarrell that Thursday night. Its reporter agreed that their small boat struck a log, but added that the boat returned to shore with everyone—including Jarrell—still aboard. Coast Guardsmen helped tow the boat ashore and said that only five people were aboard it: the captain, his helper, and three passengers.[10] Jarrell had reported that the boat carried a much larger party of pleasure seekers.

At first, government officials seemed to believe Jarrell's story. When interviewed by reporters, they provided more stories about the ship, a mixture of fact and speculation.

R. Q. Merrick, the prohibition enforcement director for New York and New Jersey, told reporters: "We had heard stories about big rum vessels which were acting as floating cabarets, but the *Herald Tribune* account is the first definite evidence that such a thing exists. There is nothing that we can do about it, so far as I can see personally, as the ship, if it is anchored 15 miles off Fire Island, is completely out of our jurisdiction, and is not violating our prohibition laws. These ships can stay 15, 30, or 50 miles off shore, and people can go out to them without violating the law, so long as these ships are not inside the United States territorial waters."[11]

Merrick insisted, however, that New Yorkers going out to the ship "apparently have more money than brains."

Other government officials agreed that the ship probably existed, but disagreed about what they could do about her. Several officials insisted that small boats carrying passengers to the vessel violated U.S. customs laws. Thus, the boats' captains and passengers could be fined and reprimanded.

A representative for the Anti-Saloon League added that the ship was certain to fail. He explained that Great Britain would order the ship to stop violating U.S. laws. The ship's patrons would also be stopped by the weather: by seasickness and winter storms. Moreover, the ship's prices were so high that few New Yorkers could afford to pay them.[12]

A top Coast Guard officer, W. V. E. Jacobs, was more skeptical. Jacobs said that his men regularly patrolled the area, and he did not believe that they could have overlooked the ship. "It is possible there is such a boat," he said, "but it is hardly probable."[13]

Other boatmen along the Atlantic Coast insisted that they never saw the ship, but few reporters believed them. News stories explained that the boatmen rarely told strangers anything about their highly profitable (and illegal) liquor trade. Typically, the *World* explained: "The fisher folk of Bay Shore, from whence the *Herald Tribune* reporter was supposed to have put out to the ship, were amazed, as they always are, when it is suggested there is rum running in their vicinity. They know nothing of her, they said."[14]

When questioned about the story, officials in Washington said the United States might ask Britain to identify the ship. British officials in the United States responded that they never heard of the ship and were surprised to learn that she was flying their flag. They promised, however, to seek more information about her. Despite their cooperation, the *New York Times* reported that the United States "might lodge an official protest to Britain."[15]

The *Herald Tribune*'s third story about the "sin ship" appeared on an inside page, without Jarrell's byline. Jarrell obviously wrote the story — and continued to lie. He reported that the Coast Guard cutter Seneca had been unable to find any trace of the seventeen-thousand-ton cabaret. He added that two more boatloads of party-goers had gone out to the liner, and that a fast rum runner had sped out to her with copies of the *Herald Tribune*.

Jarrell then explained why no one else could find the ship. Because of all the publicity, he said, the ship might have fled northward, to Rhode Island or Massachusetts, or it might "have dropped anchor 30 or 40 miles out." Jarrell added that, if the liner served only as a cabaret, its most profitable season would end by Labor Day; thus, she might already have left the area.

Other reporters continued to speculate about the ship's identity.

On Sunday, Jarrell had suggested that the ship might be the Kaiser Friedrich. The Kaiser Friedrich had been constructed about thirty-five years earlier for a German steamship line that also operated the Friedrich der Grosse. The German line, however, had refused to accept the ship from her builder because she burned too much coal during her trial runs. Jarrell continued: "The Kaiser Friedrich then became something of a nautical white elephant." It may have been used by the Russians. During the First World War, the Germans used it as a hospital ship. Later, they may have used it to house prisoners.

A Coast Guard officer speculated that the ship might be the Von Steuben. During the First World War, the Von Steuben had been named the Kronprinz Wilhelm and served as a German raider. It was captured, however, and interred in New York. After the war, the Von Steuben was sold for scrap and sailed for Baltimore.

Sources in San Francisco responded that the ship could not be the Friedrich der Grosse. The *New York Evening Post* explained that the Friedrich der Grosse "is now rusting at the bottom of the Pacific Ocean, 600 miles off the California coast." The Los Angeles Steamship Co. had purchased the ship after the war and rechristened it "[t]he City of Honolulu. . . . On its maiden voyage, it caught fire . . . half way between San Pedro and Honolulu. Several days later, it was sunk by a shell from the revenue cutter Shawnee. None of its equipment was salvaged; it was too badly burned."[16]

Reporters in Baltimore revealed that the ship could not be the Von Steuben. They found the Von Steuben in the harbor there, partly junked.

Thus the search continued. Army officers who often flew over the area reported, regrettably, that they never saw the ship. Another airplane, apparently rented by the *World,* flew along the Atlantic coastline at an altitude of twenty-five hundred feet. Visibility was good, but the crew found only a scattering of small craft. The *World* speculated that the "sin ship" "had been swallowed by the sea or had slipped over the horizon 40 miles from shore."

Similarly, other ships reaching New York "reported passing the vague spot described as the mirage ship's position without viewing anything approaching a 17,000-ton liner." One of the ships' captains said that he had heard radio reports about the vessel and "kept a sharp lookout but saw nothing." The captain of a second incoming vessel insisted that the ship was a myth. To earn a profit, he explained, a large ocean liner would have to take in at least $2,000 a day. If a floating cabaret attracted enough patrons to spend that much money, someone would see them traveling between the ship and shore.

When questioned about the story, editors at the *Herald Tribune* "upheld the authenticity of the report made by Mr. Jarrell."[17] The paper even published an editorial praising Jarrell. It compared Jarrell to Christopher Columbus and explained that, "It has been the lot of the pioneer ever to find on his return from a successful quest that those who remained at home . . . were seeking to belittle his discovery."

On Thursday, the *New York Times* said that the "sin ship" might be a prop, something created to publicize a movie. Publicists for the movie industry had fooled journalists before, and this seemed to be another of their stunts. Moreover, every newspaper in New York had received an advertisement signed, "Captain of the 12-Mile Limit Cafe." The advertisement stated, "If you want to see this ship, its rollicking crew, and its unusual equipment, go to the manager of your favorite motion picture theater and ask him to put on the picture *Wine.*"

Robert H. Cochrane, vice president of the Universal Pictures Corp., told reporters that the floating cabaret and a ship shown in the movie *Wine* were similar. Cochrane insisted, however, that Universal knew nothing else about the "sin ship." The movie *Wine* had been filmed in California months earlier, and the ship shown in the movie had not been brought to New York.[18] The advertisement was simply intended to exploit publicity given the "sin ship." The corporation thought "it would be good advertising to take advantage of a piece of good fortune."

Although unable to find the "sin ship," authorities on the East Coast captured four other rum runners that week. Their capture became front-page news, and made Jarrell's story more credible.

On Monday, the *New York Times* reported that customs agents had chased a rum runner about a mile, and that "machine gun fire from the customs boat silenced the occasional sputter of shots from the runner."[19] The customs agents chased the boat onto a beach and seized about fifty cases of whiskey. Its four-man crew escaped into a waiting automobile.

On Tuesday, customs agents captured six men and confiscated seven hundred cases of wines and liquors valued at $25,000.[20] Customs agents in a speed boat had been looking for the "sin ship." Instead, they noticed a seventy-foot submarine chaser running without lights. The *World* described the chase:

> A 30-knot pursuit ensued, but when the customs scout could not catch the fugitive, Revenue Agent Van Wie settled himself behind the machine gun and let fly 20 shots over the sub-chaser. When she did not heed the warning, he lowered his aim and fired again. He spattered the boat with clean hits but got the surprise of his smuggler-hunting career, for as the bullets struck they gave out a sharp metallic ring.[21]

The rum runners had covered their ship with armored plate. Nevertheless, the crew surrendered. The customs agents found that their bullets scarred the ship's deck and smashed her windows, but that she was in no danger of sinking. One crewman had been shot in a knee. Another said that a bullet had knocked off his hat.

When asked who employed him, the ship's captain smiled and said,

"I don't know." The *World* added that the entire crew was sober, and that the captain insisted, "I don't drink the stuff, and I won't have a man aboard who does."

At 3 a.m. Friday, Coast Guardsmen cruising off Long Island saw another long, slender craft with its lights dimmed. When ordered to halt, the craft started to slip away. The *New York Evening Post* reported: "The Coast Guards opened fire, and a moment later several bullets whizzed back across their bow. For an hour and a half, the two vessels raced northward. Then, the rum runner slowed down and came to a swaying stop. On the aft deck lay Antonio Pietro, a bullet through his chest." His five companions were captured.[22]

Two hours later, officers aboard the police boat Manhattan spotted a fifty-foot cabin cruiser named the Walter Thomas. The officers fired several warning shots, then opened fire in earnest:

> Immediately the men on the Walter Thomas began piling up cases of liquor until they had made a barricade in the stern against which the police bullets crashed ineffectively. At the same time, the two rum smugglers threw some of the liquor overboard, hoping to force the Manhattan to change its course to avoid striking the floating cases.
>
> The Walter Thomas might have escaped had not it unexpectedly struck a submerged log. The boat staggered, and the police ran alongside.[23]

Two other stories published that week seem too bizarre to be true. Both may have been invented by reporters unable to find the "sin ship" and unwilling to admit their failure—to return empty-handed.

The *New York Times* published one of the stories. It reported that a businessman had stockpiled some liquor before the war and decided to move 10 cases to his summer home in New Jersey. His automobile broke down 20 miles south of Jersey City and, to avoid arrest, the businessman decided to give $100 to anyone willing to tow his car. Instead of helping, the first motorist he tried to stop stepped on the gas. The second motorist ignored him completely. Moments later, the businessman noticed a truck near the highway. Waving his arms, the businessman hurried toward it.

The *Times*'s story continued:

> The truck driver, without waiting for him, hastened to join him. Before the New Yorker could ask assistance, the driver thrust a sealed enve-

lope into his hand, ran back to his truck, and disappeared down the road. The envelope contained two $100 bank notes.

After further tinkering with his own automobile, the businessman finally reconnected the right wire and got home, his cargo salvaged without expense, he himself $200 richer.

Neighbors told the businessman that he had been marooned in an area often used by bootleggers and frequented by highwaymen. They assumed that the truckman had been stopped before and carried a pocketful of such envelopes to bribe anyone who tried to stop him: either the police or thieves.[24]

The *New York Evening Post* published the second story. It reported that the area's bootleggers had held a convention at Union Hill, N.J., and appointed a "Bootleggers' Legal Aid Committee."[25] The *Post* claimed that the bootleggers discussed their costs, prices, efficiency, sales management, and code of ethics. The code required them to "[a]void shooting affrays with prohibition agents as much as possible."

The bootleggers were also asked to contribute to a legal aid committee and to a fund "for general purposes." "In this modern age," the presiding bootlegger explained, "there must be close cooperation."

The following Saturday, eight days after publishing Jarrell's first story, the *Herald Tribune* admitted that it was a hoax and explained how the hoax started. It had received a tip from a source "believed to be wholly reliable." The source said that a large ship was anchored beyond the twelve-mile limit, and that it was selling liquor to the public. The paper sent Jarrell out to verify the details. Jarrell had been employed by the paper since 1922 "and had always borne the reputation of being an industrious and reputable reporter."

Jarrell disappeared for two days, then wired the *Herald Tribune*'s city editor that the tip was true and that he was returning to New York. After writing the first story, Jarrell returned to Bay Shore and Fire Island to learn more about the ship. He spent two more days working on the story, but "the reports he submitted were so vague that suspicions as to the truth of his original article were aroused." With the help of prohibition agents, the paper began its own investigation of the matter. At first, its inquiry seemed to confirm Jarrell's story, "but as it developed, it soon became apparent that he had never visited the liquor-laden craft on which he said he had spent a night."

When questioned by his editors, Jarrell at first insisted that every detail was true. Gradually, however, he began to weaken and admitted "embellishment."

The *Herald Tribune*'s statement continued:

> He was given every opportunity to offer confirmation, but could not do so, except in unessential details. Still insisting that his story was fundamentally true and would "stand up," he left the office, promising to return and straighten up the matter.
>
> Instead, he sent back a written and signed confession that his article was false and admitted that "sufficient evidence has come into your hands to prove that the story of the floating cabaret" was wholly without foundation.
>
> In his confession, Jarrell further says: "In anticipation of the natural penalty for my misdemeanor, and assuring you of my sincerest regret about the whole affair, I herewith tender you my resignation as a member of the *Herald Tribune* staff, to take effect at once."
>
> Sanford Jarrell has been posted on the bulletin board of the *Herald Tribune* editorial rooms as dishonorably dismissed.[26]

How had Jarrell gotten into so much trouble? Years later, an editor in California speculated that

> Perhaps Jarrell thought . . . that his editors would know he was spoofing. But it was August in New York. Prohibition was a bore. The *Herald Trib* was a reliable newspaper. Jarrell was a reliable reporter. And indeed it was an epic lark. . . .
>
> The reporter who makes up a story so fanciful and improbable, so fraught with absurdities, that he expects it to collapse at once, in laughter, is foolish, but rarely larcenous. It is only when everyone believes him, including his own editors, that he realizes he has made a terrible mistake, and doesn't know how to get out of it.[27]

New York's other daily newspapers responded with a surprising grace. None criticized the *Herald Tribune*. Only one, the *World*, published Jarrell's confession on its front page. Similarly, the *Washington Post* published only three paragraphs of the *Herald Tribune*'s statement, then apologized to its readers. The *Post* explained that it "printed this fake story in good faith" and regretted misleading its readers.[28]

Why weren't other newspapers more critical?

The story embarrassed everyone. For an entire week, the story had fooled the press, the public, and most government officials. Other editors in New York sent their own reporters out to search for the ship and to interview the government officials. Journalists also speculated about the ship's profits, identity, and location — and published their speculation in front-page stories. To compete with Jarrell, some invented other details — perhaps entire stories — about the ship and about the area's bootleggers.

Also, other reporters and editors may have been reluctant to criticize a colleague they knew and a paper they respected. Moreover, the *Herald Tribune* had admitted its guilt and fired Jarrell. Thus there was nothing to add.

In 1962, Jarrell died in obscurity, "poisoned by fumes from a gas heater in a seedy Long Beach, California, apartment."[29] Author Tom Wolfe began to work for the *Herald Tribune* that year and found that its staff was still talking about Jarrell's story. Wolfe learned that

> He [Jarrell] was unable to find the ship, but he did find a saloon in Montauk, and he telephoned in a week's worth of the creamiest and most lurid chronicles in the annals of drunk newspapermen. The *Trib* couldn't print them fast enough. Half the city gasped; the other half headed for eastern Long Island to rent motor launches. When the hoax was revealed, the *Trib* fired the reporter, whereupon, legend has it, three other New York newspapers offered him jobs.[30]

Time magazine reported that Jarrell was offered seven other jobs. But Jarrell seemed unable to settle down. He worked for more than thirty newspapers before poor health forced him to quit.[31] A colleague said that Jarrell was writing the final draft of his autobiography. Thus, his death created another mystery. No one has found Jarrell's autobiography, not even a portion of it.

Common Themes

Hoaxes that appear in the media often share a common theme. Some hoaxes are created for similar reasons. Others are created at the same times or places. A few are accidental, and a few are created by non-journalists, by people eager to fool or embarrass the media.

For years, the reporters in some cities felt compelled to hoax. Their editors demanded exciting new stories, and there were never enough real stories to satisfy them. To survive, the reporters manufactured more sensational stories. Their editors may have suspected that the stories were fictitious but published them anyway. If a story was exposed as a hoax, the editors could respond (sometimes truthfully) that they trusted their reporters and thought the story was accurate. Then, to prove their sincerity, the editors could fire the reporters who wrote it.

Journalists created other hoaxes to beat and embarrass their rivals. In retaliation, their rivals created more hoaxes, thus starting a never-ending cycle of fakes and frauds. The hoaxes became especially common in cities such as Chicago, where the competition was fierce.

Hoaxes in the New England states were different. Weeklies and small dailies published most of the region's hoaxes. They were clever stories, created to amuse the newspapers' readers, not to beat their rivals.

The nation's radio and television stations broadcast fewer hoaxes, and most were accidental. Broadcasters seem to have been influenced by the field's changing standards, by journalists' new sense of professionalism and growing concern about their ethics and responsibilities. In addition, broadcasters feared government retaliation. The Federal Communications Commission could revoke the license of any station responsible for a frightening hoax.

The public—not the broadcasters—have called some programs "a hoax." A few entertainment programs broadcast by radio and television stations fooled the public because they used a realistic format: simulated news bulletins that seemed to describe real disasters.

Some hoaxes continue to appear in newspapers. Most are published by the nation's weeklies and appear on a single day: April Fools' Day. Even the weeklies are becoming more cautious, however. Their editors do everything possible to warn their readers that the stories are false, made up, and make-believe. Yet even the editors' most preposterous tales fool some readers, often a surprising number.

Other hoaxes are created by pranksters and propagandists. They seem to enjoy fooling the media, and a few have made a career out of it.

11 Chicago's Hoaxes: Beating (and Embarrassing) Your Rivals

HE competition in Chicago was fierce. Editors believed that more people would buy their papers if they beat their rivals—if their papers were the first to report exciting new stories. After attracting more readers, the editors also hoped to attract more advertisers, revenue they needed to survive.

The reporters who uncovered a good story were likely to be congratulated and given a byline, praise, and a raise. Rivals who missed the story were reprimanded, even fired. But there were never enough good stories to satisfy the city's editors. To ensure that they would be paid, newcomers began to create more exciting stories. They created other stories to impress the editors: to obtain (and retain) regular jobs on their staffs.

An experienced reporter recalled that an editor tore up one of his first stories and threw it on the floor. The editor rewrote the story himself, then showed it to the reporter, saying, "That's the way you should have handled it."

"But that isn't the way it happened," he responded.

"For God's sake," the editor exclaimed. "Do you think you're working on *The Ladies' Home Journal* or some Sunday-school magazine? You can't let the facts stand in the way of a good story."[1]

Other editors never told their reporters to fake, but their comments and actions encouraged the practice. One editor told a reporter, "Don't ever fake a story or anything in a story—that is, never let me catch you at it."[2] A colleague explained: "Of course a city editor will always tell a reporter he won't have any faking. Thus, if the paper gets into trouble through exaggeration, it isn't the editor's fault."[3]

Today, the newspapers in Chicago rarely publish any new hoaxes. But hoaxes continue to appear in the books written about Chicago's famous journalists and newspapers. While describing the hoaxes that newspapers published fifty or a hundred years ago, the books change some details and add others, sometimes creating entirely new stories. As a result, stories about Chicago's old hoaxes have changed and improved with age, just like stories about the Denver hoax that caused a war in China.

Chicago's bitterest and most disreputable competition began in 1900 when William Randolph Hearst rented a dilapidated building on West Madison Street and opened the *Chicago American.* Because of all the noise and confusion there, journalists called it "the Madhouse." Hearst was a good newspaperman, but a born maverick: rich, aggressive, and sometimes irresponsible. To sell more papers, he charged only a penny a copy and published the *American* every morning, evening, and Sunday. Hearst also published numerous "Extras," and some of their headlines were printed in red. Their size varied "from large to gigantic."[4]

The *American* eventually became an evening paper, and Hearst established a separate morning paper, the *Examiner.* Their editorial offices were located in the same building, yet there was an intense rivalry between them. Each day, copies of all their editions were sent to Hearst's home in California, along with copies of all their rivals'. Hearst demanded an explanation if a rival—even the other newspaper he owned—beat either the *American* or the *Examiner.*[5]

Reporters from all of the city's major newspapers accompanied the police to the scenes of serious crimes and, if the police failed to uncover any good clues, the reporters were tempted to invent some. If, for example, the reporters decided that a janitor might have murdered his mother-in-law and thrown her body into a furnace, they might discover some bones in the furnace. Two or three days later, police technicians might examine the "evidence" and discover that they were mutton bones. Until then, the bones provided good headlines, the type of thrills that readers seemed to expect from the Chicago papers.[6]

To get a good and exclusive story, other reporters occasionally hid — or even kidnapped — criminals. Reporter Bill Doherty, for instance, once found the wife of a murder victim in a saloon. Doherty bought her a drink and called his editors, who told Doherty that the woman had become a suspect in her husband's murder. They urged Doherty to hide her, to take her some place where the police and other reporters would never find her. Because the police would never look there for her, Doherty took her to his home.[7]

The suspect in another murder was captured by the police in Wisconsin. A squad from Hearst's *Examiner* sped to the town. Posing as Chicago policemen, they flashed fake badges and brought the suspect back to a Chicago hotel. The suspect gave the reporters a detailed statement, and the police and other journalists read it in the *Examiner.*[8] So their story would remain an exclusive, the reporters waited a day or two before returning their prisoner to the Chicago police.

A young reporter just learning the police beat was scooped by a more experienced rival. His rival reported that a German shepherd had been awakened by smoke and began to bark. The noise aroused several people, so everyone living in a blazing apartment building was able to escape. To verify the details, the young reporter went to the building. He found that no one in the neighborhood owned a dog, and that the fire was confined to some rubbish on a back porch.[9] Firemen estimated the damage at $4.

Another young reporter was assigned to several of Chicago's suburbs, including Oak Park. The reporter rushed from police station to fire station, and from courtroom to hospital, looking for news. Because most of the stories he found were minor, few ever appeared in print. When the reporter did find a good story, he phoned in the details and a "rewrite man" wrote the account.

The reporter finally got a murder, and it made page 27. A few days later, a minor burglary made page 1. The reporter, Robert St. John, almost ignored the burglary. There were no clues, and the loot totalled only a few hundred dollars. The burglar, however, had left a homemade ladder leaning against the house, and his shirt in an upstairs bedroom. The rewrite man took the details and created a long tale about Oak Park's "Ladder Burglar." He portrayed the burglar as a harmless eccentric, a frustrated craftsman who spent his days in a little basement workshop, constructing ladders that were masterpieces. Each night, the

craftsman carried one of his ladders to Oak Park, hoping to find someone who would appreciate his work. The burglar looked for a house
occupied by people with good taste and left his ladder as a gift, to be
admired the next day. The craftsman occasionally stole something, but
only to buy more lumber to build more ladders.

The rewriteman added that the burglar was also a frustrated nudist,
doing a slow strip tease. He apparently intended to leave one garment in
every house he robbed.

The next morning, St. John found another minor burglary: someone had stolen a ring worth $20. The rewriteman turned it into another
page 1 story, claiming that the "Ladder Burglar" was terrorizing the
suburb. This time he had left his trousers behind and was gradually
approaching complete nakedness. The entire police force, including the
reserves, was looking for a man carrying a ladder and dressed in only his
hat, shoes, socks, and underwear.

St. John was unable to find any more burglaries in Oak Park.
Rather than abandon the story, the *Daily News* reported that the burglar
had moved to Chicago, leaving his ladder, shoes, and socks at a house
there.[10]

Another young reporter, William Salisbury, seemed to enjoy creating hoaxes. Salisbury—young, ambitious, and eager to please his new
editors—never worried about the fact that he was misleading his readers.

After moving from Omaha, Salisbury applied for a job at the *Chicago Tribune,* promising its editor "a hot scoop."[11] Salisbury found a
seventy-nine-year-old man who intended to marry his housekeeper, a
woman nearly fifty years younger. The man's children were upset because they would not inherit his money. They nearly started a riot, and
some threatened to have the old man declared insane. The details were
only partially true, but Salisbury hurried back to the *Tribune* with the
story and was hired "on space." He was given some assignments and paid
according to the amount of space they filled. If he did a good job, he
might be hired as one of the *Tribune*'s full-time reporters.

The paper sent Salisbury out to cover an accident involving a street
car, and he started to leave because only three people were injured, none
seriously. Five other reporters covering the story were also "space" writers. So their stories would be published—and they would be paid—the
reporters stopped Salisbury and agreed to tell their editors that the crash
had been more sensational and that 15 people had been injured.

To obtain another job, Salisbury created another hoax. He went to Chicago's Chinatown and invented a story about its largest temple. Before leaving, he talked to a police officer on the beat and also to the officer's sergeant. Salisbury suggested that Americans angry about events occurring in China might attack the temple. To protect its big idols, the Chinese might want to move them and bury them outside the city.

Salisbury persuaded the two officers to swear that his story was true — that they had stood outside the temple, watching the move and guarding the idols' safety. In return, Salisbury made the sergeant the hero of his story. He then hurried to another paper, gave its editor the story, and added that — if the editor wanted to verify the details — he should call the sergeant.[12]

As a new reporter at a third daily, Hearst's *American,* Salisbury was asked to write about an old tugboat that sank in Lake Michigan. The boat's four-man crew swam to safety, and Salisbury wrote a careful story about their ordeal. When the story appeared in print, Salisbury barely recognized it. Someone had rewritten the story, adding details that he never dreamed of. The story reported that the sailors had risked their lives to rescue the boat's mascot, a cat. "I had thought I possessed a pretty fair imagination," Salisbury said, "but I realized that I had much to learn if I were to succeed in yellow journalism."[13]

To protect themselves from the cutthroat competition, several reporters began to cooperate: to secretly work together, even to create hoaxes together.

The reporters assigned to Chicago's County Building took turns going from office to office while their colleagues played poker. When they returned to the pressroom, they shared their notes with everyone there, and everyone called in the same stories. The system eliminated scoops, but also eliminated all the tension and stress. No one would ever be fired because they missed a story.[14]

The reporters assigned to Chicago's hotel beat developed a similar scheme: the Hotel Reporters' Association. The association concocted hoaxes so its members would always have something to write about.

One of their hoaxes described two Mexican bullfighters who were traveling to Spain via Chicago. To make the story more interesting, a reporter called a Coliseum on Michigan Avenue, saying that he represented the bullfighters and wanted to reserve the Coliseum for a bullfight some night that week. The reporter then called the chief of police, thus making it a front-page story. The chief of police said he would surround the Coliseum with an armed force, if necessary, to prevent the fight.

On another dull day, the reporters began talking about the rats seen in Chicago alleys. "We ought to get up a rat story," they agreed. The next day, all their papers published interviews with Dr. Nagushi, a famous Japanese physician. Dr. Nagushi described a cholera epidemic in the Orient and said that rats spread the disease. Dr. Nagushi added that rats caused most epidemics. However, the benefits would be temporary if only one country exterminated its rats. Dr. Nagushi explained that the rats traveled aboard ships and would soon return. Therefore, every country in the world should combine against them, starting a world-wide rat hunt.

The *Tribune*'s editors took the story seriously. For weeks after that, they interviewed doctors and other experts in the city. The experts revealed that rats also spread diphtheria, smallpox, and measles. Readers frightened by the stories attacked the city's rats. Some tore up the city's wooden sidewalks. Homeowners flooded their cellars to drown the rats. Other people tried to smoke the rats out. Their fires got out of control, destroying several barns.[15]

The reporters in Chicago also invented a fictitious witness. Editors wanted the names of everyone involved in news stories, yet some names were impossible to obtain. People often vanished before the police or reporters arrived. To satisfy their editors, reporters invented "Ignatius Z. Yelswo," a name not found in any telephone book. After that, Yelswo witnessed an amazing number of crimes and accidents. The hoax continued until the editors sent a photographer out to take Yelswo's picture. The photographer discovered that his address was a vacant lot.[16]

Editors devised similar schemes. During the First World War, an editor at the *Examiner* waited in his office every night until all his rivals printed their final editions. If their papers contained anything new — any big stories that his staff had missed — the editor clipped them out and added them to the *Examiner*'s front page. The *Examiner*'s regular editions had already been printed and transported to newsstands; nevertheless, the editor ran off a few extra copies. He sent the copies directly to his boss, William Randolph Hearst, and kept his job for years because nobody ever seemed to scoop him.[17]

Editors in Chicago created other hoaxes to embarrass the rivals they hated. Walter Howey was the *Chicago Tribune*'s city editor, and colleagues called him "a journalistic genius."[18] Howey loved the *Tribune* and considered it a great newspaper—powerful and respectable. He refused to leave—to work for Hearst—even when offered more money.

In 1917, Howey printed a two- or three-paragraph story about a Hollywood producer he knew. One of the *Tribune*'s owners, Joseph Medill Patterson, worked hard to maintain the paper's honesty and integrity, and Patterson was infuriated by the story. He considered it "press agent's stuff," free publicity that Howey had given a friend.[19] Patterson asked Howey to apologize to the *Tribune*'s readers. Howey refused, insisting that the story was newsworthy. The next morning, Patterson published an apology on the *Tribune*'s editorial pages, which he controlled.

Howey immediately resigned. He had earned $8,000 a year at the *Tribune* and accepted $35,000 to become managing editor of Hearst's *Herald and Examiner*. Hearst wanted to make the *Herald and Examiner* the greatest morning paper in the United States, and he told Howey, "Beat the *Trib*. That's your only job. Just beat the *Tribune*." To embarrass his former employer, Howey created a series of hoaxes that tricked Patterson into publicizing Hearst's newspapers and movies. In addition, the hoaxes also helped increase the *Herald and Examiner*'s circulation and prestige.

After moving to the *Herald and Examiner,* Howey learned that it owned the serial rights to a novel about a handsome young man who inherited several million dollars. A few days later, a reporter covering Chicago's hotels learned about the arrival of a mystery man—an elegant and wealthy young man from Philadelphia. Normally, the young man's family avoided publicity; nevertheless, he admitted the truth. He had to lose $1 million.

The young man explained that his family inherited a great deal of money before the adoption of a federal income tax. The money seemed to multiply, so that every branch in his family became rich. His father had died and left him some of the money, but hoped that he would remain modest about it. His father wanted him to understand that their wealth was not a sign of great intelligence or virtue. To teach him how difficult it was to lose a fortune, his father's will required him to lose $1 million within a year, but while attempting to invest it shrewdly. He could not give the money away, nor deliberately invest it in useless ventures.

The *Tribune*'s reporter checked the story and found that every detail seemed accurate. Thus, it appeared on the front page. Howey promptly leased a billboard across from Patterson's office and paid a crew of sign painters triple their normal wages to work all that night. By 4 a.m., the painters had finished. The billboard announced that Hearst's *Herald and Examiner* would serialize a novel about a young man who had to spend $1 million to inherit a fortune and marry a beautiful girl.

The *Herald and Examiner* serialized the novel for three weeks, and it increased the newspaper's circulation by thirty-two thousand a day.[20]

On March 14, 1917, another story on the *Tribune*'s front page reported that a beautiful young woman had married a penniless invalid. The story explained that Miss Phillipa Hartley of New York had married John Colfax of a North Side rooming house. Colfax was dying of "a lesion of the heart," and Miss Hartley had married him to inherit a fortune.

The story explained that Miss Hartley's uncle, Carleton Hannan of Bombay, India, was dying. Hannan's will left Miss Hartley his entire estate, nearly $5 million. But to receive it, she had to be married. If she failed to find a husband within three months after Hannan's death, she would be disinherited. The will named Dr. Gilbert H. Willis, also of Bombay, as Hannan's trustee. Willis had just arrived in Chicago and filed the documents in the city recorder's office. He then summoned Miss Hartley from New York and began looking for a husband for her: a young man suffering from tuberculosis or some other fatal disease. The groom would be paid a large sum of money but, immediately after the ceremony, would be expected to leave his bride forever.

Willis began a personal search through Chicago's lodging houses and found Colfax — unkempt, poorly clothed, and dying — in one of them: Colfax agreed at once to marry Miss Hartley, and they took out marriage license No. 75669. A preacher on the North Side performed the ceremony. The *Tribune* reported that Mr. and Mrs. Colfax then started on a taxicab honeymoon which lasted "perhaps 15 minutes." The first stop was Colfax's rooming house. After dropping him off there, Dr. Willis and Mrs. Colfax drove on, alone, to her hotel. Mrs. Colfax packed her belongings and boarded the next train back to New York.

After her departure, Willis revealed the reason for Hannan's strange will. Hannan disliked the man his sister married. His sister had since died, and Miss Hartley was the couple's only child. Hannan feared that, if Miss Hartley was not married when she inherited his fortune, her father would take it from her. So Hannan drew up a trust agreement that required Miss Hartley to get married and that left her father only $1.

Willis also explained why he wanted to find a husband for Miss Hartley as quickly as possible. Her uncle might die at any moment, and the seas were unsafe because of the First World War. If the news of Hannan's death in India failed to reach the United States within three months—and Miss Hartley were still unmarried—she would lose everything.[21]

News stories published by the city's other papers added that Miss Hartley had been heavily veiled and dressed in black. The stories also revealed her age as twenty-five. A clerk noticed three magnificent diamond rings on her long, slender fingers. When interviewed the next day, the clerk seemed disappointed because Miss Hartley had not married him. "Why didn't she tell me about it?" he lamented. "I'm single. I'm poor. I needed the money; she could forget all about me, and I'd never have any touch of conscience."[22]

The newspapers disagreed about Colfax's fate. The *Tribune* reported that Colfax was dropped off at his rooming house. The *Evening Post* said he received $1,000 but was expected to die soon.[23] The *Daily Journal* said he had moved into a hotel "with enough money to give him the comforts of life. . . . "[24]

Other newspapers were more skeptical. Several noted that Dr. Willis was their only source. The *Evening Post* wondered why, of all the places in the world, Willis filed the will in Chicago. Also, did it make any sense for Hannan to require Miss Hartley to get married? Was it, perhaps, some kind of publicity stunt?

A headline in the *Chicago Daily News* warned that it might be a hoax. The *Daily News* explained that "Colfax" might be a fictitious name. Moreover, Willis had not returned to his hotel room, and every minister interviewed by reporters denied that he had performed the ceremony. Most insisted that no minister would have performed it.[25] Yet, if the story were true, would Colfax now look for a specialist to cure his diseased heart? But was there really a Colfax? Had there really been a marriage? Or was it a hoax, a press agent's yarn?

Recent books about Chicago journalism agree that the story was a hoax and that Howey created it to embarrass the *Tribune*. Some of the books' details, however, are inconsistent or obviously mistaken. Other details are new. They appear in the books, but not in the stories published in 1917.

One of the books, *The Madhouse on Madison Street,* explains that Howey hired an actor to darken his skin and pose as an Indian prince. The book adds that the prince (not Willis) appeared at Chicago's city hall late one afternoon and announced that his sister, a 19-year-old princess, had just gotten married. To be valid, her marriage had to be recorded before midnight. The prince said that his father was an Indian ruler, and that the laws of their principality required his sister to marry by midnight or forfeit a fortune in jewels, land, and servants. The government office he needed had already closed for the day, but a reporter from the *Tribune* agreed to help, to persuade a clerk to reopen it. In return, the reporter was shown the couple's marriage certificate, and it revealed the groom's name: Gib Ekoj. The *Tribune*'s reporter raced back to his office with the story.

The book adds that a tipster called the *Tribune* later that day, complaining that Gib Ekoj had married the princess as a matter of convenience, to earn a few dollars. Now, instead of spending his wedding night with her, he was staying on skid row, in a room costing ten cents a night. A reporter found Gib Ekoj there, drunk and determined to get revenge. The groom explained that he had been a student at the University of Chicago but dropped out after becoming an alcoholic. When offered a chance to marry the princess, he had hoped to rehabilitate himself and to recoup his family's fortune. Before the wedding, he had signed some papers forfeiting any right to the princess's fortune and titles but thought they were a formality. After the ceremony, some attorneys had given him a few dollars for wine, and the princess left aboard a train.

The man sobbed that his family would lose face, and that suicide seemed to be the only answer. As reporters watched, he pulled $500, all in new $50 bills, from his robe. He would send the money to his family, he said, and drown himself in Lake Michigan.

At midnight, the book asserts, the *Tribune*'s home edition hit the streets with the story on page 1. A picture the groom had provided showed the princess seated on an elephant. Minutes later, Howey's *Herald and Examiner* hit the streets with its own exclusive. It announced that the prince and princess were advance agents for a new movie starring Marion Davies. Miss Davies was Hearst's girl friend.

Spelled backward, the prince's name was "Big Joke."[26]

The same book describes another of Howey's hoaxes, one involving a Hindu princess. While staying at a Chicago hotel, the princess supposedly told reporters that she was the daughter of a wealthy maharajah. Years earlier, she said, a band of revolutionaries had surrounded a palace where her father was staying. An American engineer was working in the palace and, as the rebels prepared to kill her father, the American smuggled him out in a bedroll.

"And that is why I am here," the princess said. The young American left the next morning. The maharajah had given him a gold ring as a remembrance, but the American refused to accept any money. After British troops restored order, the maharajah searched everywhere but was unable to find the young man. They did not even know his name, only that his home was in Chicago. Now, the maharajah had died and mentioned the American in his will. If the man showed her the ring, the princess would give him $2 million.

It was a complete scoop for the *Tribune*. Soon afterward, Hearst's film company released a film titled *The Maharajah's Daughter*.[27]

On October 31, 1921, a story from Los Angeles reported that Harry Phillips, a Mexican mine owner, was giving money to strangers.[28] Phillips had rented the best room in a Los Angeles hotel "just to wash up." He gave the hotel's bellboys $10 and $20 tips, then tossed $20 bills from its fire escapes "just to make people smile." Phillips told a bellboy that he had been away from the United States for 15 years and was disappointed by the misery he saw in Americans' faces. To cheer them up, he decided to share his money with them.

Hearst's *Herald and Examiner* added that Phillips had cashed a draft for $50,000 and boarded a train for Chicago. The *Herald and Examiner* explained that, as a youth, Phillips had sold newspapers in Chicago. People in Chicago helped him, and now he was returning to thank them.

It was a big story, and other newspapers sent their reporters out to learn more about Phillips. On Tuesday, the *Tribune* reported that Phillips had sold newspapers in front of two Chicago hotels, the Morrison and the Sherman, and might stay at one of them.[29] The hotels had already received dozens of phone calls, most of them from women asking whether Phillips had arrived. Letters addressed to Phillips were also piling up at the hotels. Most seemed to come from people who wanted some of his money.

On Friday, the *Herald and Examiner* revealed that Phillips had stopped in Omaha. He marched 150 jobless people into an exclusive restaurant there and fed them breast of guinea hen. Then, by mistake, Phillips tipped a Belgian war hero. The general was wearing his uniform, and Phillips noticed his gold braid. Mistaking the general for a hotel doorman, Phillips thrust a $10 bill into his hands.[30]

From Omaha, Phillips wired ahead to the Hotel Sherman, asking for three connecting rooms with baths and a private dining room. He also requested a large bouquet of roses and pictures of smiling girls. He tried to evade the journalists in Chicago, but a reporter from Hearst's *Herald and Examiner* managed to find and interview him. Phillips told the reporter that, while shining shoes and selling papers in Chicago eighteen years earlier, he received a telegram saying that his father had been hurt in an accident. He did not have enough money to return home, and a stranger—perhaps a bit tipsy—noticed that he seemed depressed. The stranger stuffed a bill into his hands. Phillips smiled, and the tipsy stranger stuffed another bill into his hands: a total of $25. Now, after striking it rich, he was returning to Chicago and wanted to give its residents—by absolute surprise—$1,000 for every $1 they had given him.[31]

On Saturday, other newspapers in Chicago reported that Phillips had stood up in an automobile parked outside his hotel and tossed out $5 bills and a pocketful of change. A group of newsboys swarmed around the car, clamoring, "Give me some. I'm a newsboy." As Phillips drove off, the crowd closed in over the spot, scrambling for coins that had rolled into the gutter.

The stories published in 1921 are still available in Chicago libraries, but the books written about Chicago's famous journalists and newspapers tell a much different tale. In addition, the books explain how Howey used the tale to promote the *Herald and Examiner.*

The Madhouse on Madison Street claims that Phillips was an Alaskan—a big-bearded fellow, dressed in brown corduroys and a floppy Stetson—who supposedly carried a flask of bourbon and a huge supply of dollar bills. The book adds that Phillips had struck a lode of almost pure gold and that his fortune totalled $10 million. Because he had no friends or relatives, he wanted to give it all to the people of Chicago.

The Alaskan threw away handfuls of the dollar bills, attracting large crowds and obstructing traffic. When the police warned Phillips to stop, he simply moved to another neighborhood. Finally, he was arrested and taken before a judge. In court, Phillips supposedly unbuckled a money belt containing thousands of dollars. To avoid hurting the city, he told the judge, he had talked to Walter C. Howey, editor of the *Herald and Examiner,* and Howey agreed to distribute the money for him. Each Sunday, he would give Howey several thousand of the bills, and Howey would tuck them into copies of the *Herald and Examiner,* for sale at five cents.

The next Sunday, the circulation of the *Herald and Examiner* soared. When readers opened the newspaper, dollar bills fluttered to the ground. The following Sunday, people tried to grab several copies of the paper. Phillips disappeared, and police riot squads had to be called out to maintain order.[32] The *Herald and Examiner*'s circulation more than doubled, from 400,000 to 800,000, eventually reaching a peak of 1.1 million.

A second book, *Deadlines and Monkeyshines,* claims that Phillips was an oil wildcatter and attracted a mob of twenty-five thousand people, all scrambling after his money. After being arrested for obstructing traffic, Phillips left town. He complained that the people in Chicago were not smiling, just fighting over his money. Phillips called them the "worst bunch of people I've ever seen."

This book adds that Hearst's *Herald and Examiner* defended its readers, responding that the people in Chicago were the finest in the world: that they deserved the $25,000 Phillips promised them. Since Phillips would not give them the money, the *Herald and Examiner* announced that it would.[33] It started a "Smile Contest" and distributed millions of free "Smile" coupons, each with its own serial number. The *Herald and Examiner* conducted drawings to select the winning numbers, then published the results.

In fact, the *Herald and Examiner* distributed the "Smile" coupons that fall. Thousands of new readers, anxious to learn whether the serial numbers on their coupons had won, rushed out to buy more copies of the paper.

Why do the books about Chicago's famous journalists and newspapers contain so many errors? Some books were written by the city's most famous journalists, and the journalists may have relied upon their memories of events that occurred forty or fifty years earlier. Other books were written by the journalists' successors. Their successors apparently relied upon the newsroom tales passed from one generation of journalists to the next. But while repeating the tales, journalists seem to have distorted and embellished them, so few are still accurate.

Some authors may not have cared whether the tales are accurate. They are interesting stories and, regardless of their accuracy, help describe an exciting era in Chicago journalism, an era of competition and hoaxes.

12 New England's Gentler Humor (and New York's)

HOAXES published in the New England states were unique. Many were created by editors at the region's weeklies and small dailies. The hoaxes became a regular feature in some of their papers. The characters they described appeared several times a week for years.

Unlike hoaxes published in the West, New England's hoaxes were clever rather than exaggerated, bloody, and revengeful. The editors in New England wrote their hoaxes for the fun of it, to amuse — not frighten — their readers.

Also, the editors wrote about local topics: often unusual plants, animals, fish, or people. Their stories were so amusing that other publications — larger newspapers, books, and magazines — reprinted them for years. As a result, the editors became famous, even national celebrities.

Other hoaxes were created by journalists at the region's largest and most prestigious dailies, including the *New York Times*.

One of New England's most famous journalists, Lou Stone, began to work for the *Evening Citizen* in Winsted, Connecticut, when he was only fourteen. During the following years, Stone created hundreds of stories, mostly whimsical tales about the animals and rural life around him.

As a sideline, Stone served as a correspondent for the Associated Press and a dozen major newspapers. When Stone needed some extra cash, he sent their editors telegrams describing his latest creation and asking whether they wanted to buy it. The editors discovered that people everywhere enjoyed the stories, never caring whether they were true or false. Some editors published the stories on their front page. Thus, Stone became a national celebrity, and Winsted became known as "America's hoax town."[1]

In 1895, Stone was twenty years old and needed $150. To obtain the money, he sent telegrams to the newspapers in Boston and New York, telling them that a stark naked wild man was terrorizing the countryside. Unfortunately, Stone made the story too good. After buying it from him, the editors rushed their own reporters to the scene to learn more about Winsted's "wild man." The big-city reporters did some inventing of their own, often ridiculing Winsted and its heroic hunters.

Their stories illustrate a common phenomenon in journalism. If reporters describe a monster, some of their readers will begin to hear and see it. Other readers will hide, and still others will begin to search for the monster. All their activities — their sightings and hunting expeditions — generate more stories, so the monster remains in the news for weeks.

The first stories about Winsted's "wild man" appeared on Friday, August 23, 1895. Several New York papers reported that passengers aboard a stagecoach saw the man. He lived in "Injun Meadow" and jumped out from behind a cluster of bushes, naked and making hideous noises. Farmers in the vicinity reported that their hens were stolen and their calves and lambs — even huge oxen — disappeared, apparently eaten by the wild man.[2]

Other people began to see the wild man, first in one location, then in another. Their descriptions varied, but all were truly horrible. Readers who believed the stories became afraid to leave their homes. Men began to carry guns, and farmers slept with axes under their beds.[3]

While searching for a lost hog that Saturday, Selectman R. W. Smith saw the wild man eating blackberries. The man sprang high into the air and uttered the most awful scream that Smith had ever heard, a scream filled with fear, hate, and rage. "He was 6 feet high," Smith said, "very broad and strong, and naked. His body was covered with thick skin, like the coat of a Newfoundland dog. . . . "[4]

On Sunday, five hundred armed men were expected to hunt for the wild man and then lynch him. Newspapers reported that every member of the Fourth Regiment of the Connecticut National Guard would join the hunt, and the guardsmen were practicing at a rifle range. On Monday, newspapers reported that only two hundred or three hundred men had actually joined the hunt. They surrounded Injun Meadow but found only a footprint and a hut containing an old shoe and several bones, all picked clean.

A reporter for the *New York World* ridiculed the posse's efforts. "Several false alarms were raised," the reporter said, "and during one of them Constable Gillette, who was making an enthusiastic rush for cover, got badly mixed up with a barbed-wire fence, and it took the posse 10 minutes to unravel him. Many other heroes barked their shins and sprained their ankles while executing masterly retreats from each other."[5] Some of the searchers sounded loud warwhoops, hoping that the noise would scare the wild man into the open. "It was one of these howls that stampeded Constable Gillette," the *World* reported. "Thinking that it was the work of the wild man, he made a terrific charge (he says) or retreat (others say), and then had a rough and tumble encounter with a spiked fence."

Another newspaper, the *New York Herald,* reported that only 100 armed men spent Sunday beating about Winsted's blackberry bushes. "They found footprints, they found a tame hog, they found blackberries and also weariness," the paper claimed, "but no monster, hairy or bald."[6]

A Boston paper, the *Evening Journal,* claimed that a hunter saw the wild man, and that he was seven feet tall. The man's arms reached nearly to the ground, and long white tusks protruded from his mouth. His body was covered with hair, and the hair was matted with leaves and twigs so thick that bullets would bounce off it.[7]

The following Thursday, another Boston daily reported that the wild man was a gorilla.[8] Passengers aboard a stage traveling to Winsted had seen the gorilla cross a highway, leap onto a fence, and stand on its hind legs. Its hair was coarse and black, and its glistening white teeth "would have sent shivers down the back of a New York policeman."[9]

Two women in a wagon also saw the gorilla. The women said they heard a terrible shriek. Their horses broke into a mad run, and the hairy, grinning monster made a flying leap across the road. Boston's *Evening Transcript* speculated that "[t]he gorilla probably escaped from some circus years ago."

The *World* disagreed. It doubted that the monster was a gorilla and explained that, although local residents had reported seeing the monster for years, "[t]he gorilla is a native of Africa and could not possibly stand the rigors of a Northern winter."[10]

About five hundred men and boys joined a hunting expedition that began at dawn the following Sunday. Some were on horseback, some in wagons, but most on foot. The newspapers in Boston and New York reported that there was a cry of warning, and that many of the hunters retreated, "suddenly remembering errands their wives had given them."[11] The road became a mass of men, boys, dogs, and horses, all fleeing back toward Winsted. "Behind the flying crowd some strange object was crashing through the brush, uttering a hoarse cry, half human and wholly terrible." The *World* added: "The creature seemed to be gaining on the rapidly swelling crowd, but suddenly it darted to the rear. Now and then a glimpse could be caught of a dark, hairy object racing on all fours like mad toward Patrick Danehy's farm."

The most fearless men turned to pursue the monster. While approaching Danehy's farm house, they were appalled by a frightful screech and the noise of a monster crashing toward them through the brush. The hunters stood their ground for a moment, and there was a roar of firearms. An instant later, all the hunters fled back toward the road.

To protect himself from the bullets, Danehy hid in a woodshed. Cautiously, he crawled out and peered toward a clump of trees on the edge of Injun Meadow. His eyes finally rested on a dark object, lying stark and stiff. His fear turned to anger.

"Drat the fools," he muttered. "They've shot my jackass!"

The story in another New York daily was much different, but still uncomplimentary. The *Herald* reported that four men looking for the gorilla had camped overnight in Injun Meadow. Long past midnight, one of the men was awakened by a peculiar noise. He screamed "and instantly the others awoke, seized their guns, and began blazing away." When the smoke cleared, the men saw a strange-looking animal grazing peacefully under a tree. One of the men fired again, dropping the animal in its tracks. The next morning, a farmer looking for his jackass found it dead, and there were reports that all four men might be charged with trespassing.

A posse of fifty citizens left Winsted later that Sunday, determined to bring back the gorilla, dead or alive. The *Herald* reported that they were joined by forty farmers carrying pitchforks. At about 2 p.m., the searchers discovered footprints leading into a cave "and of course there could no longer be any doubt that the circus gorilla was there." Someone suggested building a fire at the mouth of the cave, and it burned fiercely for about fifteen minutes. Suddenly, an immense beast sprang through the opening, so frightening the brave hunters "that they forgot to discharge their firearms and ran home as fast as they could."

Skeptics in Winsted thought the beast was a wildcat, but they were attending a meeting at the time, safely inside a church. The *Herald* concluded that there was no sense in offering a reward for the beast's capture. No one in Winsted dared go within a mile of its cave.[12]

Later that week, several newspapers reported a new theory, that the wild man was an insane artist who had escaped from an asylum.

Most of the reporters returned to their offices. A few days later, a writer from the New York *Recorder* announced that he had found the wild man. The *Recorder* published an exclusive picture of the ferocious beast: a stray jackass.[13]

Two months later, Lou Stone reported that someone had found a whale in a nearby pond, and that Jonah's initials were carved on its tail. The whale was so old that it fell apart and smelled horribly when taken from the water.[14]

During the next thirty-eight years, Stone also wrote about a river that ran uphill, a pig that painted landscapes, a dog that talked, and a tree that grew baked apples. Another of his stories described a windstorm that blew a sheet of paper into a typewriter, then typed the entire alphabet backward.

Other stories described the region's unusual fish. One winter, Stone reported that the line used by an ice fisherman became tangled around something in the water. The fisherman laid down on the ice and peered into the water, hoping to see the trouble. His nose was cold and red, and it apparently touched the water. A pike grabbed his nose, mistaking it for a piece of beefsteak. The man jerked his head back so quickly that he pulled the fish out onto the ice. The pike was fourteen inches long, and Stone reported that you could still see its teeth marks in the fisherman's nose.

A farmer lost his false teeth in another of Winsted's lakes. While fishing two months later, the farmer caught a big-mouthed bass and discovered that it was wearing his teeth. Stone reported that other fish had gold fillings in their teeth, and admired girls who went swimming in flashy bathing suits.

Winsted's chickens became even more famous. Stone reported that one chicken was so patriotic that it laid red, white, and blue eggs every Fourth of July. A hen hopped onto a locomotive's cowcatcher, got off in Winsted, and left an egg to pay for her ride. Another hen liked a chef so much that she laid an egg on his bed at 6:30 each morning, then cackled to wake him so he could eat the egg while it was still fresh.

Cows were another of Stone's favorite subjects. Stone described a cow shocked by an explosion. The cow's feelings were so churned up by the experience that she gave butter instead of milk. Another cow was owned by two old maids who milked it themselves. The cow became so bashful that, after being sold, it refused to let a man touch her unless he dressed in women's clothing, including a sunbonnet.

Stone also reported that an eagle sat on some turtle eggs. When the eggs hatched, the turtles were able to fly. Other stories claimed that a farmer used a vacuum cleaner to pluck his chickens, and that a bald-headed man painted a spider web on his scalp to scare away the flies. Frogs played a flute; a cat whistled "Yankee Doodle"; and a squirrel walked upright on two feet, using a twig for a cane.

Readers enjoyed the stories because they seemed so believable. The animals that Stone described thought and acted like humans. The stories were also innocent, never offending or making fun of anyone.

Several other newspapers offered Stone jobs, but he decided to remain in Winsted and died there in 1933. There were reports that Stone was putting all his stories together in a book. If so, the book was never published and the manuscript disappeared. Not even the *Evening Citizen* kept a record of all his stories. A patron who admired the stories saved a few of them and donated her scrapbook to the Winsted library. The scrapbook is all that remains of Stone's wonderful collection of animals.[15]

Some readers also believed the stories written by another New Englander, Lester Green of Prospect, Connecticut.[16] Green posed as a gentleman farmer and described the unusual plants and animals on his farm in Prospect. One of his most famous stories described a dog he trained to run away from foxes. When a fox appeared, the dog ran home with the fox in close pursuit. Green waited there and shot every fox the dog led to his doorstep. He collected enough of their pelts to make a fox cape for his wife.

Green also reported that he noticed a rabbit eating his tobacco plants and lured an entire flock of the animals around him. He taught the rabbits how to chew tobacco, and said that the hunters in Prospect failed to shoot a single one of them that season. Green explained that the rabbits hid behind hedges until the hunters approached, then spit tobacco juice in their eyes.

While butchering a pig, Green discovered a small gland in its tail and realized that it was responsible for the tail's curl. He extracted all the fluid from the gland, diluted it with alcohol, and rubbed the mixture on his wife's hair. The fluid transformed it into an instant mass of curls.

Green also described a hen that sat on some eggs in a small meadow. Green flooded the meadow, not knowing that the hen was there, and a sudden cold snap froze the water. While cutting some ice later that winter, he found the hen and her eggs trapped inside a block of it. He chipped away the ice and placed the eggs on a stove. When the eggs hatched, the chicks were wearing fur instead of feathers.

Green also described some unusual experiments. To prevent the apples from falling off his trees, he sprayed glue on the fruit early in the season. After that, the apples stuck tightly, even during wind, rain, and sleet storms. During another experiment, he crossed mosquitoes with lightning bugs so people would be able to see the mosquitoes at night.

Salesmen believed the stories and traveled to Prospect to visit Green and ask for permission to manufacture his amazing discoveries. The salesmen never found anyone named "Lester Green" in Prospect. A cartoonist named C. Louis Mortison wrote the stories and attributed his discoveries to the fictional Green. Months passed before the town's other residents learned Green's real identity. By then, the tall tales from Prospect had become famous.

Another hoax described a ghost. During the 1870s, Americans were fascinated by the idea of "spirit materialization" — the idea that the dead might reappear. A young journalist named Edward P. Mitchell witnessed a seance in Boston. In the dim light, dead Indian chieftains seemed to emerge from a cabinet, followed by other famous Americans. To poke fun at the seances, Mitchell wrote a story in the form of a letter. On December 19, 1874, his "letter" appeared on the *New York Sun*'s front page.[17] The *Sun* told its readers that the letter was written by a respected businessman and mailed from Pocock Island. The island was located seventeen miles off the coast of Maine and had 311 residents, mostly fishermen. Another of its residents, John Newbegin, had died four years earlier.

The letter explained that Newbegin had been forty-eight, without family, "and eccentric to a degree that sometimes inspired questions as to his sanity." He was an intelligent man who read a good deal and "might have attained influence in the community had it not been for his utter aimlessness of character, his indifference to fortune, and his consuming thirst for rum." Newbegin earned some money fishing and invested it in two boats. In 1870, one of the boats smuggled in some brandy, and Newbegin was found dead with an empty bottle nearby. The islanders buried him without a coroner's inquest, a burial certificate, or funeral services. Excited by a large catch of fish that summer, they soon forgot all about him.

In August of 1874, there was a heavy gale along the Atlantic coast. Members of the Naugatuck Yacht Club were returning from a summer cruise and forced to seek shelter at Pocock Island. They stayed on the island for three days. The club's members included Mr. E_____, a famous medium who was particularly successful in materializations. To relieve his friends' boredom, Mr. E_____ gave a seance in a little schoolhouse on the island, to the utter bewilderment of islanders permitted to attend.

The first form to step out of a wooden cabinet was an Indian chief. He was followed by a child whom no one recognized, a French Canadian who could not talk English, and a fat gentleman who said he was the first governor of Maine. All these figures returned to the cabinet and were seen no more. Mr. E_____ had the lights turned down still further. The door of the wooden cabinet slowly opened, and another figure emerged, holding a dead fish in his right hand. The islanders rose from their seats, exclaiming, "It is John Newbegin!" They turned and fled in terror.

Newbegin came calmly forward and turned up the solitary kerosene lamp that shed light over the proceedings. He then sat down in a chair, folded his arms, and said, "I propose to remain in the materialized condition." Since then, the letter continued, he has been a living inhabitant of Pocock Island, eating, drinking (water only), and sleeping like any other man. The yachtsmen left the very next morning, probably believing that Newbegin was a fraud hired by Mr. E_____. But the residents of Pocock Island knew that John Newbegin had come back from the land of the dead.

The idea of having a ghost join their community was not at all pleasing to the island's inhabitants. They were still a little sensitive about the subject and seemed reluctant to talk about the skeleton in their closet. Yet the islanders now realized that a spirit was not necessarily evil. They had come to accept Newbegin's presence and were quite neighborly with him.

The businessman had interviewed the dead man, and his letter continued: "I found him affable and even communicative. He is perfectly aware of his doubtful status as a being, but hopes that at some future time there may be legislation that shall correctly define his position and the position of any spirit who may follow him into the material world."

Newbegin admitted that he was glad to get back to Earth "and that he embraced the very first opportunity to be materialized." He seemed reluctant, however, to discuss the four years of his death, apparently because his memories of it were unpleasant.

Newbegin regretted the wasted years of his previous life. Indeed, his conduct during the past three months showed that his regret was genuine. He had stopped drinking, gotten back into the fishing business, and was generally respected on the island. There was a noticeable reluctance, however, to accept his debts. "In short," the letter concluded, "Mr. John Newbegin is a most respectable citizen (if a dead man can be a citizen) and has announced his intention of running for the next Legislature."

The letter speculated that Newbegin could be a pioneer, the first of a large immigration from the spirit world. A whole flock of dead people might come trooping back to Earth.

The story was widely reprinted, usually as the truth. The *Sun*'s editor was so impressed by it that he offered Mitchell a full-time job on his staff.[18]

Other New Englanders have written their autobiographies, and many are wonderful—but not accurate—storytellers. Unfortunately, even their most inaccurate stories are accepted as fact.

In 1939, Florence Finch Kelly wrote a book about her fifty-six years as a journalist. Kelly's book describes the most amazing hoax she observed during those fifty-six years. In the autumn of 1883, she claimed, a young man named "Soames" worked as the assistant telegraph editor at the *Boston Globe.* Soames wanted to go to Washington but needed more money for the trip. To earn the money, Soames spent several days at a public library and returned with a story that "would make your hair curl."

The story reported that an earthquake in the South Pacific had damaged a ship's compass. The ship's captain did not know his exact location but told a truly horrible tale. A volcano had blown an entire island into the sky. Ashes darkened the sky and covered his ship's deck. Other marvels made even the tough old captain's eyes pop from his head. The ocean bubbled with heat from the volcano, killing tons of fish, yet huge blocks of ice floated in the red-hot lava.

Soames told his editors the truth: it was an imaginary tale, but every incident he described "had happened in some volcanic eruption sometime in the past." He obtained all the details from authentic scientific sources. The *Globe* bought the story and published it on page 1. Other newspapers reprinted the story, and their competitors denounced it. They insisted that the details were so bizarre — so totally impossible — that it was obviously a hoax.

Months later, according to Kelly's account, journalists learned that a volcanic eruption had just lifted an entire island two thousand feet out of the Pacific Ocean, creating a hole one thousand feet deep. It was the greatest eruption in modern times, remarkably similar to the eruption that Soames had imagined.[19]

A book published in 1956 makes the story sound even more amazing. Frank Edwards, author of *Strangest of All,* provides this account:

> A Boston journalist named "Edward Samson" was drunk and sleeping it off on a couch in the *Globe*'s office. Samson awoke shortly after 3 a.m., drenched with perspiration. He had dreamed about the volcano with an exceptional clarity — as if watching it from a grandstand seat. Samson sat down in the deserted office, lit a candle, and wrote out the details, describing how thousands of fear-maddened natives on the island of "Pralape" fled toward the sea. The natives were trapped between the red-hot lava and the boiling sea, and the disaster ended with "a tremendous explosion that destroyed the island of Pralape in its entirety. . . . "
>
> The next day, another editor found Samson's notes and thought they were based upon a genuine cable. The *Globe* published the story beneath an 8-column banner headline. Other newspapers copied the story, and The Associated Press transmitted it to dailies as far west as San Francisco.
>
> The *Globe* failed to receive any more cables about the volcano, and its publisher demanded an explanation. Samson confessed that his notes were

based upon a dream. He was fired, of course. Then—before the *Globe* could publish a correction—it received reports of a real volcano in the Straits of Sunda off the coast of Java. As more details reached the *Globe,* its editors discovered that Samson's account, based upon a dream, was amazingly accurate.

The *Globe* promptly tossed its correction into a wastebasket, placed Samson back on its payroll, and published his picture on page 1. "In other words, the vivid and terrifying events Ed Samson was dreaming about were actually taking place at that same instant half way around the Earth from where he lay tossing on the couch in the office of the Boston *Globe.*"[20]

In 1959, Edwards published a second book, *Stranger Than Science,* and it repeats the tale.[21]

The *Globe,* however, insisted that it never employed anyone named "Edward Samson," and that its story about the volcano was based upon a cable, not a dream. The *Globe* explained that an editor named "Byron Somes" received a brief cable from London, and the cable reported that a volcanic eruption had already occurred on the island of Krakatoa in the Straits of Sunda. The paper added: "From the scant details in this story, plus information gathered at a public library, Somes wrote a series of stories about the disaster. The stories also appeared in other newspapers and, remarkably, Somes's account of the disaster came very close to the truth in its details."[22]

Thus, Kelly's autobiography misspelled Somes's name and was mistaken when it said that he wrote the story months earlier. Similarly, Edwards was mistaken when he said the story was based upon a drunken dream.

The *Globe*'s old editions are still available. Their content and eyewitness accounts also contradict other details in Edwards's books. Edwards's first book said that the editor at the *Boston Globe* was named "Edward Samson," and that Samson called the island "Pralape." The *Globe*'s editor was named "Somes," and every story in the *Globe* identified the island correctly, as "Krakatoa." Edwards claims that the *Globe* published Somes's picture and an eight-column banner headline, yet the *Globe* never published any pictures and used only one-column headlines. Edwards adds that the island blew up on August 28 and disappeared on the 29th. Eyewitnesses said that only a portion of the island blew up, and that it sank on the 27th. Edwards also claims that thousands of natives died on the island. Eyewitnesses said that thousands of people died in neighboring areas, but that Krakatoa was uninhabited.[23]

In 1910, Kenneth Roberts was a beginner at another Boston paper, the *Post*. An editor sent him to a fish market to check on a story published by another newspaper in the city. The rival's story reported that a fisherman had caught a codfish weighing a record seventy-one pounds. When Roberts reached the market, its stalls were dark and deserted. He returned to the *Post* and noticed a sign on an office wall. It insisted: "ACCURACY, ACCURACY, ACCURACY."

Roberts ignored the sign. Afraid to admit that he failed, he sat down and concocted a story about a codfish weighing seventy-one pounds and measuring five feet three inches from snout to tail. Roberts added that an eminent authority, Professor Morton Kilgallen, estimated that the cod was forty-seven years old. The professor based his estimate upon the length of the cod's whisker. "Contrary to general opinion," the professor said, "the age of a codfish is not told from looking at his teeth, although some old salts claim they can . . . tell the age of a cod by examining his molars."

Professor Kilgallen said it was often difficult to estimate a cod's age by its whisker because, when two codfish fought for a piece of food, each cod tried to nip off the other's whisker. If one succeeded, the loser became an outcast. The professor added, "I have known instances of codfish who deliberately committed suicide by swimming up on a beach and exposing themselves to the air after suffering the loss of their whiskers." Another of the cod's habits was even more unusual. Professor Kilgallen explained that, after laying her eggs, a mother cod kept them warm by breathing warm water on them.

An editor threw Roberts's story into a wastebasket, but another editor retrieved it. The next morning, it appeared on the *Post*'s front page "along with a murder . . . , a two-headed calf, and other important matters." Each week after that, Roberts wrote three more stories about Professor Kilgallen. His later stories revealed that, to reduce his utility bills, the professor connected electric eels to his lighting system. The professor also possessed a fish with false teeth, maintained an aquarium for sick fish, treated halibut for sunburn, and studied the love life of lobster.

Some readers refused to believe that crabs tunneled for great distances by biting into the earth and blowing it backward through their ears. Some also doubted that jellyfish produced their young by breaking small pieces off their own bodies. Despite their skepticism, Professor

Kilgallen became a popular figure in Boston, and the *Post* raised Roberts's salary from $18 to $20 a week.

The following February, the professor announced that he was getting married and intended to spend his honeymoon studying "the action of green bananas on the voracious grettle fish of the Gulf Stream."[24] By then, Roberts was earning $30 a week.

Another hoaxer, T. Walter Williams of the *New York Times,* was a unique figure in the world of journalism. Williams created strange characters who wandered around the world, getting into trouble everywhere. A colleague explained: "There weren't always enough interesting people around to satisfy Mr. Williams. He solved this by inventing a few." The colleague described Williams as a dignified gentleman, fond of Scotch whiskey, and fond of telling "the biggest damn tales you ever heard."[25] Williams's stories may be the only fiction that the *Times* ever knowingly published in its news columns.

Williams spent thirty-seven years along the New York waterfront, gathering shipping news for the *Times*. He was an ideal reporter for the job, having been born in England in 1865 and sailed around the world while still a youth. He left his ship for months at a time, seeking adventure on land: searching for gold in the Amazon, installing lightning rods in Central America, and helping dig the Panama Canal.

In 1899, Williams began to write for William Randolph Hearst. He moved to the *Times* in 1905. But after turning to journalism, Williams continued to think of himself as a sailor. He became friends with thousands of seamen and captains, and they saved their best stories for him, including their stories about a sea serpent.

On Feb. 11, 1934, Williams reported that the passenger ship Mauretania had sighted a sixty-five-foot serpent in the Caribbean. One of the ship's officers, S. W. Moughtin, told Williams, "It was a fine, clear afternoon. At first I thought it might be a whale or a whistling grampus thrusting its head up into the air to catch flying fish on the wing, but soon saw that it was too large. The head of the monster was about 7 feet out of the water and was fully 2 feet across."[26] The monster's head and shoulders disappeared before Moughtin could call another officer, but the ship's senior third officer saw thirty feet of it. The ship's passengers were below at the time, eating lunch.

Moughtin speculated that the monster may have been an offspring of a monster seen in 1907, or it may have been a relative of Scotland's Loch Ness monster.[27]

On February 2, the Mauretania's crew spotted a second monster in a harbor. The monster was about twenty-five feet long and fifteen feet wide, with huge fins sticking out six feet on each side. It sank below the surface before the ship's passengers were able to take a single snapshot.

On February 24, Moughtin returned to New York after a cruise to the West Indies and seemed surprised at the excitement his first story had caused. "All I can swear to," Moughtin reiterated, "is that the sea serpent I saw had a shiny, jet-black skin, and it left a long undulating wake as if it must have been at least 65 or more feet long." When asked whether he believed Moughtin's story, the ship's captain responded that Moughtin had served with him for a long time and was a very reliable officer. "Besides," the captain said, "sailors never lie."[28]

On March 10, the *Times* reported that the Mauretania had sighted another 65-foot serpent in the Caribbean.[29] After watching the serpent for a moment through binoculars, Moughtin sent word to the captain, Reginald V. Peel, and Peel watched it for about three minutes. "I do not know exactly what it was," Peel said, "and I do not wish to be mixed up in the sea serpent story business, but it was certainly 60 feet long, with four humps, and the same number of what looked to me like fins." Several passengers also saw the monster; unfortunately, it disappeared while they went below to fetch their cameras.

On March 27, the *New York Times* poked fun at its own stories. A brief article on its editorial page warned that, if the shipping line which owned the Mauretania failed to be more careful, "it may yet be haled into court for the violation of the anti-trust laws in the matter of sea serpents. Ever since the navigating officers of the Mauretania about six weeks ago first sighted the sea monster," the paper explained, "the famous British liner has never failed to make port without announcing a new glimpse of the marine wonder." The *Times* wondered whether the monster operated by special arrangement with the shipping line, and only for the Mauretania's passengers. If so, it might be a form of unfair competition, prohibited by new federal laws.[30]

Williams's other stories — more obviously tall tales — usually appeared in the *Times*'s Sunday edition. One of the stories, only a few paragraphs long, reported that a monkey at a Bronx park had learned to play a ukelele.[31] Other stories described Marmaduke M. Mizzle, a famous caraway-seed merchant. The stories told of Mizzle's adventures in strange lands, searching for strange animals with his faithful servant, an Egyptian named "Ali."

Mizzle's life was in constant danger. After feeling something cold and clammy under his head, he discovered that he was using a king cobra for a pillow. While swimming in Upper Burma, he was attacked by a swivel-eyed spotted Samba-Samba: a strange underwater reptile, about six feet long, with a single eye in the center of its head. While being chased by a rhinoceros, he ran around a tree and fell over a tiger dozing in the shade. The tiger rose with a roar, and Mizzle escaped as the rhino charged, starting a terrible battle between the two animals.

"These stories of adventure with wild animals sound unreal," Mizzle admitted, "but to men who have slept in the mud and reeds on the banks of the Upper Congo and been trodden upon by a hippopotamus before breakfast, or been chased by a red-headed spotted Bildik . . . they may sometimes appear strange, but never extraordinary—no, indeed."[32]

In 1920, Mizzle visited the circus animals at Madison Square Garden and recognized several old friends, including a Bengal tiger that had saved his life. While traveling through the jungles of India, he had been warned about a bad tiger named "Minkoll." A short time later, he heard a wild animal roaring in great pain and saw a tiger, evidently Minkoll, resting against a tree. As tears ran down its furry cheeks, the tiger pointed to his jaw. Mizzle peered into the tiger's mouth and saw that one of its back teeth was decayed. Taking out a long piece of steel wire, Mizzle fastened one end to the tooth and the other to a tree. This done, he poked the tiger with a needle. The beast gave a tremendous roar and dashed forward with a rush, tearing the tooth out by its roots. After a moment, Mizzle said, the tiger sat down on his haunches, "then he looked up at me gratefully, wagged his huge tail three times, and stalked off into the jungle. . . . "

Two years later, Mizzle was attacked by an elephant. He was fleeing in zigzag fashion, ready to fall from exhaustion. Suddenly he heard a roar and saw something dash toward the elephant. It was the grateful Minkoll, and he saved Mizzle's life. "It was an extraordinary story," Mizzle admitted. But if you went to Madison Square Garden and looked closely at the circus tiger there, you could still see the cavity where he wrenched out the decayed tooth.[33]

In 1929, Mizzle was in Peru. As his faithful servant Ali tried to wade across a river, he got in over his head, and a ten-foot alligator started for the poor Egyptian. To add to the danger, an Indian armed with a bow and arrow stepped out of the forest and started to draw on Ali. Mizzle could do nothing but stand and watch. As the alligator made a final dash for his intended victim, the Indian let fly his arrow. It missed Ali but hit the big alligator in an eye. The alligator turned and swam toward the river bank with Ali clinging to its back in desperation. Ali scampered safely ashore as Mizzle climbed a tree to hide from the Indian.[34]

A few years later, two full-grown tigers almost consumed Mizzle on the left bank of the Irawaddy River in Burma.[35] A letter from Mizzle explained that he was proceeding through a dark tropical forest. That night, he suddenly awoke and was terrified by two full-grown tigers standing close beside his little cot and gazing down at him. Fortunately, the tigers were not hungry and trotted away in the most amiable manner.

The tigers returned that afternoon, evidently hungry and intending to eat Mizzle. Just as the tigers were about to spring upon him, he heard wild shouting, and his friend—a Russian professor named Ivan Snabzhonkersotovich—rushed upon the scene. The professor and his companions had been collecting insects and were waving huge butterfly nets at the end of long bamboo rods. "These," Mizzle said, "they cast dexterously over the heads of the startled tigers, which scared the beasts so badly that they tore the netting to pieces and dashed into the forest with parts of it hanging to their heads."

Mizzle also became involved in a fight between a tiger, a hippopotamus, a crocodile, and a giant panda. In a letter from Upper Burma, the famous caraway-seed hunter explained that he had jumped into a canoe and told a native to paddle to the opposite bank. Before they could get away, a giant panda came tearing down to the bank, chased by a tiger. At the same time, a big crocodile and a hippopotamus appeared between the canoe and shore. The panda made a great jump and landed in the canoe, going clean through the bottom of it. The tiger landed on the hippo's back, and the crocodile grabbed the tiger by its tail. As the current carried them all downstream, the hippo tried to shake off the tiger, Mizzle clung to the canoe, and the panda clung to Mizzle. Just as Mizzle decided to drown, Ali pulled him from the water with the panda still clinging to his hair.[36]

Another of Williams's creations, a waterfront philosopher named Ben Fidd, had traveled the Seven Seas for nearly forty years in all kinds of sailing vessels. Now, he worked as a watchman along the New York waterfront.

In 1931, Fidd recalled his worst voyage.[37] He was aboard an old ship, ready to leave Calcutta for London. At the last minute, the captain received a cable instructing him to bring back 203 monkeys. A carpenter set to work, building cages on the ship's deck, and the next day all sorts of natives came down to the dock with monkeys they wanted to sell. A few nights after they sailed, two crewmen noticed that their caps were missing, and another crewman was struck on the head. The next morning, "they saw that nearly all the monkeys had got loose and were up aloft, having the time of their lives." In a week, the ship was a mess. The monkeys tipped over paintpots and threw potatoes at the captain. The voyage back to London lasted 104 days, and the crew nearly went mad. When they finally reached London, the owner came aboard and asked why the ship was full of monkeys. "I only brought the 203 you ordered," the captain replied.

The owner said he had cabled for two or three.

By 1941, Fidd had retired but often returned to the waterfront with his grandson. While watching the ships there, he reminisced about Thanksgiving Day aboard an American ship sailing to China. Because there was no ice to preserve meat, the ship carried a good deal of livestock, including six turkeys. The skipper and the cook were saving an especially fat bird for Thanksgiving dinner. One Sunday morning, there was a loud yell. The captain's pet turkey had blown overboard and was struggling to stay afloat. They stopped the ship, and the crew lowered a boat. As several sailors neared the turkey, an eighteen-foot shark swallowed it.

There was a tremendous commotion. The shark lashed the sea with its tail, then all of a sudden became still. The turkey had apparently stuck in the shark's gullet and was choking it. The sailors hauled the shark aboard their ship, ripped it open with a sharp knife and, sure enough, found the turkey inside, "with just a dash of life left in it." The crew revived the turkey and enjoyed it for Thanksgiving dinner, along with a large portion of rum.[38]

Fidd also described the rats he saw during his sailing days. "Sailing craft, especially the wooden ships, were full of rats," he said. "They lived in the hold and came on deck to get water. I've seen them on fine moonlight nights . . . playing hide-and-seek around the deck, just like school kids." When the ships docked, rat-catchers came aboard and caught a few sackfuls of the varmints. However, the rat-catchers always let a fair number go free so they would have more business when the ships returned.

Fidd said the rats changed ships at Singapore. Rats coming from Europe and America refused to go farther east, and rats coming from the Orient refused to go farther west. He once saw two British steamships, one bound for Japan and the other for London, docked at Singapore. At sundown, he saw rats coming down one of the ship's mooring lines. "I saw them climbing down to the pier carrying small packages which looked like nests, and some appeared to be carrying their young," he continued. When he looked at the steamer bound for London, he saw a similar procession climbing aboard it.[39]

Some readers, even other journalists, believed the stories. Another newspaper sent its reporters and photographers to the waterfront to interview Ben Fidd. Similarly, an agent asked for Mizzle's address so she could ask him to write a book.

Other New Yorkers continue to publish some hoaxes. One of the most active, Dan Rattiner, has been nicknamed the "Hoaxer of the Hamptons."[40] Each year, Rattiner publishes three or four hoaxes in the East Hampton *Summer Sun* and five sister weeklies on the east end of Long Island.

Rattiner has reported that the police chief in Bridgehampton wanted local residents to contribute raw meat to feed a killer shark roaming the area's beaches. The police chief hoped that, if people fed the shark, it would stop consuming one or two swimmers a day.

Another story revealed that the area had sunk more than an inch.[41] The Seismological Institute of New York told the *Summer Sun* that the problem seemed to be related "to the weight of the 2 million tourists who visited the East End. . . . " The institute had recorded some tremors, particularly around the Fourth of July when the largest number of tourists appeared. Now, the ground itself seemed to be collapsing. A spokesman for the institute explained that the subsoils were "simply not built to withstand the sort of influx that took place this past summer. . . . " If the trend continued, he warned, "the East End will be completely sunk by the year 2314."

A local developer called the report "hogwash" and "a plot to stop the natural growth of the area." An environmentalist took the report more seriously, but said the problem was caused by the amount of water tourists drank, not their weight. "When people drink up our water supply underground," he explained, "it moves the water above ground, creates a vacuum underneath, and causes the earth to pull down."

The County Board of Supervisors, meeting in emergency session, found a solution to the problem. The board voted 5 to 4 to prohibit fat tourists. A new law adopted by the board would go into effect the following May. By then, everyone would have ample time to become familiar with the law, "and, if necessary, lose the necessary pounds to be allowed in."[42]

Signs posted along major highways would warn tourists that "FAT VIOLATES THE LAW," and that "FAT PERSONS MUST GO HOME." Anyone found on the streets after May 1, and suspected of being overweight, would be taken to a police station and weighed. Anyone found to be overweight would be fined $1,000 and escorted from the area.

Radio and TV Hoaxes: Dolls, Monsters, and Martians

ROADCASTERS rarely create deliberate hoaxes. Those broadcasters responsible for a hoax are too likely to be criticized by their colleagues and fired by their station. In addition, the federal government may threaten to revoke their station's license.

Broadcasters are also cautious because their hoaxes are more frightening than the hoaxes published by newspapers. People trust the nation's radio and television stations, and many obtain all their news from them. The stations are also more personal than newspapers. People know their local and network newscasters, and often consider them family friends. Americans never expect the newscasters to mislead them.

A few radio and television programs have frightened the public. Most were entertainment programs that used a realistic format — simulated news bulletins to report mythical disasters. Audiences generally labeled such shows hoaxes.

The public's reaction to the programs is predictable. People frightened by a radio or television program switch to other stations to learn more about the disaster. The other stations are broadcasting their regularly scheduled programs, not denying the disaster's authenticity. As a result, people's fright turns to panic. Some begin to call the police. Telephone lines become jammed, and people unable to complete their calls become hysterical. At that point, some people begin to pray, and others flee. A few prepare to defend themselves, or they call their families for help and to say a final "good-bye." Their calls spread the panic to other people, even to people not listening to the program.

Broadcasters have created a few hoaxes for the fun of it, to fool or amuse their audiences. After the Second World War, for example, U.S. soldiers occupied Japan, and the Armed Forces Radio Service in Tokyo reported that a monster was advancing toward Tokyo. It was May 29, 1947, and an announcer for Station WVTR warned that a twenty-foot sea serpent had come ashore and was approaching the city. For an hour, the announcer continued to report that military police were battling the monster, but that small-arms fire failed to stop it.

Japanese police sounded a general alarm, and U.S. soldiers were advised to stay off the streets. Instead, soldiers grabbed machine guns, jumped into Army trucks and Jeeps, and raced through the city, searching for the monster. An hour later, the announcer reported that the monster had been stopped by soldiers using flamethrowers.[1]

The station's switchboard lit up and stayed lit up for three hours. The telephone lines to other Army agencies in Tokyo were also clogged with calls from Americans and Britons, "some of whom were frankly frightened." An employee at WVTR said that one of the calls was from Gen. Douglas MacArthur.[2]

Two years later, a radio station in Willmar, Minnesota, broadcast a similar hoax. Maurice Chargo, an announcer at Station KWLM, reported that a circus train from South Dakota had pulled into the local railroad yards, and that some of its wild animals had escaped. Chargo warned that the animals were roaming the countryside, and that parents should keep their children inside. Chargo added that a policeman had been hospitalized "with seven broken ribs suffered in fighting the wild animals."[3]

Parents rushed to the town's playgrounds to snatch up their children.[4] Other listeners bolted their doors. A whistle summoning the town's volunteer firemen sounded minutes later, "and a lot of folks thought the fire department was being called out in the fight to round up the animals." In fact, they were being called out to fight a fire at the Central Dairy Products Co.

The *Willmar Daily Tribune* reported that a policeman was hospitalized, but not because of any injuries inflicted by the animals. Rather,

"He had been ill with pneumonia. . . . "[5] No circus trains were in Willmar that night, and no wild animals roamed the countryside. The only animals aboard trains in the city were cattle headed for market.

The town's police chief wanted to arrest Chargo but was unable to find any laws he violated. The police chief also wanted Chargo taken off the air. A representative for Station KWLM responded that there was no reason "to take any such drastic action."[6] He promised that, in the future, Chargo would stick to his script.

Why did Chargo create the hoax? It was a cold, stormy night in the middle of winter, and Chargo said, "I just ran out of jokes. I got to thinking that maybe nobody listens to me."

A more humorous (and recent) hoax involved dolls dropped from an airplane.

In 1983, millions of parents lined up at toy counters to buy their children Cabbage Patch dolls, and thousands of people staged near riots to get them. Some stores were sold out, and others hired police officers to help maintain order. The manufacturer, Coleco Industries, Inc., sold the eighteen-inch dolls almost as if they were real babies. The dolls were designed by a computer, so no two looked alike. Also, each doll came with a diaper, a name, a birth certificate, and adoption papers.

As a joke, Gene Mueller and Bob Reitman at Radio Station WKTI-FM in Milwaukee, Wisconsin, announced that a B-29 bomber would drop fifteen hundred to two thousand of the dolls into the Milwaukee County Stadium at three o'clock that November afternoon.[7] They instructed their listeners to bring a catcher's mitt and an American Express credit card to the stadium's parking lot. Mueller and Reitman told people to use the catcher's mitt to grab a doll, and then to hold their credit card up to the sky so an aerial photo could record their charge number.

Wind gusts that afternoon reached thirty-seven mph, and the wind chill was seven degrees below zero. Despite the bad weather, about two dozen people went to the stadium. Some were too embarrassed to tell reporters their names. Others did not want their employers to know where they were. A thirty-two-year-old father arrived late and was unable to find any of the dolls. He looked up to see if the plane was also late and explained that his two-year-old daughter wanted a doll for Christmas.

Mueller and Reitman continued the joke the next morning but tried to make it even more ridiculous. They reported that a barge full of

Cabbage Patch dolls was anchored eight miles out in Lake Michigan with Popeye aboard. The two men advised their listeners to go to the lake with a can of spinach and swim to the barge. Once aboard the barge, they would be able to exchange the spinach for a doll.[8]

Broadcasters created other hoaxes because of competitive pressures. Some, like newspaper reporters, wanted to improve their stories, to make them more colorful and dramatic. Other broadcasters expected the hoaxes to help their careers.

During the 1930s, one of the nation's most notorious criminals, John Dillinger, escaped from an Indiana jail. Newspapers in Chicago sent their reporters to Indiana to cover the search for Dillinger. Steve Trumbull, the news director at Radio Station KYW in Chicago, placed some portable broadcasting equipment on a truck and joined them. After hearing that a farmer had seen Dillinger, Trumbull rushed to the spot. He found that it was another false alarm but went on the air anyway. Trumbull described, in vivid detail, a battle between Dillinger and the police. Gunshots being fired in the background almost drowned out his voice.

Other reporters rushed to the scene. They found that some detectives happened to be in the area, and that Trumbull had suggested they do a little harmless target shooting while he was on the air. Trumbull insisted that he never told his audience that Dillinger was surrounded. If they inferred that Dillinger "was at that moment fighting it out with the forces of law and order, it was not his fault."[9]

A more serious hoax involved a psychic who said she predicted the attempt to assassinate President Ronald Reagan.

Tamara Rand, a thirty-two-year-old psychic from Los Angeles, appeared on a Las Vegas talk show, "Dick Maurice and Company," in January 1981. On March 30, a sandy-haired young man named John Hinckley, Jr., fired six shots at President Reagan as he left a Washington hotel. The shots wounded four men, including the president. A bullet struck him in the left side, stopping only three inches from his heart.

It was a Monday afternoon, and Rand immediately announced that she had predicted Reagan would get a "thud" in the chest, with "shots all over the place." Rand said she also predicted that the gunman would be a young, fair-haired radical named "Jack Humley." She telephoned NBC's affiliate in Los Angeles with the story.

On Tuesday, Rand returned to Station KTNV in Las Vegas to "rearticulate" her January prediction. She explained that the rearticulation was necessary because she had slurred and stumbled over some words. Later that Tuesday, she again called the NBC affiliate in Los Angeles, this time saying, "I have a tape of my predictions."

Rand delivered copies of the tape to several stations, and both the ABC and NBC television networks used it during their morning news programs.[10]

On Friday, ABC and NBC admitted that they had been fooled and that Rand's tape was a fraud. The news director at KTNV had reviewed the January program and discovered that Rand had never mentioned the shooting. When employees at the station compared the January program with the tape showing Rand's predictions, they noticed that the microphone was positioned differently and that the rings on her fingers were also different.

On Sunday, Maurice admitted that the predictions were a hoax.[11] It had started, he said, as a "way of helping a friend." Maurice had expected the hoax to help Rand's career.

Other broadcasts involved Martians, and the most famous occurred on October 30, 1938, the night before Halloween. Millions of Americans are familiar with the program, but few know about the replications that caused twenty deaths in South America.

H. G. Wells published *The War of the Worlds* in 1898, and his novel described an invasion of Earth by Martians. In 1938, the novel was adapted for radio, and CBS broadcast the adaptation over a coast-to-coast chain of 151 stations. Announcements made before, during, and after the hour-long program clearly stated that it was a dramatization. Thus, the broadcast was never intended to fool the public.

A young playwright asked to write the script had almost given up. "Under no circumstances," he complained, "could it be made interesting or in any way credible to modern American ears."[12] A secretary agreed, adding, "Those old Martians are just a lot of nonsense. It's all too silly. We're going to make fools of ourselves! Absolute fools!" Even members of the cast thought the script was too weak and absurd.

The script was finished on Wednesday, and the actors rehearsed it on Thursday. The rehearsal was frenzied and confused, and the cast remained pessimistic.

The "Mercury Theatre on the Air" started routinely at 8 p.m. that

Sunday. There was a weather report followed by an orchestra playing at a Manhattan hotel. Seconds later, an announcer interrupted with a special bulletin. Explosions had been observed on the planet Mars, and unidentified objects were "moving toward the Earth with enormous velocity." Later bulletins added that a flaming object, probably a meteorite, had crashed on a farm near Grovers Mill, New Jersey.

A newsman at Grovers Mill revealed that the flaming object was not a meteorite, but a ship from outer space. It was a yellowish-white cylinder, about thirty yards in diameter. As the newsman watched, the top began to rotate like a screw, and something wiggled out. It was a huge, mechanical man, and its face was frightful. Its eyes were black, and its mouth was V-shaped, with saliva dripping from its quivering lips.

A heat ray incinerated everything around the Martian, turning the spectators to cinders. The National Guard was called out and a state of emergency declared. Americans were urged to remain calm, but the Martians destroyed Trenton, New Jersey, and marched toward New York, preceded by a cloud of poisonous black smoke.

As the Martians approached New York, bells warned the city's residents to flee. Five of the machines, as tall as skyscrapers, crossed the Hudson River "like a man wading a brook." By then, other cylinders had fallen near Buffalo, Chicago, and St. Louis.[13]

Because the "Mercury Theatre on the Air" had no sponsor, there was no commercial break for forty minutes. By then, the Martians had conquered most of the country.

A newsman rushing to the studio observed a half-dozen women and children scurrying from a theater on Third Avenue. He also noticed men dashing from nearby bars and peering up at the sky. He found that policemen had entered the glass-enclosed control room at CBS and watched in disbelief as the actors "stood stoically before the microphones, reading their scripts, ignorant of the havoc they were creating throughout the land."[14]

Social scientists estimated that six million people heard the broadcast, and that one million were disturbed or frightened by it.[15] All over the United States, listeners were calling the police, newspapers, and radio stations. Some wanted to know whether the program was real. Others wanted to know what they should do. The *New York Times* received 875 calls.

Listeners in New York feared that the city was being bombed. By 8:30, some had packed their belongings and begun to flee. A man ran into a police station, shouting that enemy planes were overhead. A woman looking for her family ran into a theater, screaming, "Get out! Get out! The city's on fire!"

The Martians supposedly landed in New Jersey, and the panic there was worse. Newspapers reported that some families ran onto the streets with wet towels and handkerchiefs wrapped around their faces as protection from the gas.[16] Other people called the police. Some wanted gas masks, but others needed ambulances and rescue squads. A single hospital in the city treated fifteen people for shock and hysteria.[17]

As the hysteria worsened, people began to insist that they saw the Martians and heard their bombs. The *Press-Scimitar* in Memphis recalled its staff to publish an "Extra" about the bombing of Chicago and St. Louis. In Concrete, Washington, an electrical failure occurred midway through the program, and listeners there blamed the Martians. A family in Missouri saw a red glow, possibly a forest fire, in the sky and also blamed the Martians.

At 8:18 p.m., the Associated Press informed the nation's news media that the program was "a studio dramatization." Similarly, a bulletin transmitted to the state police in New York stated, "Station WABC informs us that the broadcast just concluded over that station was a dramatization of a play. No cause for alarm." At 9 p.m., newscaster Gabriel Heatter presented a reassuring message over the Mutual network. At 9:30, Walter Winchell broadcast a similar message on NBC. Local stations interrupted their programs with more disclaimers.

When told that thousands of listeners had panicked, Orson Welles seemed bewildered. "How could they?" he asked. "They were told several times it wasn't real." Also, the invasion supposedly occurred a year later, and the program was narrated by a survivor who described events that had occurred in the past.

Newspaper columnists were even more amazed by the public's response. Events the program described would have taken days or even weeks to occur. The program compressed all the events into fifty minutes: falling meteorites, trips to New Jersey, meetings, warnings, land and air battles, and the invasion of New York. No one seemed to hear—or remember—the program's last half hour. It revealed that there was nothing to fear, that all the Martians were dead, killed by bacteria in the Earth's atmosphere.

Also, at the very end of the Halloween program, Welles had announced that it was the Mercury Theatre's way "of dressing up in a sheet and jumping out of a bush and saying 'Boo.' "

Why were so many people frightened? Many had tuned in late, just in time to hear the bulletins about a meteorite falling at Grovers Mill. Experts also blamed the times and the program's realistic format. In 1938, the world seemed to be on the verge of another war. Other radio programs had been interrupted by real news bulletins about the crisis in Europe, so the public was familiar with their use. In addition, some listeners—particularly the poor and the poorly educated—trusted radio and relied upon it for much of their news. Listeners also trusted experts quoted during the program—astronomers, professors, and the secretary of the interior.[18]

A magazine, *Christian Century,* said that some listeners panicked because they lacked faith in God. However, social scientists found that some listeners panicked because of their faith. Listeners who were deeply religious believed that the invasion was real because it seemed to be an "act of God" and fulfilled religious prophecies about the end of the world.

Actor John Houseman had helped found the Mercury Theatre and said that another factor, the program's "sheer technical brilliance," had also contributed to its impact. Houseman explained that the program started slowly, almost dully. After fifteen minutes, the tempo accelerated to a wild, reckless pace. By then, its credibility had been established, and people believed everything that followed. "To this day," Houseman added, "it is impossible to sit in a room and hear the scratched, worn recording of the broadcast, without feeling in the back of your neck some light draught left over from the great wind of terror that swept the nation. . . . "[19]

People who claimed they were hurt by the program filed numerous lawsuits against CBS. Women said they suffered miscarriages. Other plaintiffs said they "suffered from shock and, in some cases, heart attacks."[20] Their lawsuits totalled $750,000, but "none was substantiated, or legally proved."

Friends feared that the broadcast would destroy Welles's career. Instead, it made him a national celebrity. The broadcast also helped the "Mercury Theatre on the Air." Until then, it had been unable to find a sponsor. After "The War of the Worlds," the Campbell Soup Co. agreed to sponsor the series, but changed its name to "Campbell Playhouse."

Americans fooled by the broadcast became more skeptical of the programs they heard on radio. When Japanese planes bombed Pearl

Harbor on December 7, 1941, even some journalists thought, at first, that "it was an Orson Welles kind of hoax. . . . "²¹

Two stations in South America copied Welles's program, and the results there were even more frightening. A writer who had worked in New York suggested that a radio station in Santiago, Chile, might replicate the broadcast. Thus, on November 21, 1944, simulated news bulletins reported that Martians had landed fifteen miles south of Santiago. Later bulletins reported that the Martians defeated Chile's armed forces and destroyed Santiago's civic center.

Thousands of listeners all over Chile "were gripped by hysterical fits." The *New York Times* reported that "Chileans ran in panic into the streets, while others at home were reported to have suffered nervous upsets and heart seizures."²² The program was blamed for numerous accidents and injuries, and "some time was required to restore calm."

On February 12, 1949, a radio station in Quito, Ecuador, broadcast a second replication. A director at Station HCQRX, called "Radio Quito," rehearsed the program in secret and presented it as a genuine news story, not a dramatization.²³

The dramatization began with a musical program. An announcer interrupted with "an urgent piece of news." At that very moment, he said, something strange was happening. Later bulletins added that Martians were approaching Quito, preceded by a black cloud of deadly gases. Parts of the city were destroyed and troops massacred. The archbishop was praying for God's mercy, and Ecuadorians everywhere were fleeing. In the background, listeners could hear the clamor of church bells, the crackle of flames, and the agony of the dying. A government minister urged everyone to remain calm, but the mayor instructed women and children to flee, leaving the men "free for action and combat."

Some listeners, half-dressed and hysterical, "fled into the streets in wild displays of terror." When the broadcasters realized what was happening, they urged their listeners to remain calm and tried to assure them that the program was fictitious.²⁴

Infuriated by the hoax, rioters attacked a three-story building that housed HCQRX and Quito's leading newspaper, *Comercio*. They began throwing stones at the building, smashed its windows, and tore open its iron gates. Rioters also hurled flaming rags and papers at the building, setting it afire. About 100 people were inside, and some escaped out a rear door. Others climbed to the third floor, feeling safer there from the mob. Flames engulfed the first floor, cutting off their escape.

Police and soldiers were called to restore order. Unfortunately, they were delayed. Some had participated in a parade that morning and had been given time off that night to rest, "leaving minimal security troops on duty." Other police officers had been sent to a distant suburb to investigate reports of the Martians' landing there.[25]

After finally reaching the building, the police and soldiers used tanks and tear gas to clear a path through the rioters so firefighters could extinguish the flames. Only the front of the building remained, and rescuers found 20 bodies in the ruins.[26]

Recent radio and television programs have continued to frighten some Americans.

A Halloween program aired by a small station in Northern California scared so many listeners that it had to be stopped. In 1974, KXGO-FM in Arcata broadcast a program prepared by students at Humboldt State College. The program was titled "Orionids" and had already been broadcast over a campus radio station, but the station's signals were so weak that only people within five miles of the campus received them. KXGO reached a much larger audience and began broadcasting the program at 9 p.m. on October 31.

Simulated news bulletins reported that meteorites had fallen throughout Northern California, releasing a deadly bacteria. On-the-spot reports added that scientists were investigating the meteorites, but that Californians were becoming ill and dying. The National Guard was called out and martial law declared. It appeared that "the end of the world had come."

KXGO had publicized the program for weeks in advance and also broadcast several disclaimers. Nevertheless, "Some residents freaked out . . . , still others called the police, and others began activating the National Guard."[27] Listeners as far away as Brookings, Oregon, 120 miles to the north, called the radio station. A police dispatcher in nearby Eureka estimated that she received a hundred telephone calls, and a sheriff received two hundred more. "People were just panicked," the police dispatcher said. Because of the panic, KXGO stopped the program ten minutes before its conclusion.

An employee at the station said: "We were just astounded at the reaction. It was incredible. People just developed fear, and it fed on itself, so that some of them didn't even believe it when they heard the disclaimers."

In 1980, radio station WPFW in Washington, D.C., broadcast "Staying Alive," a program that described the likely effects of a nuclear attack against the United States. The program was based on a government report, but presented as a dramatization to promote an anti-nuclear rally scheduled in Washington later that day.

By coincidence, WPFW broadcast the dramatization shortly after 9 a.m. on April 25. A few hours earlier, U.S. forces had failed in their attempt to rescue fifty-three Americans held hostage by the Iranians. Eight helicopters had started out to rescue the hostages. Three of the helicopters developed mechanical problems. Then, at a secret landing site on an Iranian desert, the rotor blade on a fourth helicopter sliced into the fuselage of a C-130 Hercules transport. Eight Americans died, and the mission was abandoned.

Some Americans stayed up all night listening to the news. When they heard WPFW's dramatization the next morning, they thought the Iranians, or perhaps the Russians, had launched the nuclear attack in retaliation.

The dramatization began with a disclaimer, then shifted to an urgent message: "The United States is under attack! This is not a test! The United States is under attack!" Listeners could hear honking horns and wailing sirens in the background. Some immediately switched to other stations, hoping to obtain more details about the crisis. Others stumbled into basement bomb shelters or looked out their office windows, expecting to see a mushroom cloud over Washington.

One of the listeners exclaimed, "It sounded extremely realistic. Everyone turned 10 shades paler."[28] Another said, "I don't think I could ever adequately convey to you the sheer terror we felt. We became pale, our pulses raced. I really believed that we were in shock."[29]

Since then, the doomsday dramatizations have spread to television. On March 20, 1983, the NBC television network broadcast a two-hour movie, *Special Bulletin*. It was a Sunday evening, and the movie was publicized for weeks in advance. It was presented as a series of news bulletins from a fictitious television network, and the bulletins reported that terrorists, armed with a nuclear bomb, threatened to destroy Charleston, S.C. Government commandos ambushed the terrorists, but the bomb exploded, destroying the city.

NBC broadcast thirty-one disclaimers during the two-hour movie. Because the story occurred there, officials at WCIV-TV in Charleston also superimposed the word "Fiction" at the top of their picture. Despite their precautions, "Switchboards lit up in television stations across the country." NBC received thousands of calls, and its affiliates received thousands more. Some people wanted to know whether the story was real. Others complained that the program was irresponsible, frightening, and likely to give real terrorists new ideas.

WCIV received about two hundred calls in the first forty-five minutes.[30] Some calls came from people who never watched the program. Friends and relatives in other cities had called them to ask whether the story was true.

Other people called WCIV with a different complaint. They enjoyed the program but objected to the word "Fiction" being flashed at the top of their screens.

14 April Fools' Hoaxes: Pelicans, Sharks, and Baseball

By Isa Lyar and Lirpa Loof

EWSPAPERS have published thousands of hoaxes on April Fools' Day. A few weeklies continue to publish the hoaxes, but most dailies have abandoned them.

Editors fear that the hoaxes will harm their credibility, that if readers distrust the stories published on April Fools' Day, they will also distrust the stories published on other days of the year. Editors also fear that the hoaxes may frighten or inconvenience some readers, possibly causing an accident or even a serious injury. Moreover, it is difficult to create an exciting, clever, funny, new hoax every year.

The hoaxes that newspapers do publish contain facts so bizarre – so obviously impossible – that reporters rarely expect anyone to believe them. To be certain, they include silly names, such as "Isa Lyar," or the words "April Fool" spelled backward. Despite their precautions, some readers believe almost every hoax.

Most readers, even those frightened by the hoaxes, seem to enjoy them. After learning that the stories are fictitious, they become embarrassed, not angry. A minority – perhaps no more than 1 percent – complain about the stories. Because of their complaints, more and more editors are abandoning them, even on April Fools' Day.

No one knows for certain when people began to observe April Fools' Day. Some experts believe that the custom started when France adopted a new calendar in 1564. Until then, Frenchmen celebrated the New Year on March 25, and their holiday season ended on April 1. News traveled slowly in those days, and some Frenchmen continued to observe the old holiday because they failed to hear about the new one. Other Frenchmen continued to observe the old holiday because they disliked the new one. Gradually, the practice seems to have evolved into a joke.[1] However, other experts believe that April Fools' Day may have something to do with the beginning of spring, or that it started with an ancient Roman festival.

Early settlers brought the custom to America, but April Fools' Day never became an official holiday, observed by schools or governments. Instead, it remains a genuine folk holiday, observed chiefly by small boys. Pranksters send their victims on absurd errands—to buy hens' teeth or pigeons' milk, or ask their victims to find a skyhook, a left-handed monkey wrench, elbow grease, or Fallopian tubes.

During the 1920s, the Philadelphia zoo had to shut off its telephone on April 1 to avoid receiving more calls for "Miss L. E. Phant," "Mr. Lyon," and "Mr. Wolf." In a single day, officials at the New York morgue received more than a hundred calls for "Mr. Stiff."[2] Other pranksters put pepper in salt shakers, and salt in sugar bowls, or they pinned cards saying "April Fool" or "Kick Me" on their victim's back.

Clearly the practice is declining. In England, the decline started more than 100 years ago.[3] Today, the decline in April fooling is also noticeable in the United States. Most Americans—not just journalists—have stopped observing the day.

There are exceptions, however. In 1984, a story published by an Illinois daily created a national sensation. The *Eldorado Daily Journal* announced an exciting new contest "to recognize and honor the American summer tradition, Daylight Saving Time."[4] Bob Ellis, the newspaper's managing editor, reported that the contest would be open to everyone. "The rules of the contest are simple," Ellis said. "Beginning with the first day of Daylight Savings Time this year, those entering the contest must begin saving daylight. Whoever saves the most daylight . . . will be awarded prizes."

Only pure daylight was allowed. Ellis warned that, "No pre-dawn light or twilight will be accepted." Daylight from cloudy days was acceptable, but moonlight was strictly prohibited. Any moonlight mixed in with a contestant's daylight would bring immediate disqualification. Contestants could store their daylight in any type of container and, after accumulating enough to win, would have to bring it to the *Journal*'s office.

Ellis hoped the contest would become an annual event and promised, "All entries will be donated to less fortunate nations that do not observe Daylight Saving Time." He announced the rules early because "it seemed appropriate to coordinate the announcement with Sunday, April 1, 'All Fools' Day.' "

Before writing the story, Ellis decided upon two tactics. First, he would write the story in a serious manner, "hopefully just like any other news story, so that the reader would get well into the content before realizing that he had 'been had.' " Second, he would keep the story a secret. Ellis told no one, not even his own employees. "It was fun," he said. "Typing and giggling, like a naughty child writing a dirty word on the wall."[5]

Ellis was stunned by the response. He was relaxing at home when the first call came, from CBS in San Francisco; they wanted to interview him for a live national radio broadcast. An hour later, it was NBC in New York—again, a live national radio program. After that, Ellis "heard from every section of the nation." His story appeared in a Chicago newspaper and on a Dallas television station. An acquaintance heard it on a radio station while vacationing in Florida.

Why did Ellis write the story? It was a light-hearted jest, he said, "a change of pace from the usual and often gloomy side of the news." Ellis believes that readers hunger for even a small tidbit of encouragement and optimism. He wrote the story, he said, so that, for one glorious, fleeting journalistic second, his readers "could laugh at the world, and me, and perhaps even at themselves, with reckless abandon. And feel good. And therein lies the worth of such a diversion."

A New Orleans paper, the *Picayune,* began publishing April Fools' stories more than a hundred years ago but never provided any clues indicating that its stories were fictitious.

In 1876, the *Daily Picayune* reported that "the entire front of the City Hall had toppled to the Earth."[6] For nearly twenty minutes before the accident, a night watchman heard a slight cracking. When the noise grew louder, he hurried inside to warn three or four clerks who slept in their offices. The watchman's warning came not a moment too soon. For hardly had the clerks rushed into the streets when portions of the front wall began to totter and collapse. It was a narrow escape, and one for which the *Daily Picayune* sincerely congratulated the young gentlemen.

In 1887, the same paper reported the discovery of an Aztec ship buried in the muddy shores of Lake Pontchartrain. Workers found the ship while digging the foundation for a lighthouse. At first, they thought it was a cypress stump. Then, clearing away the earth, they discovered that it was a block of wood carved into the shape of a dragon, the emblem of an Aztec god.[7] The excavation continued until they uncovered the forward part of an Indian canoe.

How had the ship gotten there? The *Daily Picayune* speculated that huge fleets of Aztec warships had once sailed on the Gulf of Mexico and up the Mississippi River. Some experts believed the Aztecs traveled as far north as the shores of Lake Michigan and started settlements in the rich agricultural heart of North America. Sometime later, savage hordes of North American Indians drove the Aztecs southward, burning their cities. Because the cities were built of wood, all traces of the Aztec civilization in North America vanished.

In 1891, the *Daily Picayune* reported that an enormous meteorite had fallen upon the city, causing a terrific explosion. The paper said that people had seen an immense glare of fire in the sky and heard the hissing of flames. The meteorite—black and 8 feet in height—fell almost directly in front of the city's water works. Its surface was pitted, apparently by the heat as it passed through the Earth's atmosphere.

Readers in New Orleans rushed to the city's water works to see the meteorite but found only what appeared to be a huge boulder—a sample of iron ore discarded after an exposition in the city.[8]

An Illinois paper, the *Daily Journal* in Kankakee, began publishing April Fools' hoaxes in 1952. It abandoned the hoaxes during the early 1960s, then resumed their publication in 1965 because its readers asked for "something cheerful in the paper."[9]

One of the *Journal's* first hoaxes reported that drillers struck oil on the south lawn of the Kankakee County Courthouse.[10] A photograph showed the drilling rig, and a caption explained: "Work began at 10 a.m. About 2 p.m., workmen withdrew the drill bit, dropped a huge rock down the 3,000-foot hole, and heard it splash into what is believed to be a vast underground oil pool." Loof Lirpa, a Venezuelan expert in charge of the drilling, announced that the well had been completed in a few hours because underground rock formations "are easily penetrated only on this day of the year."

Loof Lirpa (or Lirpa Loof) reappeared in all the *Journal*'s stories. Spelled backward, his name is "A-p-r-i-l F-o-o-l."

In 1967, a photograph on the *Journal*'s front page showed workers trying to lift a strange object—possibly a flying saucer—from the Kankakee River.[11] A witness, Isa Lyar, told reporters that he was fishing from the bridge. He heard a whistling sound, looked up, and saw the object approaching. Lyar said the object appeared to be a flying saucer but was moving slowly and seemed to be wobbling. It struck the bridge, bounced off, and plunged into the water. It was the first report of an unidentified flying object ever crashing in Illinois, but officials at the Adler Planetarium in Chicago said UFO sightings normally increased during the period from March 29 through April 2. They called it "the concentric lirpa loof effect."

By noon the next day, the *Journal* had received 263 telephone calls about the story. Most callers were skeptical, but some thought the story might be true. A woman said she stayed up all night "worrying about whoever was aboard that UFO." Another reader warned other citizens, "If you see little people, don't shoot at them. I don't want anybody from outer space mad at Kankakee."[12]

In 1968, the *Sunday Journal* reported that a film crew planned to produce a popular television series in the Kankakee River State Park. The paper added that the director wanted to hire local residents for several roles and would begin the auditions at 9 a.m. Monday. In the meantime, the film crew planned "a gala birthday party for Lirpa Loof, the show's chief cameraman, whose birthday is April 1."

On Monday, reporters spotted about fifty cars stopped near the park. Most of the drivers seemed to be in their late teens or early twenties, and they were waiting to apply for the jobs as "extras."[13]

A year later, the paper revealed that a space capsule, thought to be Russian, had landed in Kankakee after miscalculating during reentry. The Russian government had not commented about the capsule, but a photograph showed the Russians' familiar hammer and sickle painted on its side. Three cosmonauts were still inside, and one was thought to be Lirpa Loof, who had been missing for a year.[14]

Some readers rushed to the spot to look at the ship, but a twelve-year-old boy realized that it was "all wet." He recognized the capsule as a U.S. Gemini.

Other April Fools' stories published by the *Journal* described giant frogs, a dinosaur, and a volcano. The paper also revealed plans for a huge athletic stadium expected to house a high school hockey team, the Chicago Bears football team, and two Chicago baseball teams. The stadium would be forty stories high and include one drinking fountain and two men's rooms.

The *Journal*'s editors insisted that they were not trying to fool their readers, only to "surprise and tickle" them.

How did readers respond? About one out of every hundred people who called the newspaper disliked its stories.[15] One reader said he was sick, sick, sick of Lirpa Loof, who had become a tired joke. A woman said she was insulted by the story about the Russian spacecraft and shocked by the *Journal*'s "sick sense of humor." A third critic insisted that "[h]umor belongs in the comic section, not on the front page."

Other readers defended the paper. They called its stories "clever," "refreshing," "great fun," and "a pleasant diversion." One of the readers explained that April Fools' Day "is the only day of the year when we can laugh at ourselves and each other in an inoffensive manner." Another added, "In these times of hardship, war, distrust, and suspicion, we, the people need to have a laugh or two."

A third daily, the *Kokomo* (Ind.) *Tribune,* described an underwater monster in Wildcat Creek. A boy said the monster—at least fifteen, possibly twenty-five feet long—"raised its head out of the water and hissed at me." A farmer reported finding the half-eaten carcass of a cow. "There were no animal tracks," the farmer said. "Only what appeared to be an impression on the ground, as if something had slithered into the water after eating part of the cow." The police brought out their tommy guns. An officer said, "We believe that an ordinary police pistol might be enough to kill this monster, but we're taking no chances."[16]

A few years later, the *Tribune* announced plans to save money by closing Kokomo's police station from six each evening until six each morning.[17] The paper reported that the police planned to install an automatic answering device to record the complaints they received at night.

When a desk sergeant reported for duty the next morning, he would replay the tape and assign officers to answer the complaints.

The police expected to save even more money by screening the complaints. "Since many of the complaints will be several hours old by the time they are checked, there will be no need to answer them," the paper explained. It admitted, however, that "[t]here will be a problem on what to do in the case of a woman who calls in and says her husband has threatened to shoot her or some member of the family." An experienced police officer provided the solution. In that case, he said, "We will check the hospitals and the coroner, and if they don't have any record of any trouble, then we will know that nothing happened."

A story published in 1963 revealed plans for a nudist camp in Kokomo.[18] Two years later, the *Tribune* reported that the city planned to increase its property taxes and use the money to build "a modern and handsomely furnished health and social club for local public officials and retired public officials."[19] "There has been a great need for a facility such as this," one of the officials insisted. "Our public officials are hard-working individuals who deserve a convenient place for recreation." Another official agreed, adding, "We believe the idea will be well received by our citizens. It will mean an increase in taxes, but this is well accepted by people when they realize that it is for a good thing."

Each of the *Tribune*'s hoaxes began on its front page and was continued on an inside page. Moreover, it ended with a confession. Typically, a story about a local gymnasium that might be converted into a helicopter factory concluded: "If you have read this far you must realize by now that we are only kidding. This is April 1."

Two Florida dailies created unusual animals for their April Fools' editions.

The *Sunday News-Journal* in Daytona Beach reported that Sam P. Suggins, a tourist from Georgia, had discovered a talking pelican.[20] Suggins said he had been walking along a dock "and all of a sudden I heard someone ask, 'Catch any fish?'" When Suggins turned to answer, no one was there, only a goofy-looking pelican sitting on a post.

"I tell you, it was downright spooky," Suggins said.

Suggins offered the pelican some food, and it hopped on his shoulder. When Suggins tried to shoo it away, the pelican resisted. Suggins continued: "I put him down on the dock and walked away, and he followed me. He didn't say anything, but every time I took a step he would." Suddenly, Suggins realized that the pelican might be a rare and valuable bird.

They walked to Suggins's pickup truck and, when he opened the door, the pelican hopped in. Suggins drove to his motel, but the pelican refused to talk to the manager. For ten minutes, Suggins tried to get the pelican to say something, but it remained silent. "Just sat there pickin' his feathers," Suggins said. The manager began looking at Suggins "kinda funny" and suggested that he take the pelican to the Humane Society. When they got there, Suggins realized that the pelican was not very smart. While looking at a puppy, it said "Kitty."

Experts at the U.S. Pelican Center at Canaveral National Seashore said they had received unsubstantiated reports that sailors taught pelicans to talk. Sailors kept the pelicans aboard their ships, just as other people kept parrots and parakeets.

The *News-Journal* printed a series of asterisks beneath the story, then added another paragraph suggesting: "This is your official April Fools' kit, especially for your friends who tend to believe everything they read. Simply cut this article out above the asterisks and have fun Sunday, April Fools' Day."

Another Florida daily, the *Orlando Sentinel,* discovered a tiny walrus that ate cockroaches.[21] In 1984, the *Sentinel's* Sunday magazine reported that the Tasmanian Mock Walrus (TMW) seemed to be a perfect pet. "Although homely," the story said, "it's quite lovable, resembling in temperament a hamster or a tame white rat." The TMW was four inches long and purred like a cat. It did not have to be walked or bathed and could easily be trained to use a litter box. Moreover, a single TMW could eliminate all the cockroaches in an average-sized house. Just turn it loose and let it go.

An Orlando couple said they had worked on a sheep ranch in Tasmania, a large island southeast of Australia, and smuggled four TMWs—one male and three females—into the United States. The couple wanted to establish a TMW ranch in their back yard but had been unable to obtain a license and the necessary zoning variances. For sixteen months, they had been battling the City of Orlando. They suspected that the local pest-control industry was afraid of competition from the TMW and pressured the city into refusing their request. However, a representative for the Orlando Zoning Commission denied that pest-control companies exerted any pressure in the case.

The story contained several clues suggesting that it was fictitious. It described a *mock* walrus and ended with this quotation: "If you ask me, that's a pretty cruel hoax."

Despite the clues, "plenty of readers did not get the joke." That Sunday, dozens of people tried to call the family that raised the TMW. On Monday, readers called the *Orlando Sentinel.* Reporter Dean Johnson found that "[t]he public wanted this story to be true."[22] After being told that it was a joke, no one became angry, Johnson said. Instead, "they'd just say things like, 'You got me,' or 'I've been had.'"

Weekly newspapers continue to publish some April Fools' stories. In 1981, the *Herald-News* in Roscommon, Michigan, reported that three lakes in northern Michigan had been selected for a bold new experiment, "an in-depth study into the breeding and habits of several species of fresh-water sharks."[23] The *Herald-News* (circulation four thousand) revealed that researchers planned to release two thousand young sharks in the lakes. The sharks would range in size from three to five feet, and there would be three species: blue shark, hammerhead shark, and a limited number of great white shark. It would be the first time that sharks had been placed in fresh-water lakes, and the federal government was spending $1.3 million on the project.

A representative for the National Biological Foundation said the lakes near Roscommon were perfect for the experiment, since researchers wanted to determine whether the fresh-water sharks could survive in the changeable climate of northern Michigan. The real test would be whether the sharks could survive during the winter months. The representative added that there would probably be a noticeable decline in other species of fish in the lakes as the sharks began to feed. "These are a newly bred species," he explained. "We don't exactly know what their feeding habits will be, but we expect the sharks will eat about 20 pounds of fish each per day, more as they get older."

County officials opposed the experiment "citing possible danger to fishermen and swimmers." Pat Doherty, a member of the County Commission, told the *Herald-News* that little could be done to prevent it. "The program is being conducted under federal regulation," Doherty said. "We can complain, but no one has to listen."

Fishermen would not be allowed to catch the sharks. Furthermore, both fishermen and swimmers would have to venture into the lakes at their own risk. A spokesman for the National Biological Foundation explained, "We can't be responsible for people if they are attacked. Besides, anyone foolish enough to believe all this deserves to be eaten."

For readers who continued to believe the story, the final sentence added, "Doherty also noted that April 1 is a foolish time to be telling fishy stories."

Weeks later, a copy of the story—without the final paragraph—circulated in Detroit auto plants. Fishermen working in the plants believed the story, and some were infuriated by it.

In 1983, another Michigan weekly, the *Durand Express,* warned that "a chemical known to cause death" had been found in the city's water lines. The paper (circulation 2,365) said the chemical was dihydrogen oxide. "Inhaling the chemical nearly always results in death," it explained, "and vapors from it cause severe blistering of the skin which can be fatal if extensive."[24]

The story's final paragraph revealed the chemical's formula: H_2O (water). People who inhale it drown; people exposed to its vapor (steam) suffer severe burns.

One year later, the *Durand Express* reported, "The giant Japanese auto and truck manufacturing firm, Nissan, may be taking steps to build a huge truck and car assembly plant just north of the Durand city limits."[25] The paper claimed that the huge complex would employ thousands of workers, and General Motors feared that Nissan would pay higher wages to recruit its most skilled employees. The story's final paragraph added that the full details would "be announced by Nissan Sunday, April 1."

Unemployed auto workers believed the story and hoped they might obtain jobs at the new plant. Farmers also believed the story, and some were delighted to learn that Nissan would pay $10,000 an acre for their land. A reporter for a Flint daily exposed the story as a hoax. He doubted that Nissan would build a plant in Durand, or conduct its press conference on a Sunday, April 1.

The weekly's editor, Owen Rood, responded: "I'm just fun-loving . . . I'm not trying to hurt anyone." Rood, 62, thought he exaggerated enough while writing the story so his readers would realize it was a hoax. Despite his good intentions, Rood lost several subscribers and advertisers, and he decided that the hoax would probably be his last.[26]

The copublisher of a Connecticut weekly, the *Gazette,* created another "little, absolutely irresponsible, untrue, fabricated, never-happened, made-up story."[27] He reported that his small weekly had been purchased by a large daily. Each paragraph contained more clues to tip off readers that it was a hoax. Finally, the story announced that the weekly's new owners planned to expand its news staff "by cutting it in half—literally, at the waist; this would create twice as many reporters although, of course, they would be half their former height."

Who could swallow such a tale? "Virtually our entire readership, that's who," he said.

One year later, the *Gazette* announced that it had been purchased by the Soviet news agency TASS. "It was the first expansion of the Communist media giant outside of the Iron Curtain," the paper reported. The new publisher, Vydonch U. Kissov, "promised that his paper would be thoroughly red." He also promised to provide a new delivery system— cruise missiles.

In 1985, the *Rivereast News Bulletin* in Glastonbury, Connecticut, devoted an entire page to ten stories, all April Fools' hoaxes.[28] One story revealed plans to tear out four hundred miles of the city's sidewalks. Another revealed plans to transform a tavern into the state's largest adult bookstore.

Experts devised a plan to eliminate the area's overcrowded classrooms. "It's very simple, really," explained a representative for the Board of Education. "Families will not be allowed to have more than .75 children per household over the next 15 years." The representative admitted that school officials had not yet determined how a family could limit itself to .75 children; a computer, however, had calculated that it was the ideal figure. The representative added that families unhappy about the limitation could move, perhaps to California.

The limitation would not go into effect for ten months, and the *News Bulletin* suggested that parents who wanted larger families "might want to get started this afternoon."

A huge headline at the bottom of the page asked, "Have you figured this out yet? . . . APRIL FOOL!" James Hallas, the *News Bulletin*'s editor, said, "Reader response was very favorable."[29] The paper has a circulation of more than thirty thousand, and Hallas received only three complaints. Those three, however, "were exceedingly vocal."

Other hoaxes appear in magazines, and *Sports Illustrated* published one of the most successful. The hoax was written by George Plimpton and revealed that the New York Mets had found a young pitcher with an amazing fastball. Another player said, "You can hardly see the blur of it as it goes by. As for hitting the thing, frankly, I just don't think it's humanly possible." To be certain they were not all crazy, the Mets brought in a radar gun. Previously, the fastest speed recorded for a baseball had been 103 mph. Now, the machine revealed that the pitcher's fastball traveled 168 mph.[30]

The pitcher was a right-hander—a six-foot-four, twenty-eight-year-old mystic named Hayden (Sidd) Finch. The Mets were reluctant to talk about Finch; in fact, they knew little about him. Finch had attended Harvard, dropped out, and spent some time in the Himalayas. While in Tibet, he learned a trick that enabled him to throw a baseball with complete accuracy and enormous speed.

The Mets invited Finch to their spring training camp, but he insisted upon complete secrecy. Finch reportedly slept on yak fur and spoke fluent Sanskrit. He had almost no belongings—a knapsack, a few clothes, a bowl, a small rug, and a French horn. Finch was also an expert horn player and seemed unable to decide between a career as a baseball player and a career as a musician. He promised to decide and to inform the Mets of his decision "on or around April 1."

On April 8, *Sports Illustrated* reported that Finch had lost the pinpoint accuracy required to throw his astonishing fastball. After a press conference, he gave a gallant wave "and walked away, very much alone."[31]

Few readers noticed an obscure clue in the magazine's first story. An introductory paragraph stated: "He's a pitcher, part yogi and part recluse. Impressively liberated from our opulent life-style, Sidd's deciding about yoga—and his future in baseball." When strung together, the first letter taken from each word spelled "H-a-p-p-y A-p-r-i-l F-o-o-l-s D-a-y."

On April 15, *Sports Illustrated* admitted that its story was a hoax, and it became one of the most talked about stories in the magazine's history.[32] Managing editor Mark Mulvoy said he published it "in the spirit of fun." The magazine publishes five hundred stories a year, and Mulvoy said, "If you can't have fun with one of them, then I think this world is some odd place."

Readers called it a "masterful job" and a "memorable piece of fiction." Another stated: "You lousy, rotten, good-for-nothing blankey-blanks. You got me hook, line and sinker—and I loved it." But a critic wrote: "I have concluded that April Fools' Day will come again, but not your magazine. Cancel my subscription immediately."

Other journalists complained that the hoax was inappropriate "at a time when, according to recent studies, the public has increasing doubts about the credibility of journalism."[33] The sports editor of a major daily insisted that the hoax was "a marvelous idea—for a high school newspaper." He explained that: "[p]eople don't catch it, no matter how obvious we think it is. All it does is cause grief and misunderstanding."

Other sports writers considered the story a good joke and said the critics were taking it too seriously. They could not understand how anyone believed the story. The baseball writer for an Ohio daily explained, "Anybody who knows anything about sports, or physiology, or just has much common sense at all—you gotta know the story was phony."

Newspapers and magazines also occasionally "touch up" photographs published on April Fools' Day. In 1935, the New York *Daily Mirror* published a photograph showing a train wreck. The train was a toy, and a caption revealed the joke.[34]

In 1954, the *Lockport* (N.Y.) *Union-Sun and Journal* published a photograph of a huge ocean liner that entered a small inlet eight miles away.[35] A caption said the ship docked there because of a strike in New York City. The caption did not mention April Fools' Day, but included other clues indicating that the story was fictitious. Despite the clues, state police reported a steady stream of traffic headed for the inlet. The cars were filled with sightseers eager to see the liner.

In Texas, the *Galveston News* published a photograph showing mounds of canned coffee. The caption said: "The Monument Food Store at 25th and Broadway is doing something about the price of coffee, as can be noted by the picture above. For one day only, L. Irpaloof, proprietor, is offering assorted brands of coffee at 33 cents a pound." Irpaloof explained, "I won't make any money on this deal, but I expect to have a lot of fun, and I can't think of any better way to throw away money." Spelled backward, L. Irpaloof's name was "A-p-r-i-l F-o-o-l." Moreover, Irpaloof added, "The sale has been set for April Fools' Day, if that means anything to you—and it should!"[36]

The next day, scores of bargain-hunting housewives searched for the store and its owner.

Other newspapers have continued to publish photographs of famous buildings that collapsed. In 1933, the *Capital Times* in Madison, Wisconsin, reported that an explosion had blown the dome off the state capitol, and a photograph showed the ruins.[37] A story reported that "Wisconsin's beautiful $8 million capitol was in ruins today, following a series of mysterious explosions which blasted the majestic dome from its base. . . . " The first explosion had occurred at 7:30 that morning, rocking the dome and shattering windows throughout the city. Two smaller blasts "sent showers of granite chips down upon the heads of pedestrians." Three more explosions followed in rapid succession, toppling the dome from its supports. Miraculously, hundreds of pedestrians and motorists in the vicinity escaped serious injury and death.

What caused the blasts? According to the *Capital Times*, "Authorities were considering the possibility that large quantities of gas, generated through many weeks of verbose debate in the Senate and Assembly chambers, had in some way been ignited, causing the first blast." Hot air that had also seeped into other rooms in the capitol caused the subsequent blasts.

The story's final paragraph added two words: "April Fool."

In 1976, the *Patriot* in Harrisburg, Pennsylvania, published a similar photograph. It showed part of Pennsylvania's capitol in ruins, and a caption explained: "Custodian A. F. Day said the blast occurred during a joint House-Senate session addressed by Hubert Humphrey and Gov. Milton Shapp. . . . Day attributed the explosion to an abnormal expansion of hot air which usually is absorbed by acoustic seats in the chamber."[38]

The *Patriot* had published April Fools' jokes for years. But in 1976, it was accused of "confusing fun with irresponsibility."[39] Some readers failed to understand the joke. They apparently believed that the capitol was damaged, and that some people inside it were injured or killed. Other readers were infuriated by the *Patriot*'s reference to the hot air generated by two popular politicians, Gov. Shapp and Hubert Humphrey.

Two days later, the paper apologized, saying, "Clever or not, there won't be another one."

Radio and television stations create fewer hoaxes on April Fools' Day. An exception, a radio station in Hawaii, created a sensation in 1959. Hawaii had just been admitted as the nation's 50th state, and a disc jockey said the government would refund all the taxes that Hawaiians had paid during the past year.

The media in Europe, including the countries' radio and television stations, create hoaxes more frequently. In 1913, a newspaper in Rheims,

France, startled its readers by reporting that a German balloon—a Zeppelin dirigible—had landed nearby after losing both its propellers.[40] Enormous crowds hurried to the spot but saw no Zeppelin. Then someone remembered the date: April 1.

In 1924, a newspaper in Turkey reported that a fish weighing fourteen hundred pounds had been caught in a nearby stream. The following morning, the newspaper admitted that it had been "an April Fools' fish."[41]

Radio stations in Britain have reported that the white cliffs of Dover were turning green, and that searchers were looking for the iceberg that sank the Titanic. In 1957, a television announcer revealed that farmers were harvesting a huge crop of spaghetti. A film showed the announcer walking through an orchard, with spaghetti clearly sprouting from its trees.

A Manchester newspaper, the *Guardian,* reported in 1981 that British scientists "developed a machine to control the weather."[42] As a result, Britain would enjoy longer summers "with rainfall only at night." By manipulating a few knobs on a control panel, the scientists would also be able to provide snow for every Christmas.

Journalists seem to lose their sense of humor when other people play April Fools' jokes upon them. In 1915, an employee of the *Boston Morning Globe* cut the newspaper's price in half. At the last minute, and without attracting anyone's attention, he changed the price marked on the paper's front page from "Two Cents Per Copy" to "One Cent." About sixty thousand copies were published before anyone noticed the error.[43]

During the 1980s, a scholar at Boston University announced that the custom of playing April Fools' jokes had begun during the Roman Empire. Professor Joseph Boskin explained that fools and court jesters told Emperor Constantine that they could rule the Roman Empire more effectively than he could.[44] Constantine was amused by their claim and agreed to let his jesters rule one day each year. He appointed a jester named Kugel to serve as king for a day, and Kugel insisted that only the absurd would be allowed.

Boskin added that the custom of April Fooling is beneficial since it allows people to act foolishly, without fear of criticism. However, Boskin noted that the practice is becoming less common, partly because "people are afraid to seem foolish." Boskin complained that humor is passing from the common people to comedians and talk show hosts. "Nobody should have to turn on Johnny Carson to be able to laugh," he said. "People should be able to turn themselves on."

The Associated Press transmitted Boskin's story to news media across the country. Two weeks later, Boskin admitted that he had played an April Fools' joke on the media and that portions of his story were a hoax. Boskin said he made up the details about the origin of April Fools' Day and about the jester named Kugel, but that his other statements about April Fools' Day were accurate.[45]

A representative for Boston University failed to see any humor in the story. He apologized to the media, saying, "We regret that something that originated as a story on humor has now proved humorless." Some newspapers that had used the story published either corrections or apologies.

15 Hoaxing the Hoaxers: Fooling the Media for Fun and Publicity

OTHER Americans created hoaxes to fool the media. Moreover, they succeeded more often (and more easily) than almost anyone realizes.

The media are easy to fool because they depend upon other people. Reporters cannot find, investigate, and write every story by themselves. Instead, they rely upon a variety of tipsters to inform them about stories that seem to be newsworthy.

Anyone can call their local paper and tell its staff about a story. Some callers are obvious crackpots, and reporters dismiss them after a question or two. Others are more persuasive, and it may take a considerable amount of time and effort to check their stories. A few are liars, but so convincing that reporters believe the stories they provide. Some of their stories are so good that reporters are eager to publish them.[1]

Why would anyone want to fool the media? Most people are seeking publicity. Others think it is fun, or they may want revenge—to embarrass the media or someone they dislike. People also know that there is no legal penalty for lying to the media. The journalists fooled by a hoax may criticize the people responsible for it. But some Americans enjoy the publicity, even unfavorable publicity, and hope that other people will laugh at the media, not them.

For years, people in public relations seemed to think that fooling the media was part of their job. To obtain free publicity for their clients, publicists created unusual stunts and stories, the types that reporters were most likely to use.

Reporters resent giving free publicity to publicists, whom they feel should be paying for advertisements. The reporters fooled by a hoax are also humiliated. Colleagues may wonder why they failed to determine the truth. Editors may ask them to write a public confession, a correction that explains how they were fooled.

To avoid being fooled, reporters become skeptics, questioning almost everything they are told. Nevertheless, a few sources continue to fool them — and say that it is easy.

Residents of Colorado created an unusual hoax because they liked an editor and wanted him to have a good time. Horace Greeley began to publish the *New York Tribune* in 1841 and printed a weekly edition for readers in the West. Greeley's *Tribune* became famous because of its editorial page, not because of its coverage of the news. Greeley was a humanitarian who wanted to abolish slavery and help the poor. Readers realized that he cared about them, and they appreciated his concern.

While returning from a trip to California, Greeley stopped in Denver, and the citizens there received him "with all the honor the infant city could command." He wanted to investigate reports about the discovery of gold in Colorado, and some miners learned that he planned to visit their camp. They promptly salted the diggings for him. The miners took down an old shotgun, replaced the pellets in several shells with gold dust, and fired the shells into a pit.

Greeley reached their camp early the next morning, and the miners showed him samples of the gold they had found. He went down into the pit himself, rolled up his sleeves, and asked for a pan and shovel. After receiving the necessary instructions, he sifted through some dirt like a professional. When he finished, the bottom of his pan was covered with gold. The miners slapped him on his shoulders in regular Western fashion and told him to try again. He did and found even more gold. He poured the gold into a bag, then declared, "Gentlemen, I have worked with my own hands and seen with my own eyes, and the news of your rich discovery shall go all over the world, as far as my paper can waft it."

Greeley returned to New York and advised his readers to "Go West." Pioneers in Colorado said that his wonderful stories and sincere advice caused the state's first great boom.[2]

Other Americans created hoaxes that swindled the media and their audiences, often exploiting their generosity. The hoaxes are remarkably similar. Reporters receive a phone call—an anonymous tip—about a family that just moved to the area. The family is poor and hungry, and the husband is unemployed. There are several children, and one or two are sick, or they may be the victims of a serious crime or accident.

It is a wonderful story for journalists, especially at Christmas. Editors place the story on their front page, and readers donate food, money, and clothing. The family disappears a few days later, moving on to another city and another newspaper.

During the 1960s, newspapers in California reported that "[s]ome bad guy did his best to spoil the camping honeymoon of a Vietnamese war veteran. . . . " The veteran had served two tours in Vietnam and was seriously wounded when he parachuted onto a mine "which curtailed use of his legs and destroyed a lung." Now he was twenty-one and had just gotten married. The newlyweds were spending their honeymoon at Shasta Lake and left everything—their tent, sleeping bags, cooking gear, stove, and clothing—near the lake while searching for a camp site. When they returned, "almost everything was gone, except some clothing and a slashed sleeping bag." Californians were outraged by the insult to a wounded hero and gave the couple food, money, and new camping gear.

A few days later, another photograph showed the hero being led away in handcuffs. He had deserted from the Marine Corps and was captured after authorities recognized his picture in a newspaper.[3] He was never wounded, they said, and never served in Vietnam.

Iowans heard a similar appeal and may still wonder about its authenticity. On December 30, 1981, the *Des Moines Register* published an anonymous letter from a thirty-six-year-old man who said he intended to kill himself. The man explained that he was unemployed, and that his wife and two girls were not eligible for Aid to Dependent Children because he was alive, able bodied, and living at home. The Iowa Legislature had recently changed the requirements for ADC, so families with both parents living at home could no longer receive it.

The man explained: "The hurt in my little girls' faces because Santa forgot them this year, the thought of another jobless year, no way to pay the rent next week, I'm sorry I can't deal with it anymore." He added that his problems were common, that hundreds of people were on welfare, and that some were pawning their radios and watches "just to get a few dollars to buy gas to job-hunt some more."

The *Des Moines Register* had no way of determining whether the letter was authentic; nevertheless, its editor published a response on the front page. "Scores of thousands of Iowans read your letter in this morning's *Register,*" he said. "They want to help you. They don't know who you are, and neither do I. But I do know this: There is a job waiting for you. And clothes for your family. And Christmas gifts for your little girls. There is medical care if you need it. There is hope. There is life."[4]

The letter may have been written by someone poor and desperate, or it may have been a hoax. But regardless of the letter's authenticity, more than eighty thousand Iowans were unemployed that Christmas; thus, the feelings it expressed were real, felt by the unemployed and their families. The letter forced people to think about the problem, and about what they could do to help.

Other hoaxes, created for the fun of it, involved fake athletes. A hoax staged in 1941 involved the creation of an entire team.

Morris Newburger was a partner in a Wall Street brokerage firm and noticed that the major Sunday papers rarely published any stories about the football teams at small colleges. So Newburger created a fictitious college, Plainfield Teachers in Newark, New Jersey. On September 27, 1941, Newburger called the *New York Herald Tribune* and told its sports writers that Plainfield's team had defeated Benson Institute by a score of 20-0. Newburger also called the Associated Press, the United Press, and the *New York Times.* Their sports writers were swamped with hundreds of scores being phoned in from all over the country, and published the results without checking them. A week later, newspapers reported that Plainfield had walloped the equally mythical Scott by a score of 12-0.

Newburger created a mythical halfback for his team, a full-blooded Chinese student named John Chung. Newburger told sports writers that Chung weighed 212 pounds and gained an average of 7.9 yards each time he carried the ball. During one game, Chung scored both of Plainfield's touchdowns. During another game, he scored on a forty-seven-yard run, dragging five tacklers over the goal line with him.

Plainfield won seven straight games that fall, and a fictitious sports information director flooded the media with more news releases about the team.⁵ They reported that Chung ate wild rice between halves and that, after suffering a minor injury, he was carried off the field in a rickshaw.

Too many people learned about the hoax and began telling their friends. Both the *Herald Tribune* and *Time* magazine began investigating rumors about it. On November 17, *Time* reported that "Plainfield and its opponents were nonexistent."⁶

When questioned by reporters, Newburger begged them to let him finish the season. Plainfield had not lost a game and was scheduled to play (and defeat) Appalachian Normal that Saturday. When his pleas failed, Newburger issued a final news release. It announced that Plainfield's coach had canceled the team's remaining games because six of its fifteen players, including Chung, flunked their midterm exams.

A nineteen-year-old college student created a similar hoax. The student was from Canada and, for nearly a year, sent the *Welland* (Ont.) *Tribune* stories about a fictitious soccer team. The student described himself as the star in every game, and his final stories claimed that the team was invited to a World Cup tournament in Australia. By then, a Canadian news service was transmitting the stories to other newspapers.

A soccer writer became suspicious and called Australia. He discovered that no tournament was being held there. All the stories datelined "SYDNEY, Australia" were coming from Welland.⁷

Another student helped newspapers report on track and field meets at Cornell. The student suddenly realized "that there always has to be one boy who is last in every event."⁸ To avoid embarrassing the real losers, the student invented a fictitious character named "Johnny Tsal." After that, he reported that Tsal ran last in every major track meet.

People in show business, from P. T. Barnum to Hollywood stars, created other hoaxes to publicize their movies and careers. Some stars asked press agents for help, but Barnum never needed any help. He was the greatest showman in American history and regularly used the media to publicize his attractions. In 1834, he bought a slave named Joice Heth and claimed that she was 161 years old. While exhibiting Heth on Broadway, Barnum also claimed that she had been owned by George Washington's father and had been present when Washington was born.

Some New Yorkers doubted Barnum's claims. To encourage the debate, Barnum mailed anonymous letters to the city's newspapers. Some of the letters praised Barnum, but others denounced him. A historian explained that "Barnum cared little whether editors attacked or praised him so long as they spelled his name correctly. He knew that attention, and especially controversial attention, created gate receipts."[9] As the dispute continued, more New Yorkers went to see Heth, and they increased Barnum's receipts to $1,500 a week.

When Heth died, an autopsy revealed that she was only 80 or 90 years old. Barnum had paid $1,000 for Heth and immediately complained that he was swindled.

Barnum also exhibited a mermaid. To publicize it, he mailed more letters to the papers in New York. One of the first letters, postmarked "Montgomery, Ala.," reported that a man there possessed a remarkable curiosity—a mermaid found in the Feejee Islands. Subsequent letters from Charleston, South Carolina, and Washington, D.C., described the sensation the mermaid caused there. One of Barnum's employees posed as the mermaid's owner and actually showed it to some editors in Philadelphia. By the time Barnum placed the mermaid on display in New York, it was already famous.

The "mermaid" was part monkey and part fish, sewn together so cleverly that not even Barnum could find the seams.[10] Barnum described it as "an ugly dried-up, black-looking . . . specimen, about 3 feet long." Its mouth was open, its tail turned over "and its arms thrown up, giving it the appearance of having died in great agony."

Years later, a press agent in Baltimore actually hanged an elephant. The press agent represented a wild animal show and, even before the show opened, bombarded the newspapers in Baltimore with stories. Baltimore's most famous journalist, H. L. Mencken, recalled that the stories described "battles between tigers and boa constrictors, the birth of giraffes, the sayings of a baboon who could speak Swahili, and so on."[11]

When attendance lagged, the press agent told reporters that an elephant had become so ornery that it would have to die. Ordinarily, the elephant would have been shot, but that would attract little attention. Looking mangy and feeble, the poor beast was taken to Baltimore's railroad yards. Its legs were tied together and a heavy rope looped around its neck. In a few minutes, a railroad crane lifted the elephant into the air. "He took it very quietly and was pronounced dead in half an hour," Mencken said.

The hanging attracted a large crowd, and attendance at the show increased after that.

The late Harry Reichenbach claimed that he was paid $1,500 a week, more than any other publicity man in the country. To generate more publicity for his clients, he regularly staged practical jokes that fooled both the media and the public.

In 1917, Reichenbach learned that a small art store in Brooklyn was in trouble. The store's owner had imported copies of a nude painting drawn by a Frenchman and titled *September Morn*. The store failed to sell a single copy. To help its owner, Reichenbach placed a copy of *September Morn* in the store's display window, then went out and hired forty or fifty children at $1 apiece.

An anonymous tipster informed Anthony Comstock about the painting. The tipster complained that crowds of little children gathered outside the store to stare at it. Comstock was a powerful crusader who devoted forty years of his life to fighting obscenity. He hurried to the scene and was horrified by the sight, "a mob of little children pressing around the display window, looking at the naked lady." The art dealer was arrested, and newspapers reported the story. Soon, the entire nation was talking about *September Morn*.

Because of the publicity, Americans reportedly bought seven million copies of the painting. An oil millionaire paid $10,000 for the original "which, before Mr. Reichenbach took action, had been worth about 35 cents."[12]

Another man registered at a New York hotel, hoisted a live lion into his room, then called down to the desk for five pounds of raw meat. The man had registered as "T. R. Zan," and the stunt helped publicize a new movie – *Tarzan*.

While walking across a bridge in Camden, New Jersey, another journalist noticed an attractive young woman climbing over the handrail. When he tried to stop her, the woman fought back, screaming that she was going to throw herself into the river. A policeman tackled the woman, but she continued to scream: "My unborn child! You do not understand! I must die. My unborn child!" After being taken to a police station, the woman refused to reveal her identity but repeated the words, "My unborn child!"

The story remained in the news for days. Then reporters learned that she was a New York show girl, paid to publicize a new movie titled *My Unborn Child.* "Never," said one journalist, "were so many astute editors so completely taken in by such an obvious publicity stunt."[13]

Other stunts backfired. After working as city editor at the *Los Angeles Examiner,* James Richardson turned to publicity. He was employed by a Hollywood studio that wanted to provide "a big publicity buildup" for an attractive young starlet.[14] Richardson talked to the starlet and learned that her parents had separated when she was born. She lived with her father and had never met her mother.

Richardson decided to help the starlet, and the studio's publicity department churned out the story:

Starlet Starts Search
For Mother She's Never Known

Newspapers everywhere published the story. The starlet's mother called from Philadelphia and, at the studio's expense, boarded the next train to Hollywood. Photographers were at the station when she arrived, snapping pictures of the mother and daughter meeting, weeping, and kissing.

Richardson received a raise. A week later, the starlet's mother was arrested after being caught trying to buy dope. Fortunately, she gave the police a fake name. Fearing that they would all be ruined, Richardson called a friend on the narcotics squad. The police agreed to release "Mom" because she was only a user. In return, Richardson placed her on the next train back to Philadelphia.

Another hoax started on a Sunday evening, July 18, 1920. A man walking through New York's Central Park noticed a black silk handbag on the ground near a lake. He also found a black hat trimmed with an expensive black feather.[15] Police opened the handbag and found fifty cents, a room number at a New York hotel, and a slip of paper marked "Onda, Miss Yuki, 563. Washington, D.C."

The police assumed that the woman drowned herself. Using lanterns and rowboats, they dragged practically every square inch of the lake but failed to find her. The lake was about ten feet deep, and the police feared that her body had become wedged between some rocks.

Reporters learned that a young woman named Yuki Onda had registered at the Pennsylvania Hotel. She left the hotel shortly before 9 p.m. that Sunday and told a clerk she felt ill. She never returned, and employees at the hotel knew little about her. Newspapers reported that she was "believed to be connected with a wealthy Japanese family in Washington, D.C."[16] The police, however, were unable to find her home or family there.

While searching her hotel room, the police found a letter that seemed to explain why she committed suicide. The letter was addressed to a man named "Pierre" and expressed sorrow "that she had accepted the attention of an American suitor." The letter added that he might never see her again.[17]

The police, equipped with spotlights and grappling hooks, returned to the lake and dragged it again that Monday night.[18] They failed to uncover any trace of the young beauty, and detectives speculated that she may have been kidnapped.

A movie critic for the *New York World* discovered that, "Yuki did not commit suicide in New York at all." Instead, she had returned to Japan and married a prince.[19] The critic suggested that the police looking for her should "drop in at the Astor Theatre some afternoon this week and witness a photoplay titled *The Breath of the Gods.*" He had gone there to review the movie and noticed that "Yuki Onda" was the name of its leading character.

The district attorney was outraged by the stunt and promised to take "drastic measures" to prevent publicists from creating other hoaxes that involved the police. He told reporters that whoever staged the hoax was guilty of disorderly conduct, and that whoever left the fake suicide note in the hotel room was guilty of forgery in the third degree.

Police searched for the man who said he found the woman's hat and purse in Central Park, but his address was a fake. The district attorney then subpoenaed four publicists from the Universal Film Company. Two of them refused to answer his questions "on the grounds that it might tend to incriminate and degrade them."[20]

The district attorney also questioned Harry Reichenbach, the famous publicist. Reichenbach denied knowing anything about the hoax. He had publicized the French painting *September Morn* and also admitted being responsible for the lion hoisted into the Belleclaire Hotel. Reichenbach insisted, however, that the lion was harmless. "Well, that old lion was about 100 years old and couldn't hurt anyone," he said. "He had one foot in the grave and the other on a banana peel. He was so bad that we had to feed him milk and cut up his meat. All I was afraid of was he would die while the stunt was on."

A year later, on August 17, 1921, a carrier pigeon, wet and exhausted, appeared in Columbus Circle, New York. A police officer took the pigeon to the West 47th Street Station at about 10 p.m., and a lieutenant there read a message attached to one of its legs:

> Notify Dan Singer, Belleclaire Hotel.
> I am lost in Hoodoo Mountains,
> Yellowstone Park. Send help, provisions,
> and pack-horses.

The note was signed "Heller" and dated August 13. The lieutenant immediately called the Belleclaire Hotel and found a man named Daniel J. Singer in a room there.

"My God!" Singer exclaimed. "Probably Heller is dead by now!" Singer rushed to the police station and identified the lost man as Edmund H. Heller, a famous explorer, naturalist, and cameraman. Heller had left New York 10 days earlier to photograph the wild animals in Yellowstone Park and to gather material for a lecture tour.

While at the police station, Singer also identified the carrier pigeon. "It was a veteran," he said. Heller had taken the carrier pigeon to Yellowstone and also on an earlier expedition to Africa.

Newspapers everywhere published the story. The *New York World* reported that a policeman had "snatched the bird from the path of an approaching automobile."[21] The *World* added that the bird had flown more than 2,000 miles in four days. Now, too exhausted to consume any food or water, it "lay motionless on an improvised bed in the police station." The *Chicago Tribune* noted that the pigeon's twenty-four hundred-mile flight was "believed to have broken all records. . . ."[22]

The *New York Times* was more skeptical. It reported that the carrier pigeon had flopped down in front of a restaurant in Columbus Circle "from somewhere—coat pocket or the heavens."[23] The *Times* added that the Belleclaire Hotel "may be remembered as the hotel from which one T. R. Zan and a pet lion were expelled not so long ago, the unfortunate man and his beast having been forced to find refuge in the movies." It also reported that carrier pigeons roost at night. To travel two thousand miles in a few days (an obvious record), the bird would have to fly as fast as an airplane.

When queried by reporters, the superintendent of Yellowstone National Park responded by telegraph: "Edmund Heller is here. There is no foundation whatever for the report that he is or has been lost."[24]

The truth (like the original hoax) was transmitted across the country. The *San Francisco Chronicle* placed the story on its front page: "There was general agreement . . . today that the homing pigeon which flew into Columbus Circle — and incidentally into all the newspapers — with a message from Yellowstone Park . . . had flown from the hands of some joker."[25]

The hoax was staged to advertise Heller's lectures, apparently without his knowledge.[26] Heller repudiated the story, and his signature on the note was exposed as a forgery. Subpoenas were issued for three other men, including Singer.[27] Singer disappeared, but reporters learned that he had helped arrange Heller's lectures.

Another hoax, staged to win a bet, made monkeys out of the media in Georgia. On July 7, 1953, newspapers in Atlanta reported that dozens of people had seen a mysterious object moving silently over the city. The object appeared at about 7 p.m., and one spectator said it looked like a huge ice cream cone floating through the sky. Other people said it was "funnel-shaped" and looked like a miniature rocket ship. A woman insisted that it made absolutely no noise "and was all lit up with bright green, yellow, and pink colors."[28]

A man who saw the object streak above his home added, "It appeared to be at an altitude of from 2,500 to 3,000 feet. It was going exceedingly fast — faster than any jet airplane I have ever seen in the city." Another man estimated that the object was traveling only forty miles an hour, and a woman said it was low, not more than thirty feet above the ground. "The strangest things were the lights," the woman continued. "From one section came a green light, and from another a pink light. Others showed gold and yellow." She did not think the object came from another planet, but feared "it was something the Russians developed."[29]

Experts were baffled. The object did not seem to be a rocket and moved too slowly to be a comet.

Late that Tuesday night, three young men found a Martian. Edward

Watters, a twenty-eight-year-old barber, served as their spokesman. Watters explained that they were out "honky tonking," but not drinking. "It was a little after 11 o'clock," he said. He was driving a pickup truck fifty or sixty miles an hour on U.S. 78 and was two or three miles from Austell, Ga. As the men topped a rise in the road, one yelled for him to stop.

"Right there in the middle of the highway was this thing, glowing red all over," Watters exclaimed. It was a flying saucer, waist high and about half as wide as the road. Three or four little man-like creatures ran toward it. Two or three jumped on top of the flying saucer and sank out of sight. Watters slammed on the truck's brakes and skidded seventy feet, striking and killing a naked, hairless male. It was twenty-one inches tall and weighed four pounds.

The flying saucer rose into the air and zoomed away. A county policeman stopped at the scene, and a bank teller confirmed Watters's story. The bank teller was driving along the same road, about a half mile away, and told reporters that he saw a bright object taking off into space.[30]

More than twenty-five newspaper reporters, broadcasters, photographers, and newsreel cameramen questioned and took pictures of the three men and their space-man. Watters stored the space-man in a refrigerator and told the reporters that a caller offered him $5,000 for it.

The three men brought the space-man to an Atlanta newspaper, the *Constitution,* and its editors asked scientists at Emory University to examine the corpse. The scientists concluded that "[t]he animal definitely is a monkey. It is not from outer space." The monkey's hair had been removed and its tail chopped off. Razor marks indicated that it was shaved. Its death was caused by a blow on the head. There was no evidence that it was struck by a truck.[31]

The state crime lab confiscated the body, and an autopsy proved that it was a young monkey. The corpse was placed on display in the State Patrol building, and "several hundred people trooped by to look at it."

A reporter persuaded Watters to confess, "convincing him that anybody smart enough to pull a gag like that ought to get full credit for it." Watters explained that he had bet a friend $10 that he could get his picture published by a newspaper. To win, he paid a pet shop $50 for the monkey, took it home, and shaved it. Watters denied hurting the monkey, however. He had been shaving people for twelve years, he said, and never hurt anyone. After shaving the monkey, he hit its head with a bottle and cut off its tail.

Warrants were sworn out for the men's arrest, and Watters pleaded guilty to a charge of placing a carcass on a highway: a state health and sanitation law designed to keep dead cats and dogs off public roads. The judge fined Watters $40 and warned all three men to avoid any more monkey business.

On July 10, the *Constitution* published a picture of Watters trimming a customer's hair. Thus, Watters won the $10 bet, but seemed surprised that anyone had ever believed his story. "I thought people were smarter than that," he said.[32]

Other Americans continue to fool the media, often because journalists fail to check every fact.

In 1983, the weather on the first day of spring was awful. It was raining and windy in New York, with some flooding. That afternoon, a man called about forty newspapers, news services, and radio and television stations in the city, saying that the National Weather Service had just issued a "typhoon watch." The man identified himself as "Robert Parker of the Weather Service" and explained that the typhoon watch was caused by an unusual combination of meteorological factors.

Some radio and television stations broadcast the story, and United Press International transmitted an "Urgent" bulletin to all its clients. Quoting Parker, UPI's bulletin stated, "The National Weather Service says that, for the first time in history, a 'typhoon watch' has been issued for the New York metropolitan area."[33]

Other reporters rushed to their dictionaries and learned that typhoons are tropical cyclones formed only in the Pacific Ocean, primarily the Southern China Sea. Similar storms in the Atlantic Ocean are called hurricanes, but the hurricane season would not begin until June 1. When questioned by reporters, a genuine spokesman at the National Weather Service insisted, "There is absolutely no possibility of typhoons in this area."[34]

Another hoax involved a cure for acne. Joseph Skaggs, a journalism professor at New York's School of Visual Arts, believes that the media will fall for just about any zany story. To prove it, Skaggs spent $3,000 to rent an office and run off dozens of press releases. The press releases identified him as Joseph Gregor, a forty-year-old Ph.D. from

South America. They added that Gregor had formulated some new pills made from pulverized cockroaches. The pills cured acne, anemia, allergies, and a variety of other ailments, including the miseries of nuclear fallout.

Every major news organization in New York was invited to a press conference, but only five reporters showed up, including one from United Press International. Skaggs's friends and students posed as his patients and swore that the pills worked. One of the students explained that she suffered from lots of allergies and colds "but since taking this I haven't had one."

The story appeared in "the *Washington Star,* the *Philadelphia Inquirer,* the *Pittsburgh Press,* and about 175 other newspapers around the country, courtesy of the United Press International wire service."[35] When it was exposed as a hoax, journalists admitted, "We don't know of any defense against people who lie and get others to substantiate their lies."[36]

Skaggs has been staging hoaxes for twenty years and claims that he never had a failure. "It is easy to fool the media," Skaggs says. He believes that the media will use anything sensational, sexy, or funny — and can be fooled because they fail to check the facts.

A professional hoaxer created another story that remained in the news for six years. The hoaxer, Alan Abel, has made his living "thinking up practical jokes and teaching others how to pull them off."[37]

Abel started his most successful hoax in 1959 — a crusade to clothe animals. He created a fictitious organization, the Society for Indecency to Naked Animals (SINA). Memberships were free, and Abel claimed that fifty thousand people joined the organization. It objected to naked animals that appeared in public. However, it exempted animals that flew or swam, or that were lower than four inches or shorter than six inches.

SINA's telephone number was "MOrality 1-1963," and it had an impressive mailing address in New York: 507 Fifth Ave. A twelve-by-eighteen-inch sign on a door there read

> SINA NATIONAL HEADQUARTERS
> G. Clifford Prout Jr., President
> Alan Abel, Vice-President

Abel told everyone that SINA's great crusade had been started by G. Clifford Prout, Sr., an eccentric business consultant who wanted to communicate with animals. Abel added that he met Prout's son, G. C.

Prout Jr., at a party in St. Louis and decided to devote his life to the cause.

The press and public "gobbled it up."[38] Abel appeared on Walter Cronkite's "CBS News" and on NBC's "Today" show. After that, he was invited to chat with Jack Paar, Art Linkletter, and Johnny Carson.

In 1962, Abel visited San Francisco, posing as Prout. The *San Francisco Chronicle* published four front-page stories about his visit. The stories were light-hearted, perhaps even comical in tone; nevertheless, they failed to clearly expose the crusade as a hoax. The first story reported that G. Clifford Prout, Jr., the president of SINA, had slipped into San Francisco, hoping to clothe the "vital areas" of naked animals there. The *Chronicle* added that SINA had designed bikinis for stallions, half-slips for cows, and knickers for bulldogs.[39] Free patterns were available for people who wanted to make the garments for their pets. The patterns came in three sizes: small, medium, and large.

The *Chronicle* added that SINA's headquarters in New York was also planning comfort stations for animals and distributed emergency instructions on how people should respond if they saw a naked animal. It recommended that people should immediately cover the animal's "vital areas" with a shawl, blanket, or anything else handy "and call your nearest SINA chapter."

On Aug. 14, the *Chronicle* reported that Prout declared San Francisco a "moral disaster area." Prout estimated that 463,000 naked animals were on the loose in San Francisco and warned that there was a definite correlation between the city's high rates of alcoholism and suicide and the size of its undressed animal population.[40] Prout explained that the sight of so many naked animals triggered the moral deterioration of the entire human population.

Prout also found a shocking amount of nudity in a children's playground at Golden Gate Park. "There, in all their splendor," the *Chronicle* reported, "were naked rabbits, nude goats, sheep dressed only in the wool God gave them, and some chickens and ducks in nothing but feathers." Prout slipped a pair of drawers over a goat and tried to hitch a pair of panties on a fawn.

A year later, in 1963, pickets from SINA paraded in front of the White House. They wanted President Kennedy's wife, Jacqueline, to clothe her horse.[41]

Some Americans followed Abel's advice. They clothed their pets and formed SINA chapters in their communities. The members of a chapter in Columbus, Ohio, appeared in a Fourth of July parade, on a float full of clothed animals.[42]

In 1966, Abel wrote a book about SINA, *The Great American Hoax*. "Basically," he said, "SINA was my way of protesting against hypocrisy, censorship, and extremism.[43] He complained that defenders of the nation's morality "were so busy censoring bikini-clad women, outspoken books and films, and classic statues, they overlooked the most prurient shocker: naked and lewd animals. So why not censor them too?"[44]

Abel could never afford to rent an entire office on New York's Fifth Avenue. Instead, he had rented a door—only the door—of a broom closet. He placed SINA's name on the door and kept it locked.

In 1985, Abel staged another hoax. Phil Donahue was discussing gay senior citizens during a live broadcast from New York. Within minutes, "it was obvious something was profoundly amiss." A reporter covering the program for the *New York Post* noticed that "[p]eople were sweating, and some seemed weak. Donahue, busy discussing facts with the panel, could not see his audience's worsening condition."[45] A young woman rose, swayed, and dropped to the ground directly in front of a camera. The show continued until six more spectators, apparently overcome by the heat, also collapsed, forcing the evacuation of the entire studio audience.

Abel explained that he headed an organization named FAINT (Fight Against Idiotic Neurotic TV) and had organized the faintings to protest the poor quality of programs on television. He wanted to "raise the consciousness of the public by going unconscious."[46]

Other hoaxes involved fraudulent advertisements, often for nonexistent jobs. In 1912, an advertisement published in New York announced that a real estate dealer, Herbert A. Sherman, needed two hundred laborers. By seven that morning, four hundred men were waiting outside his office. Many had been without work for weeks. Sherman had not placed the advertisement and did not know who had. When told the advertisement was a hoax, some men shrugged and left. Others refused to believe that it was a hoax and refused to leave. The crowd continued to grow until someone called the police, and they hustled the men outside.

Later that morning, a crowd of better-dressed men tried to apply for the twenty jobs as Sherman's clerks and stenographers. Another two hundred men gathered at Sherman's second office, hoping to obtain the jobs as his coachmen. He spent the morning turning them away.[47]

Similar hoaxes continue to mislead the poor and jobless. Two Florida dailies published advertisements promising to pay laborers $7.50 and $9.25 an hour. Two hundred men showed up at one location and one hundred at another "all awaiting jobs that didn't exist."[48] It was a cruel hoax, an unemployed welder said. "It was something I've never seen before, some of the despair in people's faces. They were so desperate they would have done almost anything to find work."

Other phony advertisements were published in Chicago, Detroit, Tulsa, and Milwaukee. The unemployment rate in Milwaukee exceeded ten percent, and hundreds of people applied for jobs at a company offering "top wages" and "liberal fringe benefits." The company existed, but the jobs did not.[49] "It was cruel," a newspaper executive said. "The people most damaged by it were the people most desperate for work."

Another advertising fake excited the entire country. News stories reported that a young man eloped with a pretty young woman. She was the daughter of a wealthy Pittsburgh merchant, and her parents were furious. The honeymooners had boarded a train for the West, and the bride's father was chasing them with a gun. The honeymooners stopped at the best hotel in Cleveland. Smiling and happy, they talked to reporters there.

Papa immediately boarded a midnight train for Cleveland, but the honeymooners left — apparently for St. Louis — before he arrived. After reaching Cleveland, Papa fumed and fussed, then hired a special train to rush him to St. Louis. The young couple stopped there just long enough to talk with reporters, then left "for the South." They appeared in St. Paul, Minnesota, moved on to Chicago, then disappeared.

Reporters everywhere began to watch for the couple. The reporters wanted to learn why Papa was so mad. His new son-in-law seemed to be a respectable young man. His daughter was old enough to get married, and their marriage ceremony had been a legitimate one.

Most readers sympathized with the young lovers and wondered why Papa hated the young man. Was he a bigamist or a thief? Was it his politics or religion? Papa finally explained that the young man was in the soap business. He had raised his daughter in the best society in Pittsburgh and did not want her to marry a soap man.

The young man worked for a soap factory near Buffalo, and the officials there revealed that he was paid more than $10,000 a year. The officials also revealed that their company planned to announce a new venture, one that involved more than $500,000. They hoped that the brainy young man would return soon. They could not do anything without his help.

When the honeymooners reappeared, the public demanded an explanation: to know more about the couple and the groom's $500,000 venture. Thus newspapers were forced to report—as news—the company's plans to introduce a new brand of soap. Because of all the publicity, the entire country had become interested in the soap before the company produced the first bar.[50]

Other hoaxers wanted to become rich or famous. An anonymous tipster called a Chicago newspaper and told a reporter about a boy who had been walking along Lake Michigan. One of the boy's feet slipped between two boulders, and he was unable to free it. The waves were giving him a terrific pounding, and firemen were unable to pry the boulders apart. The caller said that a smart cop went over to a patrol wagon, removed a wheel, and grabbed a handful of grease. After smearing the grease over the boy's leg, he told the boy to relax and then pulled him free. The caller did not know the patrolman's name but had noticed that his badge number was "9797."

The police department identified the patrolman, and the reporter expected a story about his heroism to appear on page 1. Before the story's publication, the reporter received a second call, and the second caller said that a firemen, not a policeman, rescued the boy. The reporter rushed to the fire station and found a lieutenant there soaking his legs in hot water. His dripping clothes, still smeared with grease, were piled nearby.

The reporter also found the patrolman. His clothes were dry, and other officers speculated that he had made the first call, describing himself as the hero "when he didn't even go near the water."[51]

In 1965, another tipster collected almost $10,000 from the CBS television network. The tipster was an ex-convict and had been in a federal prison with Jimmy Hoffa. Hoffa had disappeared, and the ex-convict promised—but failed—to give CBS information about the location of his body.

Three months after Patty Hearst's kidnapping, another ex-convict told the *Los Angeles Times* that he could arrange an interview with her. The ex-convict said that Patty Hearst was in Hong Kong, and the *Times* flew him there, first class. The ex-convict arranged a meeting for 7 p.m. that Friday. The meeting was postponed until Saturday, then until 4 p.m. Sunday. After a third cancellation, the ex-convict explained that Hong Kong was too hot for Patty. However, they could meet her in Bangkok.

The ex-convict fooled the *Times* because "he seemed knowledgeable, and his story checked out." The *Times*'s reporters were skeptical, but said that the only way to determine for sure whether he was telling the truth was to go to Hong Kong. The trip cost the *Times* about $15,000; however, the ex-convict did not seem to be motivated by the money, nor by the publicity. He enjoyed the excitement.[52]

Another hoax seemed to promote a cause: women's need for legalized abortions. The story described an Iowan, a young mother too poor to pay for a late abortion. In desperation, she tried to perform the abortion on herself, with a butcher knife. She failed and died.

Jacquelyn Mitchard, a writer for the *Capital Times* in Madison, Wisconsin, heard the story and thought it sounded genuine. Another woman offered to arrange a telephone interview with the victim's sister, and Mitchard noticed that the sister sounded odd. However, Mitchard had interviewed a great many odd-sounding people and said that most of them "turned out to be dead on the level."

A week after the story's publication, Mitchard received a call from a doctor at the Centers for Disease Control. To verify the story, he and Mitchard began calling the coroners in Iowa, Illinois, and Wisconsin. None knew anything about the case. Growing more suspicious, they obtained the sister's phone number. After tracking her down, they located a woman who "was neither dead nor on the level." When Mitchard asked the woman why she lied, "she laughed."[53]

Larry Speakes staged another hoax to trap two White House reporters. Speakes was President Ronald Reagan's press spokesman, and he suspected that reporters were looking at the private papers on his aides' desks. To catch them, Speakes left two fake memos on the desks. One of the memos proposed moving the press corps from the White House to a building next door. The second memo proposed announcing—during the half-time at a football game—President Reagan's decision to run for a second term. The football game was scheduled for New

Year's Day, and the memo explained: "Half-time audiences are one of the biggest audiences of any television shows. Half-time audiences are the most representative audiences. One pitfall is going to be that the football league people feel their game is being politicized."

Speakes disclosed the hoax at a routine press briefing. He planted the memos, he said, because one reporter was looking through White House desks "even while you're sitting there."[54] Speakes added that two reporters "bit like snakes." One of the reporters stole a memo from a secretary's desk, and another sat on a desk until she was able to read both memos. The reporters spent two days telephoning people all over the White House, trying to find someone willing to confirm the details.

Neither memo was published, and Speakes never identified the reporters.

A Change in Ethics: Firing the Guilty

HE news media no longer publish many hoaxes, not even on April Fools' Day. When a fictitious story does appear in the media, it is usually because of an unintentional error, or because a nonjournalist may have misled the media.

The nation's laws have not changed. There are still no laws that make it a crime to fool the public. Everything else has changed, however — the media, their reporters, publishers, and audiences. From a peak of 2,200, the number of daily newspapers in the United States has fallen to about 1,650. Only fifty cities still have two or more daily newspapers that compete with one another. Because there is less competition, there is less need for journalists to find — or manufacture — exclusive stories.

Journalism has also become more respectable. Most people entering the field are college graduates from middle-class families. Their wages and working conditions have improved, and many think of their work as a *profession,* not a mere job. Increasingly, journalists also think of themselves as public servants, with a responsibility to report the news as fully, fairly, and accurately as possible. They worry more about their image, and fear that a hoax might harm their credibility. Thus journalists have become more responsible, but less fun-loving and carefree.

The nation's great press barons have also disappeared. One of the last, William Randolph Hearst, died in 1951. Newspapers formerly owned by the press barons have failed or been purchased by large corporations called chains. The chains have acquired more than 70 percent of the nation's

daily papers, and some appoint business people—not journalists—to manage their properties. Many of the new
publishers seem to be more interested in their newspapers'
profits than in their content. Few want to raise hell—to publish scoops, stunts, hoaxes, and other colorful stories of
doubtful authenticity. Rather, the chains and their new managers dislike controversy and sensationalism. Thus their
newspapers have become more alike—more responsible, cautious, and colorless.

Advances in science and education also discourage the
publication of hoaxes. Americans are more sophisticated and
better informed than ever before. Television enables people to
watch events as they occur, even those in distant countries. As
a result, people are harder to fool. Moreover, genuine discoveries—space shuttles and artificial hearts, for example—are
more exciting than anything journalists might create. The advances in science and technology have also eliminated journalists' need to create hoaxes. Using computers and satellites,
newspapers everywhere receive more information than they
can publish. Important stories arrive in minutes. If a journalist did create a hoax, others—using the new means of communication—could easily expose it as fictitious.

Similarly, the journalists who create a hoax no longer are
rewarded for their creativity. Instead, most are fired. The
media's new owners and managers fear that a hoax would
anger the public. The people frightened or inconvenienced by
a hoax might cancel their subscriptions to a newspaper, or
might file thousands of lawsuits against it, claiming that they
suffered some physical or psychological harm.

The media have become so cautious that some are reluctant to air even legitimate stories likely to frighten the public.
In 1971, for example, broadcasters were notified that the
United States was being attacked with nuclear weapons. The
broadcasters were supposed to inform their listeners. Instead,
most continued their regular programming.

A routine test of the nation's Emergency Broadcast System was scheduled for February 20, 1971. At 9:30 that Saturday morning, a civilian employee at the National Emergency
Warning Center in Colorado transmitted the wrong tape.[1]

Instead of transmitting a test tape, he transmitted an emergency alert that was supposed to be used only after another country had launched a nuclear attack. Broadcasters at twenty-five hundred radio and television stations were told that the president had declared a national emergency, and that their normal programming should cease immediately. The alert included the proper code word, "HATEFULNESS," which meant that it was real.

If it had been real, most Americans would never have learned about it. Fearing a hoax, most stations ignored it. A spot check revealed that only four of sixteen stations in West Virginia went off the air.[2] In San Francisco, the system "seemed to break down completely."[3] Not a single station there went off the air, nor any of the twenty-one stations in Atlanta.[4]

A few hoaxes continue to appear in the media. But today, most are the work of a single individual trying to fool everyone—a newspaper's editors as well as its readers. The competition to obtain good jobs remains fierce, and young journalists are tempted to create some hoaxes to help their careers. The *Washington Post* published the most famous example. Janet Cooke, a young reporter at the *Post,* wrote about an eight-year-old black child addicted to heroin. Cooke's story appeared on the paper's front page and won a Pulitzer Prize. Its editors returned the prize after learning that Cooke had invented the eight-year-old, partly to dramatize the problem of drug addiction in Washington's slums. The *Post* fired Cooke, then published an eighteen-thousand-word explanation and apology.

Even the Chicago papers now fire journalists responsible for a hoax. In 1951, for example, Chicago's *Herald-American* reported that a local woman expected five or six babies. It was August 21, and reporter Hugh S. Stewart told his editors that the woman was five months pregnant, and that her babies were due in a month or two. He added that experienced doctors had been called in for consultations but disagreed about the number of babies the woman was carrying. Using stethoscopes, all the doctors easily detected the heart beats of five babies. Some doctors thought they detected the heart beats of six.

"There is no record in any country of six babies surviving," Stewart wrote. Nevertheless, the quintuplets' chances of survival seemed excellent. Experts explained that there had been great advances in the science of pediatrics and obstetrics. Moreover, Chicago was "far advanced in its facilities for handling multiple births."[5]

Stewart claimed that the number of women having multiple births was increasing, and that scientists believed that the release of atomic energy was a factor. He explained that a mysterious factor caused an increase in the number of males born during wars. The increase in births — and in multiple births — seemed to be "nature's way of compensating for the tremendous slaughter of global conflict."

A second story, published two days later, reported that medical experts were still debating whether the woman would have five or six babies. The experts were also debating the best way of determining the correct number. Stethoscopes were safe but inaccurate. X-rays might settle the matter, but doctors feared that the frequent use of X-rays might harm the unborn infants. They did not want to take any X-rays until just before the babies' birth. There would be less danger then, and the X-rays would be of great help "in the admittedly desperate fight to deliver the infants safely and assure their survival."[6]

The *Herald-American* published a third — and more suspicious — story on August 26. It reported that the birth of six babies would not set a record after all.[7] The story explained that, in 1866, a Chicago woman had given birth to sextuplets, and that all six had survived. The details, however, were hazy. Chicago's Great Fire of 1871 had "swallowed up records registered by the attending physician, Dr. James Edward." Moreover, the children had not been told about their multiple births "till their mother revealed it on her death bed." (The story failed to explain how the mother had, for years, hidden that fact from six brothers and sisters, all born on the same day.)

Six months later, the *Herald-American* admitted that its

story was a hoax. It had been fooled by a trusted member of its own staff, reporter Hugh Stewart.[8] The paper's editors explained that, for months, Stewart had concealed the fraud "under a blanket of ingenious fabrications. . . . "

The *Herald-American* described Stewart as a "quiet, studious, highly regarded newsman." He had been hired as the newspaper's science and medical writer, and his stories were careful, conservative, and authentic. Moreover, he had a knack for making technical subjects clear to readers. In August, he told an editor that confidential sources informed him about the woman. Stewart added that he would be ruined if he revealed the sources' identity. He could not tell anyone, not even his editor.

During the following months, Stewart kept his editors informed about the woman's progress. He told them that specialists had been called in, but that the woman had developed a cyst, and the births were delayed. "Gradually," the editors admitted, "a sickening suspicion became conviction — a seasoned mature newsman had 'cracked up' and fallen for the lure of a false 'news beat.' " They had been duped, their readers misinformed.

After hours of grilling, Stewart admitted that the story "was purely a product of his imagination." He was fired, and the *Herald-American* apologized for its error.

In 1985, another Chicago daily, the *Sun-Times,* fired a reporter accused of writing a more unusual hoax. On November 18, reporter Wade Roberts described five Texans as they watched a football game between the Chicago Bears and the Dallas Cowboys. Roberts said the Texans were in a bar located off a dusty farm road near Eden, a small town 240 miles from Dallas. A man named Jefferson Davis Bonner owned the bar, and folks around Eden called it Bonner's. It was a spartan place, with a concrete floor and walls of corrugated metal.

One of the Texans, Les Smalley, had made a bet with his wife. She hated football, and they agreed that—if the Cowboys won—she would not bother him for the rest of the season. But if the Cowboys lost, he could not watch another game until the Super Bowl.

Roberts described the Texans as their mood changed from confidence to despair. The Bears scored the first touchdown and went on to win the game by a score of 44–0. The Texans promptly hoisted their bottles and toasted the victors. "We hate gettin' whupped," one said, "but them Bears are one hell of a team."

Smalley disappeared into an outhouse. "Boys," he said later, "been thinkin' 'bout gettin' me a divorce."[9]

Mike Royko, a columnist at another Chicago daily, the *Tribune,* called it a fine piece of writing, "one of the better stories of its kind I've ever read." Nevertheless, Royko questioned the story's authenticity. If you called the deputy sheriff stationed in Eden, Royko explained, "[h]e will tell you flatly that there is no such bar as Bonner's." Nobody living in Eden was named Jefferson Davis Bonner. None of the Texans mentioned in Roberts's story lived in or near Eden.[10]

"We're pretty small," the deputy said. "And everybody knows everybody." Eden had a population of five hundred. The entire county had a population of only thirty-five hundred.

Roberts's editors asked him to confirm the story's authenticity, and an editor traveled to Texas with him. They were unable to find Bonner's or any of the Texans mentioned in the story. After two days in Texas, Roberts was offered a chance to resign. He refused and was fired.[11]

A story involving a Boston broadcaster demonstrates, perhaps even more dramatically, the change in media ethics. Some journalists no longer tolerate hoaxes, not even on April Fools' Day.

The broadcaster, Homer "Skip" Cilley, worked as executive producer of the evening news at Channel 7 (WNAC-TV) in Boston. It was April 1, 1980, and Cilley wanted a little fun—an outrageous story for the "kicker," the last story on the station's 6 p.m. newscast.

Near the end of the newscast, the anchorman announced, "Ladies and gentlemen, we've just gotten word of a volcano erupting in Milton." Channel 7's cameras shifted to a reporter who said lava was flowing down a ski resort, the

Great Blue Hill, and into the nearby towns of Milton and Quincy.[12] The station then broadcast film of a real volcano, Mt. St. Helens in Washington. Other film clips, all old and taken out of context, showed the governor and the president. Both seemed to be talking about the volcano in Milton.

The entire story lasted about ninety seconds. At the end, the reporter held up a card saying, "April Fool."

Many viewers, especially those in Milton and Quincy, missed the joke. The police in Milton said they normally received about a hundred calls during an eight-hour shift. That night, they received a hundred calls in an hour. Other viewers called a Civil Defense agency, asking whether they should abandon their homes.

The station fired Cilley and explained that he "failed to exercise good news judgment." In addition, Cilley had violated station and Federal Communications Commission rules by misleading his audience about the film.

The FCC announced that it would investigate the incident. A representative for the FCC explained: "If a situation like this causes serious harm to a number of people, or a serious possibility of harm, then it becomes an important matter, the kind for which a station could lose its license."[13]

Other hoaxes are created by the media's part-time employees, by freelancers, and by other people eager to get their stories into print. Some do not realize that the rules have changed and that the media no longer want hoaxes. Others have written stories so silly that they never expected anyone to believe them, especially not their editors.

One of the silliest stories originated in Winsted, Connecticut, where it was reported that a bio-chemist there had manufactured a patriotic pickle, one that was red, white, and blue and had fifty stars. In addition, the bio-chemist had developed yellow pickles with purple polka dots, and green-and-blue pickles with a brown tweed. The *Waterbury* (Conn.) *Republican* published the story, and United Press International transmitted it to other newspapers across the United States.

Two correspondents were fired. They admitted creating

the story, but insisted that it was not a hoax. "It was a tongue-in-cheek article," one said.[14] They had wanted "to lighten people's lives," and thought that their story was so absurd that no one would believe it.

Other stories are more serious, and more difficult to verify. Typically, they continue to describe the events occurring in distant countries. Every newspaper is vulnerable, even the best. On December 20, 1981, for instance, the *New York Times* published an exciting story about life in Cambodia. The story was written by Christopher Jones, a 24-year-old freelance writer. Jones described the Cambodians' guerrilla war against Vietnamese troops who occupied their country. His story began in Bangkok, the capital of neighboring Thailand. Jones wrote that he had been picked up at a hotel there and set off in an air-conditioned minibus. He was taken to a Khmer Rouge camp crowded with guerrillas who were smiling and puffing on marijuana cigarettes. Some of the soldiers were mere children, separated from their families at the age of twelve. Two days later, Jones was awakened by gunfire. It was 3:45 a.m., he said, and a Vietnamese division was only five miles away. He was evacuated to another camp and saw several Khmer Rouge soldiers at its entrance, "proudly photographing four severed heads." A raiding party had brought the heads in that morning.

After that, Jones said, he frequently heard the sounds of military action and witnessed one battle. Tracers flashed, mortars thumped, and Vietnamese helicopters hovered overhead. "Then I heard the grinding drone of tanks, growing louder," Jones wrote. "A volley of machine-gun bullets flung up pebbles and red dirt all around us. A mortar shell landed somewhere behind."[15] Fortunately, the Khmer Rouge were able to disable several of the tanks, stopping the attack.

Five weeks later, the *Washington Post* reported that Khmer Rouge officials in Bangkok insisted that Jones had neither visited the guerrillas nor interviewed any of the people quoted in his report.[16] Moreover, Jones's story included material taken from a novel published in 1930.

Embarrassed, the *Times* announced that it would investigate the matter. On February 22, the paper agreed that

Jones's story was a hoax.[17] It had found him in Spain. After three days of questioning, he admitted that his article was fictitious. He said he had made up the story because he could not afford to travel to Cambodia. He spent several weeks concocting it in Spain, using his imagination, maps, and other secondary sources. To make the story more credible, Jones also forged his expense account.

An editorial in the *Times* complained that Jones's story was not merely an error, but a hoax, "a false and partly plagiarized tale. . . . " The paper explained that Jones had combined old interviews with many fake new ones, and that he did it so well "that no Cambodian experts challenged the account until the plagiarism . . . was discovered."[18] Executive editor A. M. Rosenthal admitted that the *Times* had erred by failing to show Jones's story to experts on Cambodia. Another editor added that nothing in the story had seemed inconsistent. Moreover, it had been impossible to check the quotations that Jones attributed to rebels in the Cambodian mountains.

Critics responded that Jones's story was filled with errors, and that the *Times* should have detected them.[19] Before submitting his story to the *New York Times,* it turned out, Jones had tried to sell it to *Time* magazine. *Time* checked the story with its bureau in Bangkok and "decided we didn't like the sound of it." Other experts also questioned Jones's accuracy, especially his reference to Khmer Rouge soldiers smoking marijuana and drinking liquor, "practices strictly forbidden by their notoriously effective code of discipline."

Why did the *New York Times* publish the story? A critic explained that "Jones's piece was, after all, a good story, full of adventure and colorful description."[20]

Other hoaxes, perhaps a majority of those now appearing in the media, are created by nonjournalists, usually for fun or profit. People seeking publicity have always tried to trick the media into publishing their stories. Increasingly, nonjournalists are also trying to swindle the media, selling them exclusive stories such as Hitler's "diaries." The diaries were crude forgeries, yet the media bid $3 million for them.

The problem is certain to continue. Why? Journalists are vulnerable to misinformation and always will be. Journalists cannot determine the truth of every story they publish, nor check every detail. They receive too many stories, and a single story may contain hundreds of details. Some of the stories arrive moments before their deadlines, and some describe the events occurring in distant countries. As a result, journalists are forced to rely upon their sources. Unfortunately, some sources fail to observe or remember important details, others are mistaken, and still others lie—convincingly.

In 1975, for example, the Boston *Globe* reported that Soviet leader Leonid Brezhnev was flying to Boston to be treated for leukemia.[21] Someone at the Sidney Farber Cancer Center in Boston had prepared a fake admission card for Brezhnev. Other employees saw the card, and rumors about his visit spread through the city. The *Globe* tried to check the story and, because no one denied its authenticity, published a front-page exclusive.[22]

A New Yorker named Joey Skaggs has been even more successful. Skaggs seems to have made a career out of fooling the media, and his stories illustrate their continued vulnerability to misinformation. Skaggs recently appeared on ABC's "Good Morning America" program to describe a new diet. To guarantee its success, he said, Americans trying to lose weight would be able to hire enforcers—strongmen—to watch them twenty-four hours a day. If people following the diet tried to eat too much, the strongmen would physically restrain them.

Skaggs's earlier hoaxes involved bordellos for dogs, sperm banks for rock stars, and condominiums for fish. Journalists believed—and reported—every one of them.[23]

A few Americans seem to want hoaxes. They clearly want to be entertained, not informed, and so turn to television. Like the media's old hoaxes, television's entertainment programs enable people to relax and to momentarily forget their problems.

Other Americans turn to the nation's tabloids. These appeal to the alienated, the poorly educated, and especially the elderly. Typically, the tabloids publish stories about astrology, celebrities, and UFOs. Other stories resemble the hoaxes that other newspapers published a hundred years ago. They describe unusual babies, monsters, and Martians. In addition, the stories occur in distant areas, often India, Africa, or South America.

But the tabloids' stories tend to be reassuring rather than frightening. They describe the wonders of science and medicine, including miraculous new diets, and drugs that cure baldness and cancer. They rarely report more depressing stories about crimes, accidents, or wars. Thus they provide an escape; after reading them, people feel better about themselves and about the amazing world around them.

Typically, the *Weekly World News* reported that a baby girl vanished from her crib in the jungles of Sumatra, kidnapped by an orangutan ape.[24] Villagers found the orangutan—a 125-pound female—and a marksman armed with a dart gun fired a tranquilizer at it. In a few minutes, rescuers were able to retrieve the baby, still clutched safely in the ape's hairy arm. The baby suffered no ill effects, and was as fit and healthy as any normal baby.

Another of the tabloids' stories reported that a woman in South Africa "had a close encounter of the intimate kind with a space traveler from a distant planet."[25] She was "a stunning woman of 46" when her unusual love affair began. Gazing up at the African sky one night, the woman saw a huge spaceship and a handsome man looking down at her from one of its windows. Eighteen months later, the ship returned and the handsome stranger stepped out. Knowing no fear, the woman flew into his arms, and they became lovers.

The woman, now seventy-three, had learned the true meaning of love while mating with the alien. She gave birth to a son, half human, half alien: "Ayling, who lives with his father, Akon, on the planet Meton."

APPENDIX

Ben Franklin's Parable against Persecution

1. And it came to pass after these Things, that Abraham sat in the Door of his Tent, about the going down of the Sun.

2. And behold a Man, bowed with Age, came from the Way of the Wilderness, leaning on a Staff.

3. And Abraham arose and met him, and said unto him, Turn in, I pray thee, and wash thy Feet, and tarry all Night, and thou shalt arise early on the Morrow, and go on thy Way.

4. And the Man said, Nay, for I will abide under this Tree.

5. But Abraham pressed him greatly; so he turned and they went into the Tent; and Abraham baked unleavened Bread, and they did eat.

6. And when Abraham saw that the Man blessed not God, he said unto him, Wherefore dost thou not worship the most high God, Creator of Heaven and Earth?

7. And the Man answered and said, I do not worship the God thou speakest of; neither do I call upon his Name; for I have made to myself a God, which abideth always in mine House, and provideth me with all Things.

8. And Abraham's Zeal was kindled against the Man; and he arose, and fell upon him, and drove him forth with Blows into the Wilderness.

9. And at Midnight God called unto Abraham, saying, Abraham, where is the Stranger?

10. And Abraham answered and said, Lord, he would not worship thee, neither would he call upon thy Name; therefore have I driven him out from before my face into the Wilderness.

11. And God said, Have I born with him these hundred ninety and eight Years, and nourished him, and clothed him, notwithstanding his Rebellion against me, and couldst not thou, that art thyself a Sinner, bear with him one Night?

12. And Abraham said, Let not the Anger of my Lord wax hot against his Servant. Lo, I have sinned; forgive me, I pray Thee:

13. And Abraham arose and went forth into the Wilderness, and sought diligently for the Man, and found him, and returned with him to his Tent; and when he had entreated him kindly, he sent him away on the Morrow with Gifts.

14. And God spake again unto Abraham, saying, For this thy Sin shall thy Seed be afflicted four Hundred Years in a strange Land:

15. But for thy Repentance will I deliver them; and they shall come forth with Power, and with Gladness of Heart, and with much Substance.

NOTES

INTRODUCTION

1. George S. Turnbull, *History of Oregon Newspapers* (Portland, Ore.: Binfords & Mort, Publishers, 1939), p. 55.
2. Fred Fedler, "Mrs. O'Leary's Cow and Other Newspaper Tales about the Chicago Fire of 1871," *American Journalism* (vol. 3, no. 1, 1986), pp. 24–38.
3. John Myers Myers, *Print in a Wild Land* (Garden City, N.Y.: Doubleday & Co., Inc., 1967), p. 76.
4. Bill Hosokawa, *Thunder in the Rockies* (New York: William Morrow & Co., Inc., 1976), p. 22.
5. Howard Ziff, "New Breed," *Editor and Publisher* (October 27, 1979), p. 5.
6. Burton Rascoe, *Before I Forget* (Garden City, N.Y.: Doubleday, Doran & Co., Inc., 1937), p. 238.
7. Franc B. Wilkie, *Personal Reminiscences of 35 Years of Journalism* (Chicago: F.J. Schulte & Co., Publisher, 1891), p. 131.
8. Paul Lancaster, "Faking It," *American Heritage* (October-November 1982), p. 55.
9. Will Irwin, *The Making of a Reporter* (New York: G.P. Putnam's Sons, 1942), p. 52.
10. Robert St. John, *This Was My World* (Garden City, N.Y.: Doubleday & Co., Inc., 1953), p. 130.
11. Ishbel Ross, *Ladies of the Press* (New York: Harper & Brothers, 1936), pp. 299–300.
12. Piers Brendon, *The Life and Death of the Press Barons* (New York: Atheneum, 1983), p. 1.
13. Stephen Longstreet, *We All Went to Paris* (New York: The Macmillan Company, 1972), p. 176. See also Eric Hawkins with Robert N. Sturdevant, *Hawkins of the Paris Herald* (New York: Simon and Schuster, 1963), p. 17.
14. Al Sicherman, "A Dinner in the Spirit of Wrong Way Corrigan," *Minneapolis Tribune,* June 1, 1984, p. 1K.

CHAPTER 1

1. Bernard Fay, *Franklin: The Apostle of Modern Times* (Boston: Little, Brown, and Company, 1929), p. 44.
2. Frank Luther Mott and Chester E. Jorgenson, *Benjamin Franklin* (New York: American Book Company, 1936), pp. 96–111.
3. Benjamin Franklin, *Satires and Bagatelles* (Detroit: Fine Book Circle, 1937), pp. 22–24.
4. Alfred Owen Aldridge, *Benjamin Franklin: Philosopher and Man* (Philadelphia: J.B. Lippincott Co.), 1965, p. 89.
5. Richard E. Amacher, *Franklin's Wit and Folly* (New Brunswick, N.J.: Rutgers University Press, 1953), p. 80.

6. Franklin, *Satires and Bagatelles,* pp. 9–11. See also Mott and Jorgenson, *Benjamin Franklin,* pp. 190–193.

7. P. M. Zall, ed., *Ben Franklin Laughing* (Berkeley: University of California Press, 1980), p. 94.

8. James A. Sappenfield, *A Sweet Instruction* (Carbondale: Southern Illinois University Press, 1973), p. 65.

9. Max Hall, *Benjamin Franklin and Polly Baker* (Chapel Hill: University of North Carolina Press, 1960).

10. *Ibid.,* p. 41.

11. Fay, *Franklin,* pp. 161–162.

12. Benjamin Franklin, *The Bagatelles from Passy* (New York: The Eakins Press, 1967), pp. 19–21. See also Mott and Jorgenson, *Benjamin Franklin,* pp. 379–380; Franklin, *Satires and Bagatelles,* pp. 116–117; and Amacher, *Franklin's Wit and Folly,* pp. 72–74.

13. Herbert W. Schneider, ed., *Benjamin Franklin: The Autobiography and Selections From His Other Writings* (New York: The Liberal Arts Press, 1952), pp. 184–187.

14. Franklin, *Satire and Bagatelles,* pp. 61–62.

15. Amacher, *Franklin's Wit and Folly,* p. 76.

16. Franklin, *Satires and Bagatelles,* pp. 68–70.

17. Fay, *Franklin,* p. 477.

CHAPTER 2

1. Julian Symons, *The Tell-Tale Heart* (London: Faber & Faber, 1978), p. 88.

2. Mary E. Phillips, *Edgar Allan Poe the Man,* vol. 1 (Chicago: The John C. Winston Co., 1926), p. 1,194.

3. Una Pope-Hennessy, *Edgar Allan Poe* (London: Macmillan and Co., Ltd., 1934), p. 193.

4. Edgar Allan Poe, *The Works of the Late Edgar Allan Poe,* vol. 3 (New York: Redfield, 1858), p. 126.

5. Arthur Hobson Quinn, *Edgar Allan Poe: A Critical Biography* (New York: Cooper Square Publishers, Inc., 1969), p. 226.

6. Poe, *Works* vol. 3, p. 122.

7. Frank M. O'Brien, *The Story of the Sun* (New York: D. Appleton and Company, 1928), pp. 98–99.

8. Symons, *Tell-Tale Heart,* p. 88.

9. Pope-Hennessy, *Poe,* p. 233.

10. Edgar Allan Poe, *Doings of Gotham* (Pottsville, Penn.: Jacob E. Spannuth, Publisher, 1929), p. 33.

11. Quinn, *Poe,* p. 596.

12. David Sinclair, *Edgar Allan Poe* (London: J.M. Dent & Sons Ltd., 1977), p. 217.

13. John H. Ingram, *Edgar Allan Poe: His Life, Letters, and Opinions* (New York: AMS Press, Inc., 1965), p. 276.

14. Quinn, *Poe,* p. 264.

15. Phillips, *Poe,* p. 1,192.

CHAPTER 3

1. Mark Twain, *The Autobiography of Mark Twain*, ed. Charles Neider (New York: Harper & Row, Publishers, 1959), p. 102.

2. "The Passing of a Pioneer," *The* (San Francisco) *Examiner*, January 22, 1893, p. 15. (After the *Enterprise* ceased publication, its most famous writers and editors were asked to reminisce about their experiences, and their articles provide some of the best descriptions of the paper.)

3. George D. Lyman, *The Saga of the Comstock Lode* (New York: Charles Scribner's Sons, 1934), p. 208.

4. Wells Drury, *An Editor on the Comstock Lode* (Palo Alto, Calif.: Pacific Books, 1936), p. 216.

5. Rollin M. Daggett, "Daggett's Recollections," *The Examiner*, January 22, 1893, p. 15.

6. Arthur McEwen, "In the Heroic Days," *The Examiner*, January 22, 1893, p. 15.

7. DeLancey Ferguson, "The Petrified Truth," *The Colophon* (vol. 2, no. 2, Winter 1937), p. 195.

8. Dan De Quille, *A History of the Comstock Silver Lode & Mines* (Virginia, Nev.: F. Boegle, 1889). Reprint (New York: Arno Press, Inc., 1973), pp. 52–54.

9. Mark Twain, *Roughing It*, vol. 1 (New York: P. F. Collier & Son Company, 1913), p. 250.

10. Twain, *Roughing It*, vol. 2, p. 22.

11. Drury, *An Editor on the Comstock Lode*, pp. 212–214.

12. *History of Nevada* (Oakland, Calif.: Thompson & West, 1881), pp. 292–294.

13. Lucius Beebe, *Comstock Commotion* (Stanford: Stanford University Press, 1954), p. 80.

14. Dan De Quille, "Mark Twain Takes a Lesson in the Manly Art," *Golden Era*, May 1, 1864.

15. William R. Gillis, *Memories of Mark Twain and Steve Gillis*, 2nd ed. (Sonora, Calif.: The Banner, 1924), pp. 78–79.

16. Dan De Quille, "Salad Days of Mark Twain," *The Examiner*, March 19, 1893, p. 1.

17. Mark Twain, *The Washoe Giant in San Francisco* (San Francisco: George Fields, 1938), pp. 50–53.

18. De Quille, "Salad Days of Mark Twain," p. 1.

19. Dan De Quille, *The Big Bonanza* (New York: Thomas Y. Crowell Company, 1947), p. 18.

20. For the best summary of De Quille's hoaxes, see C. Grant Loomis, "The Tall Tales of Dan De Quille," *Western Folklore* (vol. 5, no. 1, January 1946), pp. 26–71.

21. Fred H. Hart, *The Sazerac Lying Club* (San Francisco: Henry Keller & Co., 1878), pp. 77–79.

22. Mark Twain, "A Washoe Joke," *San Francisco Bulletin*, October 15, 1862.

23. Albert Bigelow Paine, *Mark Twain*, vol. 1 (New York: Harper & Brothers Publishers, 1912), p. 211.

24. Mark Twain, *Early Tales & Sketches*, vol. 1, ed. Edgar Marquess Branch and Robert H. Hirst, with the assistance of Harriet Elinor Smith (Berkeley: University of California Press, 1979), pp. 246–247.

25. Mark Twain, "The Latest Sensation," *San Francisco Bulletin*, October 31, 1863.

26. *Ibid.*

27. Dan De Quille, "Reporting with Mark Twain," *California Illustrated Magazine,* July 1893, p. 173.

28. *Ibid.,* p. 171.

29. Mark Twain, *Sketches New and Old,* vol. 19 of *The Writings of Mark Twain* (New York: Harper & Brothers, 1875; Grosse Pointe, Mich.: Scholarly Press, [n.d.]), p. 324.

30. Mark Twain, *Autobiography,* pp. 112–118.

31. Paul Fatout, *Mark Twain in Virginia City* (Port Washington, N.Y.: Kennikat Press, 1973), pp. 197–198.

32. Gillis, *Memories of Mark Twain and Steve Gillis,* pp. 104–106.

33. DeLancy Ferguson, "Mark Twain's Comstock Duel: The Birth of a Legend," *American Literature* (vol. 14, March 1942), pp. 66–70. See also Ivan Benson, *Mark Twain's Western Years* (Stanford: Stanford University Press, 1938), pp. 106–112.

34. Lyman, *The Saga of the Comstock Lode,* pp. 293–304.

35. Richard G. Lillard, "Dan De Quille, Comstock Reporter and Humorist," *Pacific Historical Review* (vol. 13, no. 3, September 1944), p. 258.

36. Oscar Lewis, "Introduction" in De Quille, *The Big Bonanza.*

CHAPTER 4

1. Locke apparently never wrote his autobiography. The most detailed account of his life appears in William N. Griggs, *The Celebrated "Moon Story"* (New York: Bunnell and Price, 1852), pp. 40–45.

2. Phineas T. Barnum, "The Great Moon Hoax," in *Great Hoaxes of All Time,* ed. Robert Medill McBride and Neil Pritchie (New York: Robert M. McBride, 1956), p. 280.

3. Copies of the *New York Sun* are available on microfilm at major libraries. Locke's "Moon Story" has also been reprinted in several books. It is most easily available in *Henry J. Raymond and the New York Press,* published in 1870 and reprinted (New York: ARNO Press and The New York Times) in 1970. The complete "Moon Story" also appears in a rare book, *The Moon Hoax,* by Richard Adams Locke (New York: William Gowans, 1859). Two other books provide detailed accounts of the hoax but do not reprint the entire story. The best (but rarest) source is Griggs, *The Celebrated "Moon Story."* The second is by Frank M. O'Brien, *The Story of the Sun,* new ed. (New York: Appleton 1928).

4. Griggs, *The Celebrated "Moon Story,"* p. 23.

5. Richard Adams Locke, *The Moon Hoax* (New York: William Gowans, 1859), pp. 60–63.

6. Frederic Hudson, *Journalism in the United States* (New York: Harper & Brothers, Publishers, 1873), p. 422.

7. Wm. N. Griggs, "Locke among the Moonlings," *Southern Quarterly Review* (October 1853), pp. 502–504.

8. Griggs, *Celebrated "Moon Story,"* pp. 32–35.

9. "Locke among the Moonlings," pp. 502–504.

10. Griggs, *Celebrated "Moon Story,"* p. 19.

11. O'Brien, *Story of the Sun,* p. 39.

12. Robert W. Jones, *Journalism in the United States* (New York: Dutton, 1947), p. 235.

13. Richard A. Practor, "The Lunar Hoax," *Belgravia* (vol. 30, 1876), pp. 177–178.

14. Griggs, *Celebrated "Moon Story,"* pp. 40–45.

15. Poe, *Works,* vol. 3, p. 122.

16. *Ibid.,* pp. 122–125.

17. Griggs, *Celebrated "Moon Story,"* pp. 37–39.

18. George R. Price discusses other factors that contributed to the success of the *"Moon Story"* in "The Day They Discovered Men on the Moon," *Popular Science* (vol. 173, no. 1, July 1958), p. 64.

CHAPTER 5

1. "Railways and Revolvers in Georgia," *The* (London) *Times,* October 15, 1856, p. 9.

2. Untitled editorial column, *The Times,* October 16, 1856, p. 6.

3. H. C. W., letter, "Railways and Revolvers in Georgia," *The Times,* October 18, 1856, p. 8.

4. A New-Englander, untitled letter, *The Times,* October 18, 1856, p. 8.

5. John Arrowsmith, letter, "Railways and Revolvers in Georgia," *The Times,* October 24, 1856, p. 7.

6. "The American Yarn" from *The Examiner,* reprinted in *The Times,* October 27, 1856, p. 8.

7. Editorial column, "A Prodigious Hoax," *New York Times,* November 1, 1856, p. 4.

8. Editorial column, "The Hoax of *The* (London) *Times,*" *New York Times,* November 8, 1856, p. 4.

9. *"The Times* 'Hoax,' " *Daily Picayune,* November 16, 1856, p. 1.

10. A New-Englander, letter, "Railways and Revolvers in Georgia," *The Times,* October 29, 1856, p. 10.

11. John P. King, letter, "The Georgian Horrors," *The Times,* November 22, 1856, p. 10.

12. R. R. Cuyler, untitled letter, *The Times,* December 10, 1856, p. 9.

13. E. Molyneux, letter, "Railways and Revolvers in Georgia," *The Times,* December 10, 1856, p. 9.

14. R. R. Cuyler, letter, "The Great Arrowsmith Hoax," *New York Times,* November 24, 1856, p. 1. Reprinted from the *Savannah Republican.*

15. Editorial column, "The Arrowsmith Hoax," *New York Times,* December 8, 1856, p. 4.

16. Untitled editorial column, *The Times,* December 11, 1856, p. 6.

17. John Arrowsmith, letter, "Railways and Revolvers in Georgia," *The Times,* December 13, 1856, p. 9.

18. Untitled editorial column, *The Times,* December 13, 1856, p. 8.

19. Editorial column, "The Arrowsmith Hoax," *New York Times,* January 5, 1857, p. 4.

20. Fairplay, untitled letter, *The Times,* December 15, 1856, p. 10.

21. One Who Has Traveled on all the Railways of the United States, letter, "Railways and Revolvers Once More," *The Times,* December 19, 1856, p. 5.

22. T. S., letter, "Railways and Revolvers in Georgia," *The Times,* December 15, 1856, p. 10.

23. R. R. Cuyler, letter, "Railways and Revolvers in Georgia," *The Times,* February 18, 1857, p. 12.

24. John Arrowsmith, letter, "Railways and Revolvers in Georgia," *The Times,* February 20, 1857, p. 8.

CHAPTER 6

1. "AWFUL CALAMITY," *New York Herald,* November 9, 1874, p. 1.
2. T. B. Connery, "A Famous Newspaper Hoax," *Harper's Weekly,* June 3, 1893, p. 534.
3. Don C. Seitz, *The James Gordon Bennetts* (Indianapolis: The Bobbs-Merrill Company, Publishers), 1928, p. 13.
4. Joseph I. C. Clarke, *My Life and Memories* (New York: Dodd, Mead and Company, 1925), p. 162.
5. Connery, "A Famous Newspaper Hoax," p. 535.
6. *Ibid.*
7. Clarke, *My Life and Memories,* p. 161.
8. "A Heartless Hoax," *New York Daily Tribune,* November 10, 1874, p. 5.
9. "A Mother Frantic with Fear," *New York Daily Tribune,* November 10, 1874, p. 5.
10. "Practical Jokes," *New York Times,* November 10, 1874, p. 4.
11. "Letter to the Editor," *New York Times,* November 10, 1874, p. 4.
12. Connery, "A Famous Newspaper Hoax," p. 535.
13. Clarke, *My Life and Memories,* p. 163.
14. Seitz, *The James Gordon Bennetts,* p. 338.

CHAPTER 7

1. Charles Sanford Diehl, *The Staff Correspondent* (San Antonio: The Clegg Co., 1931), pp. 69–70.
2. Justin E. Walsh, *To Print the News and Raise Hell!* (Chapel Hill: University of North Carolina Press, 1968), p. 9.
3. "BURNED ALIVE," *Chicago Times,* February 13, 1875, p. 1.
4. "Are Our Lives to Be Longer Imperilled by Reckless Managers!" *Chicago Times,* February 14, 1875, p. 6.
5. J. H. McVicker, "To the Editor," *Chicago Times,* February 14, 1875, p. 6.
6. R. M. Hooley, "To the Editor," *Chicago Times,* February 14, 1875, p. 6.
7. J. H. McVicker, "The Journalistic Can-Can," *Milwaukee Sentinel,* February 19, 1875, p. 7.
8. " 'Supposititious' Journalism," *Chicago Tribune,* February 15, 1875, p. 8.
9. "The *'Times'* Fabrication," *Chicago Tribune,* February 14, 1875, p. 13.
10. "Indignation at Aurora," *Chicago Tribune,* February 15, 1875, p. 8.
11. "BURNED ALIVE," *Chicago Tribune,* February 21, 1875, p. 13.
12. "Feeling at South Bend," *Chicago Tribune,* February 15, 1875, p. 8.
13. "False Pretenses," *Chicago Tribune,* February 14, 1875, p. 2.
14. Walsh, *To Print the News,* p. 9.
15. Robert Hardy Andrews, *A Corner of Chicago* (Boston: Little, Brown and Company, 1963), p. 70.
16. Diehl, *Staff Correspondent,* p. 70.
17. "571 Dead Bodies Found in Ruins," *Chicago Tribune,* December 31, 1903, p. 2.
18. "Curtain Held by Board," *Chicago Tribune,* January 3, 1904, p. 1.
19. "Left to Chance and Shut Exits at the Iroquois," *Chicago Tribune,* January 7, 1904, p. 1.

CHAPTER 8

1. "Old Wall Must Go," *Denver Sunday Post,* June 25, 1899, p. 6.
2. "Chicago to Demolish the Old Chinese Wall," *Denver Sunday Times,* June 25, 1899, p. 5.
3. "Builds Highway of Chinese Wall," *Denver Republican,* June 25, 1899, p. 20.
4. "Plan to Raze Chinese Wall," *Chicago Tribune,* June 26, 1899, p. 2.
5. "Will China's Wall Come Down," *New York Times,* June 27, 1899, p. 1.
6. Harry Lee Wilber, "A Fake That Rocked the World," *North American Review* (vol. 247, no. 1, March 1939), pp. 21–26.
7. Harry Lee Wilber, "A Fake That Rocked the World," reprinted in *Great Hoaxes of All Time,* ed. Robert Medill McBride and Neil Pritchie (New York: Robert M. McBride Co., 1956), p. 10.
8. Mark Muldavin, "The Fake That Made Violent History," in *The Double Dealers,* ed. Alexander Klein (Philadelphia: J.B. Lippincott Co., 1958), p. 303.
9. Harry Lee Wilber, "A Fake That Rocked the World," *Denver Westerners Roundup* (June 1970), p. 25.
10. Ronald Schiller, "China's Great Wall of Wonder," *Reader's Digest* (July 1982), p. 73.
11. Frances Melrose, "4 Denver Reporters Blamed for Fueling the Boxer Rebellion," *Rocky Mountain News,* November 4, 1984, p. 30.
12. William J. Duiker, *Cultures in Collision* (San Rafael, Calif.: Presidio Press, 1978), p. 3.
13. See, for example, "The Awful Pekin Massacre," *Denver Sunday Post,* July 9, 1900, p. 16. See also *Denver Post,* June 24, 1900, p. 2.

CHAPTER 9

1. Carl Bode, *Mencken* (Carbondale: Southern Illinois University Press, 1969), p. 4.
2. "A Neglected Anniversary," *New York Evening Mail,* December 28, 1917. The entire hoax, plus Mencken's later confessions, have been widely reprinted and may be more easily available in any of these books: H. L. Mencken, *The Bathtub Hoax and Other Blasts and Bravos* (New York: Alfred A. Knopf, 1958); Vilhjalmur Stefansson, *Adventures in Error* (Detroit: Gale Research Company, 1970); P. J. Wingate, *H. L. Mencken's Un-Neglected Anniversary* (Hockessin, Del.: Holly Press, 1980).
3. Willis Thornton, *Fable, Fact and History* (Philadelphia: Chilton Company, Publishers, 1957), p. 69.
4. H. L. Mencken, "Melancholy Reflections," *Chicago Sunday Tribune,* May 23, 1926, Part 8, p. 1.
5. *Ibid.*
6. H. L. Mencken, "Hymn to the Truth," *Chicago Sunday Tribune,* July 25, 1926, Part 7, p. 1.
7. H. L. Mencken, "Hymn to the Truth" in *Bathtub Hoax,* p. 17.
8. *Ibid.,* p. 19.
9. H. L. Mencken, *Prejudices: Sixth Series* (New York: Alfred A. Knopf, 1927), p. 195.
10. Fairfax Downey, "Bathtubs, Early Americana," *Scribner's,* October 1926, p. 440.
11. Carroll Dulaney, "Baltimore Day by Day," *Baltimore News,* March 16, 1929, p. 1.

12. Arthur Train, *Puritan's Progress* (New York: Charles Scribner's Sons, 1931), p. 51.

13. "The Bathtub Wins Wider Patronage," *New York Times,* August 4, 1935, p. 10E.

14. Bergen Evans, *The Natural History of Nonsense* (London: Michael Joseph Ltd., 1947), p. 247.

15. Beverly Smith, "The Curious Case of the President's Bathtub," *Saturday Evening Post,* August 23, 1952, p. 91.

16. Theo Lippman, Jr., "Roger Mudd, Meet H. L. Mencken," *Baltimore Sun,* January 12, 1976, p. 8A.

17. P. J. Wingate, "The Myth of Fillmore's Bathtub," *Washington Post,* January 4, 1977, p. 13A.

18. Paul Vandervoort, "Who Invented the Bathtub?" *Saturday Evening Post,* November 13, 1943, p. 58.

19. Wingate, "The Myth of Fillmore's Bathtub," p. 13A.

20. Smith, "The Curious Case of the Presidential Bathtub," p. 25.

21. *Ibid.,* p. 94.

22. Lippman, "Roger Mudd, Meet H. L. Mencken," p. 8A.

23. Daniel J. Boorstin, *The Americans: The Democratic Experience* (New York: Random House, 1973), p. 353.

24. Paul F. Boller, Jr., *Presidential Anecdotes* (New York: Oxford University Press, 1981), p. 111.

25. Paul F. Boller, Jr., *Presidential Anecdotes* (New York: Penguin Books, 1982), p. 111.

CHAPTER 10

1. Sanford Jarrell, "New Yorkers Drink Sumptuously on 17,000-Ton Floating Cafe at Anchor 15 Miles off Fire Island," *Herald Tribune,* August 16, 1924, p. 1.

2. *Ibid.,* p. 2.

3. "Floating Wet Palace Believed Supply Ship for Rum Row Craft," *New York Evening Post,* August 16, 1924, p. 1.

4. "Rum-Jazz Ship Not Even Sighted by Marine Patrol," *World,* August 17, 1924, p. 1.

5. "Sea Jazz Palace Eludes Search of Cutter and Plane," *World,* August 18, 1924, Section 2, Page 1.

6. Sanford Jarrell, "U.S. Orders Coast Guard to Ferret Out Cabaret Ship," *Herald Tribune,* August 17, 1924, p. 1.

7. "Coast Guard Acts to Close Cabaret 15 Miles out at Sea," *New York Times,* August 17, 1924, p. 1.

8. *Ibid.*

9. "Rum-Jazz Ship Not Even Sighted by Marine Patrol," p. 1.

10. *Ibid.,* p. 13.

11. Jarrell, "U.S. Orders Coast Guard to Ferret Out Cabaret Ship," p. 8.

12. "Coast Guard Acts to Close Cabaret 15 Miles out at Sea," p. 1.

13. "'Rum-Jazz Ship' Not Even Sighted by Marine Patrol," p. 1.

14. *Ibid.,* p. 13.

15. "Coast Guard Acts to Close Cabaret 15 Miles out at Sea," p. 1.

16. "Floating Rum Oasis Not Ex-German Ship," *New York Evening Post,* August 18, 1924, p. 3.

17. "Movie Covets Cafe Ship," *New York Times,* August 21, 1924, p. 15.

18. *Ibid.*

19. "Beach Whisky Boat to Escape Shots," *New York Times,* August 18, 1924, p. 15.

20. "Rum Runner Riddled; Crew, Cargo Seized," *New York Evening Post,* August 19, 1924, p. 3.

21. "Armored Rum Ship Captured," *World,* August 20, 1924, Section 2, p. 1.

22. "Rum Chasers Shoot One in Fights at Sea," *New York Evening Post,* August 22, 1924, p. 4.

23. *Ibid.*

24. "Beach Whisky Boat to Escape Shots," p. 15.

25. "Bootleggers' Code of Ethics Adopted at Their Convention," *New York Evening Post,* August 21, 1924, p. 9.

26. "Reporter Admits 'Sea Cabaret' Story Untrue," *Herald Tribune,* August 23, 1924, p. 1.

27. Jack Smith, "The Great Gambling Ship Hoax and How It Was Blown Out of the Water," *Los Angeles Times,* July 11, 1984, Part V, p. 1.

28. "Story of Sea Cabaret Untrue, Writer Admits," *Washington Post,* August 23, 1924, p. 4.

29. "The Great Sin Ship," *Time,* February 9, 1962, p. 63.

30. John Chancellor and Walter R. Mears, *The News Business* (New York: Harper & Row, Publishers, 1983), p. 125.

31. "The Great Sin Ship," p. 63.

CHAPTER 11

1. St. John, *This Was My World,* p. 146.

2. Rascoe, *Before I Forget,* p. 236.

3. William Salisbury, *The Career of a Journalist* (New York: B.W. Dodge & Company, 1908), p. 143.

4. Joseph Gies, *The Colonel of Chicago* (New York: E.P. Dutton, 1979), p. 34.

5. St. John, *This Was My World,* p. 151.

6. Vincent Starrett, *Born in a Bookshop* (Norman: University of Oklahoma Press, 1965), pp. 100–101.

7. Bill Doherty, *Crime Reporter* (New York: Exposition Press, 1964), pp. 174–175.

8. John J. McPhaul, *Deadlines and Monkeyshines* (Westport, Conn.: Greenwood Press, Publishers, 1962), p. 228.

9. Doherty, *Crime Reporter,* p. 15.

10. St. John, *This Was My World,* pp. 131–133.

11. Salisbury, *The Career of a Journalist,* pp. 94–97.

12. *Ibid.,* pp. 135–138.

13. *Ibid.,* pp. 152–153.

14. St. John, *This Was My World,* pp. 151–152.

15. McPhaul, *Deadlines and Monkeyshines,* pp. 91–92.

16. *Ibid.,* p. 92.

17. Robert J. Casey, *Bob Casey's Grand Slam* (Indianapolis: Bobbs-Merrill Co., Inc., 1962), p. 14.

18. Rascoe, *Before I Forget,* p. 235.

19. *Ibid.,* pp. 243–245. See also George Murray, *The Madhouse on Madison Street* (Chicago: Follett Publishing Company, 1965), pp. 223–231.

20. Murray, *Madhouse on Madison Street,* pp. 120-123.

21. "Girl Weds Man Near Death to Get Big Estate," *Chicago Tribune,* March 14, 1917, p. 1.

22. "$5,000,000 Marriage to Sick Man Mystery," *Chicago Daily News,* March 14, 1917, p. 3.

23. "Marries Dying Man to Obtain Fortune of About $5,000,000," *Chicago Evening Post,* March 14, 1917, p. 5.

24. "Weds Dying Man to Win $5,000,000," *Daily Journal,* March 14, 1917, p. 1.

25. "$5,000,000 Marriage to Sick Man Mystery," p. 3.

26. Murray, *Madhouse on Madison Street,* pp. 126-131.

27. Casey, *Bob Casey's Grand Slam,* pp. 16-17.

28. " 'Old Friends' Await Gold Smiles Man," *Chicago Herald and Examiner,* October 31, 1921, p. 8.

29. "Rain Today? Money, Maybe Chicago's 'Scotty' Is Due," *Chicago Tribune,* November 1, 1921, p. 18.

30. " 'Dollar Smiles' Man Runs Away," *Herald and Examiner,* November 4, 1921, p. 1.

31. "Smile Hunter Here, But Gives Away No Money," *Herald and Examiner,* November 5, 1921, p. 9.

32. Murray, *Madhouse on Madison Street,* pp. 132-139.

33. McPhaul, *Deadlines and Monkeyshines,* pp. 223-224.

CHAPTER 12

1. The Stone scrapbook, Beardsley and Memorial Library, Winsted, Connecticut.

2. "To Round Up a Wild Man," *New York World,* August 23, 1895, p. 2.

3. "Fresh Bones Found," *Boston Evening Journal,* August 26, 1895, p. 11.

4. "Didn't Get the Wild Man," *New York World,* August 26, 1895, p. 5.

5. *Ibid.*

6. "That Wild Man Wasn't at Home," *New York Herald,* August 26, 1895, p. 5.

7. "Fresh Bones Found," p. 11.

8. "Wild Man Is a Gorilla," *Boston Evening Transcript,* August 29, 1895, p. 1.

9. "Say It Is a Gorilla," *New York World,* August 30, 1895, p. 8.

10. *Ibid.*

11. "Braving the Wild Man," *New York World,* September 2, 1895, p. 2.

12. "Hunted a Gorilla, Killed a Jackass," *New York Herald,* September 2, 1895, p. 7.

13. "When Winsted Was 'Hoax Town,' " *Coronet* (June 1949), p. 59. See also the Stone scrapbook, Beardsley and Memorial Library, Winsted, Connecticut.

14. " 'The Winsted Liar,' " a News-Fictionist Whose Fame Is in 'Whoppers,' " *Literary Digest* (September 11, 1920), p. 62. See also "Why Nature Now Goes Back to Normalcy in Winsted," *Library Digest* (April 1, 1933), p. 22.

15. Letter from Beardsley and Memorial Library, Winsted, Connecticut, October 22, 1983.

16. Ben C. Clough, ed., *The American Imagination at Work* (New York: Alfred A. Knopf, 1947), p. 317.

17. "Back from That Bourne," *New York Sun,* December 19, 1874, p. 1.

18. Edward P. Mitchell, *Memoirs of an Editor* (New York: Charles Scribner's Sons, 1924), p. 119.

19. Florence Finch Kelly, *Flowing Stream* (New York: E.P. Dutton & Co., Inc., 1939), p. 200.

20. Frank Edwards, *Strangest of All* (New York: Citadel Press, 1956), p. 127.

21. Frank Edwards, *Stranger Than Science* (New York: Lyle Stuart, 1959), p. 59.

22. Letter from *Boston Globe,* including a clipping from an "Ask the Globe " column, February 13, 1986.

23. Daily stories about the disaster began to appear on the front page of the *Boston Globe* on August 29, 1883. See also E. W. Sturdy, "The Volcanic Eruption of Krakatoa," *Atlantic Monthly* (September 1884), p. 385; E. Metzger, "Gleanings from the Reports concerning the Eruption of Krakatoa," *Nature* (January 10, 1884), p. 242; "The Eruption of Krakatoa," *Nature* (January 17, 1884), p. 268.

24. Kenneth Roberts, *I Wanted to Write* (Garden City, N.Y.: Doubleday & Company, Inc., 1949), p. 34.

25. George Britt, ed., *Shoeleather and Printers' Ink* (New York: Quadrangle, 1974), p. 263. See also "T. Walter Williams of *The Times* Dies," *New York Times,* November 10, 1942, p. 27.

26. T. Walter Williams, "*Mauretania* Sights Sea Serpent; Entry in the Ship's Log Proves It," *New York Times,* February 11, 1934, p. 3.

27. "Monster Stirs Disputes," *New York Times,* February 11, 1934, p. 3.

28. T. Walter Williams, "Ship's Officer Sticks to Sea Serpent Yarn, but Says Artist Failed Reproducing Sketch," *New York Times,* February 24, 1934, p. 15.

29. T. Walter Williams, "New Sea Serpent Reported by Ship," *New York Times,* March 10, 1934, p. 15.

30. "Sea-Serpent Monopoly Undesirable," *New York Times,* March 27, 1934, p. 20.

31. "Zoo Monkey Learns to Play a Ukelele," *New York Times,* February 19, 1917, p. 6.

32. "Finds an Old Friend behind Circus Bars," *New York Times,* April 11, 1920, Section II, p. 6.

33. *Ibid.*

34. T. Walter Williams, "Tonka Beans Draw Marmaduke Mizzle," *New York Times,* May 12, 1929, Section II, p. 5.

35. T. Walter Williams, "Singing Spiders Irk Mizzle in Jungle," *New York Times,* November 22, 1931, Section II, p. 6.

36. T. Walter Williams, "Famous Explorer Found to Be Alive," *New York Times,* May 21, 1933, Section II, p. 2.

37. T. Walter Williams, "Old Salt Deplores Modern Sea Ways," *New York Times,* June 28, 1931, Section II, p. 5.

38. "Ben Fidd's Turkey-Eating Shark Rises as a Thanksgiving Ghost," *New York Times,* November 2, 1941, p. 12.

39. T. Walter Williams, "Ancient Mariner a Battery Visitor," *New York Times,* August 24, 1941, p. 36.

40. "Hoaxer of the Hamptons," *Time* (August 4, 1975), p. 57.

41. "The East End Is Sinking," *Dan's Papers* (October 14, 1983), p. 1.

42. "Fat Tourists to be Turned Back in 84," *Dan's Papers* (October 14, 1983), p. 4.

CHAPTER 13

1. "Mike Monster," *Newsweek* (June 9, 1947), p. 63.

2. " 'Monster' in Tokyo," *New York Times,* May 30, 1947, p. 4.

3. "Just Like Orson Welles," *Willmar Daily Tribune,* February 9, 1949, p. 2.

4. "Martians and Wild Animals," *Time* (February 29, 1949), p. 46.

5. "Just Like Orson Welles," p. 2.

6. "Things Are Back to Normal Again after 'Animal Scare,' " *Willmar Daily Tribune,* February 11, 1949, p. 2.

7. "Doll Joke Taken Seriously," *Milwaukee Sentinel,* November 30, 1983, p. 11.

8. "Dolls Don't Fall from Heaven," *Milwaukee Journal,* November 30, 1983, Part 2, p. 1.

9. St. John, *This Was My World,* p. 164.

10. George Stein, "How TV Shows May Have Fallen for a Psychic Hoax," *Orlando Sentinel,* April 4, 1981, p. 12-A.

11. "Psychic Prediction of Shooting Was All a Hoax, TV Host Admits," *Orlando Sentinel,* April 6, 1981, p. 4-A. See also "Prediction on Shooting Acknowledged as Hoax," *New York Times,* April 6, 1981, p. B13.

12. John Houseman, "Panic: The Men from Mars," in *Grand Deception,* ed. Alexander Klein (London: Faber and Faber Limited), p. 29.

13. Howard Koch, *The Panic Broadcast* (Boston: Little Brown and Co., 1970), pp. 33–80.

14. Ben Gross, *I Looked and I Listened* (New York: Random House, 1954), p. 200.

15. Hadley Cantril, "The Invasion from Mars," in *The Process and Effects of Mass Communication,* rev. ed., ed. Wilbur Schramm and Donald F. Roberts (Urbana: University of Illinois Press, 1971), p. 580.

16. "Radio Listeners in Panic, Taking War Drama as Fact," *New York Times,* October 31, 1938, p. 1.

17. *Ibid.,* p. 4.

18. Cantril, "Invasion from Mars," pp. 582–583.

19. Houseman, "Panic," p. 84.

20. William S. Paley, *As It Happened* (Garden City, N.Y.: Doubleday & Co., Inc., 1979), p. 112.

21. A. A. Dornfeld, *Behind the Front Page* (Chicago: Academy Chicago Publishers, 1983), p. 187.

22. " 'Martian Invasion' Terrorizes Chile," *New York Times,* November 14, 1944, p. 1. See also "Those Men from Mars," *Newsweek* (November 29, 1944), p. 89.

23. Jorge Fernandez, *Transito a la Libertad* (Quito, Ecuador: Editorial El Comercio, 1956), p. 161.

24. " 'Mars Raiders' Cause Quito Panic; Mob Burns Radio Plant, Kills 15," *New York Times,* February 14, 1949, p. 1.

25. "Martians and Wild Animals," p. 46.

26. "20 Dead in the Quito Riot," *New York Times,* February 15, 1949, p. 15.

27. "The Night the World Ended, Disaster on the Northcoast," (Arcata, Calif.) *Union,* November 1, 1974, p. 1. See also "Arcata Radio Station Terrifies Listeners," *Sacramento Bee,* November 1, 1974, p. B1.

28. Stephanie Mansfield and Art Harris, "A New 'War of the Worlds' Frightens FM Listeners Here," *Washington Post,* April 26, 1980, p. A17.

29. Marc Gunther, "Pacifica: Radio's Outlet for the Outrageous," *Washington Journalism Review* (May 1983), p. 43.

30. "Nuclear Terrorism Show Sets Off Flurry of Yelps and Yawns," *Orlando Sentinel,* March 31, 1983. See also Salley Bedell, "Nuclear-Terror Show on NBC Is Criticized," *New York Times,* March 22, 1983, p. C15.

CHAPTER 14

1. Maymie R. Krythe, *All About American Holidays* (New York: Harper & Row, Publishers, 1962), p. 66.
2. "April Fool Jokers Active," *New York Times*, April 2, 1928, p. 2.
3. Jane M. Hatch, *The American Book of Days*, 3d ed. (New York: The H. W. Wilson Company, 1978), p. 314.
4. "Journal Announces New Contest," *Eldorado Daily Journal*, March 31, 1984.
5. Letter from Bob Ellis, managing editor of the *Eldorado Daily Journal*, April 8, 1984. See also Bob Ellis, "My opinion," *Eldorado Daily Journal*, April 10, 1984.
6. "A PUBLIC CALAMITY," *Daily Picayune*, April 1, 1876.
7. "A BURIED BOAT," *Daily Picayune*, April 1, 1887.
8. Thomas Ewing Dabney, *One Hundred Great Years* (Baton Rouge: Louisiana State University, 1944), p. 287.
9. "Voice of the People," *Daily Journal*, April 6, 1975.
10. Photograph, "Oil for the Courthouse Lamps," *Daily Journal*, April 1, 1957.
11. "Lirpa Loof Theory Probed in Saucer Crash Here," *Daily Journal*, March 30, 1967.
12. "Lirpa Loof Strikes Again; *Journal* Phones Are Busy," *Daily Journal*, April 1, 1967.
13. "It Was a Fun Morning at State Park," *Daily Journal*, April 1, 1968.
14. "Spacecraft Lands Safely in Kankakee," *Daily Journal*, April 1, 1969.
15. "Voice of the People."
16. "Apparition in Wildcat Stirs Fright," *Kokomo Tribune*, April 1, 1952.
17. Ken Atwell, "Change in Policemen's Hours Planned as Taxsaving Measure," *Kokomo Tribune*, April 1, 1959.
18. "West Side Tract Selected for Nudist Camp," *Kokomo Tribune*, April 1, 1963.
19. "New Tax to Be Levied to Construct Public Officials' Health Club Here," *Kokomo Tribune*, April 1, 1965.
20. John Carter, "Sam Talks to a Pelican," *Daytona Beach Sunday News-Journal*, March 31, 1979.
21. Dean Johnson, "Small Wonder," *Florida Magazine* in *Orlando Sentinel*, April 1, 1984, p. 10.
22. Dean Johnson, "If Today's News Is Beyond Belief, Don't Believe It," *Orlando Sentinel*, April 1, 1985, p. D-1.
23. "Lakes Chosen for Bold Experiment," *Herald-News*, April 2, 1981, p. 1.
24. "Chemical Known to Cause Death Is in City Water Mains," *Durand Express*, March 31, 1983, p. 1.
25. "Nissan Plans Plant North of Durand," *Durand Express*, March 29, 1984, p. 1.
26. Robert Sherefkin, "Rood Joke," *Washington Journalism Review* (June 1984), p. 13.
27. David Holahan, "Rediscovering April Fools' Day," *Orlando Sentinel*, April 1, 1984, p. G-10.
28. "Regional News Roundup," *Rivereast News Bulletin*, April 1, 1985, p. 21.
29. Letter from James Hallas, editor of the *Rivereast News Bulletin*, October 1, 1985.
30. George Plimpton, "The Curious Case of Sidd Finch," *Sports Illustrated* (April 1, 1985), p. 59.
31. "The End of the Affair," *Sports Illustrated* (April 8, 1985), p. 27.
32. "Letter from the Publisher," *Sports Illustrated* (April 15, 1985), p. 4.
33. Mark Fitzgerald, "An April Fools' Day Hoax," *Editor and Publisher* (April 20, 1985), p. 7.

34. Photograph, *Daily Mirror,* April 1, 1935, pp. 18–19.
35. "April Fool Stunts Get Big Play," *Editor and Publisher* (April 10, 1954), p. 52.
36. *Ibid.*
37. Photograph, "Dome Topples Off Statehouse," *Capital Times,* April 1, 1933, p. 1.
38. Photograph, "Blast Rips East Extension of State Capitol," *Patriot,* April 1, 1976, p. 1.
39. "Darts and Laurels," *Columbia Journalism Review* (July-August 1976), p. 5.
40. "Riot over Paper's April 1 Joke," *Editor and Publisher* (April 5, 1913), p. 2.
41. "Turks Adopt April Fool," *New York Times,* April 6, 1924, p. 22.
42. "FUTURES Agenda Extra," *Manchester Guardian,* April 1, 1981, p. 11.
43. "Plays Joke on Globe," *Editor and Publisher* (April 10, 1915), p. 898.
44. "Go ahead. Be a fool. It's okay today," *Orlando Sentinel,* April 1, 1983, p. A-8.
45. "Professor Says April Fools' Story a Joke," *Orlando Sentinel,* April 17, 1983, p. A-18.

CHAPTER 15

1. David Shaw, *Journalism Today* (New York: Harper's College Press, 1977), p. 109.
2. Alice Polk Hill, *Tales of the Colorado Pioneers* (Denver: Pierson & Gardner, 1884), pp. 29–32.
3. From the author's collection of press clippings, compiled while working for a newspaper in California.
4. "Iowans Respond to Letter of Despair," *Minneapolis Star,* December 31, 1981, p. 1.
5. Lloyd Mann, "Undefeated and Undetected," in Alexander Klein, ed. *Grand Deception* (London: Faber and Faber Limited 1956), pp. 204–206.
6. "Sports Page Error," *Time* (November 17, 1941), p. 74. See also Bob Cooke, "Plainfield's Phantom Football Team," *Reader's Digest* (December 1974), p. 233.
7. John Consoli, "Canadian Papers Hoaxed on Phony Soccer Tourney," *Editor and Publisher* (March 27, 1982), p. 13.
8. H. Allen Smith, *The Compleat Practical Joker* (Garden City: Doubleday & Company, 1953), p. 136.
9. Alfred McClung Lee, *The Daily Newspaper in America* (New York: Macmillan Company, 1947), pp. 429–430.
10. Waldo R. Browne, ed., *Barnum's Own Story* (Gloucester, Mass.: Peter Smith, 1972), pp. 109–116.
11. H.L. Mencken, *A Choice of Days* (New York: Alfred A. Knopf, 1980), pp. 163–165.
12. Smith, *The Compleat Practical Joker,* p. 108.
13. St. John, *This Was My World,* pp. 220–221.
14. James H. Richardson, *For the Life of Me* (New York: G.P. Putnam's Sons, 1954), pp. 127–131.
15. "Drag Park Lake for Body of Supposed Suicide," *New York World,* July 19, 1920, p. 1.
16. "Drag Lake to Find Body of Missing Girl," *Evening Telegram,* July 19, 1920, p. 1.
17. "Japanese Beauty Believed Suicide," *New York American,* July 20, 1920, p. 4.
18. "Searchlights Aid in Search for Girl's Body," *Evening Telegram,* July 21, 1920, p. 20.
19. "Miss Onda Drowned? No, She's Flickering," *New York World,* July 26, 1920, p. 13.
20. "Swann Elated over Shaming Movie Men," *New York Herald,* July 31, 1920, p. 7.

21. "Pigeon Brings Call for Help 2,000 Miles," *New York World*, August 18, 1921, p. 1.

22. "Pigeon Bears 'Lost' Message to Gotham from Yellowstone," *Chicago Tribune*, August 18, 1921, p. 1.

23. "Breathless Pigeon Brings a Help Call," *New York Times*, August 18, 1921, p. 17.

24. "Squab Loses Credit for the World's Record Flight of 2,000 Miles," *New York World*, August 19, 1921.

25. "Heller Message Is Fake, Say Experts," *San Francisco Chronicle*, August 19, 1921, p. 1.

26. Leon Nelson Flint, *The Conscience of the Newspaper* (New York: D. Appleton-Century Company, 1925), p. 41.

27. "May Prosecute Joker for Pigeon Note Hoax," *New York Times*, August 26, 1921, p. 13.

28. " 'Cone-Shaped Rocket' Puzzles Scores Here," *Atlanta Constitution*, July 7, 1953, p. 1.

29. "Tinfoiled Triangle Teases Steaming Skywatchers Here," *Atlanta Journal*, July 7, 1953, p. 1.

30. Katherine Barnwell, "Just a Monkey, Experts Say of Tiny 'Martian,' " *Atlanta Constitution*, July 9, 1953, p. 1.

31. *Ibid.*, p. 12.

32. Katherine Barnwell, "Monkey-Hoaxer Pays a $40 Fine: Surprised Any Folks Were Fooled," *Atlanta Constitution*, July 10, 1953, p. 1.

33. "Day by Day," *New York Times*, March 22, 1983.

34. Jonathan Susskind, "New York Fails to Fall for Typhoon-alert Hoax," *Orlando Sentinel*, March 22, 1983, p. A-5.

35. "A Kafkaesque Tale of Health Faddists Eating Cockroaches," *Wall Street Journal*, September 28, 1981, p. 1.

36. "Press Hoodwinked Again," *Editor and Publisher* (October 3, 1981), p. 8.

37. Brenda Woods, "Hoaxer Is Serious about Joking," *Chicago Tribune*, February 20, 1978, Section II, p. 3.

38. Alan Abel, *The Great American Hoax* (New York: Trident Press, 1966), p. vii.

39. George Draper, "Crusade against Naked Animals," *San Francisco Chronicle*, August 13, 1962, p. 1.

40. George Draper, "City Called 'Moral Disaster Area,' " *San Francisco Chronicle*, August 14, 1962, p. 1.

41. "Pickets Ask Pony Pants," *Washington Daily News*, March 5, 1963, p. 1.

42. Abel, *Great American Hoax*, p. xii.

43. *Ibid.*

44. *Ibid.*

45. Richard Laermer, "A Dislike of Hype," *Editor and Publisher* (March 30, 1985), p. 44.

46. "Fainting Foolery Disturbs Donahue," *Orlando Sentinel*, February 3, 1985, p. A-5.

47. "Needy Men Victims of a Cruel Hoax," *New York Times*, January 23, 1912, p. 6.

48. "Phony-Jobs Ad Tricks 300 into Applying," *Orlando Sentinel*, June 9, 1982, p. B-1.

49. "Major Dailies Burned by Fake Help Wanted Ads," *Editor and Publisher* (February 5, 1983), p. 9.

50. "Famous Fakes," *Editor and Publisher* (April 2, 1910), p. 6.

51. Bill Doherty, *Crime Reporter* (New York: Exposition Press, 1964), pp. 20–21.

52. Shaw, *Journalism Today*, pp. 98–114.

53. Jacquelyn Mitchard, "Pursuing the Truth Can Be Risky Business," *Capital Times,* June 29, 1982, p. 17.

54. "Speakes Pulls Hoax on D.C. Press Corps," *Editor and Publisher* (December 10, 1983), p. 13.

EPILOGUE

1. "The Bomb and the Broadcasters," *Broadcasting* (March 1, 1971), p. 47.

2. "False Emergency Alert Throws Stations off Air," *Atlanta Constitution,* February 21, 1971, p. 20-A.

3. "If This Had Been a Real Attack Alert . . . Forget It!" *San Francisco Examiner,* February 21, 1971, p. 22A.

4. "National Alert Unnoticed Here," *Atlanta Constitution,* February 21, 1971, p. 1.

5. Hugh S. Stewart, "Mother Here Expects 5 or 6 Babies," *Chicago Herald-American,* August 21, 1951, p. 1.

6. Hugh S. Stewart, "Can X-Ray Tell What Stork Will Bring to Chicago?" *Chicago Herald-American,* August 23, 1951, p. 1.

7. Hugh S. Stewart, "Sextuplets in '66 Born Here," *Chicago Herald-American,* August 26, 1951, p. 3.

8. "Reporter Admits Baby Story Hoax," *Chicago Herald-American,* February 7, 1952, p. 1.

9. Wade Roberts, "Best — Bar None," *Chicago Sun-Times,* November 18, 1985, p. 6.

10. Mike Royko, "Texas Horror! Bar Vanishes!" *Chicago Tribune,* November 28, 1985, p. 3.

11. Mark Fitzgerald, "Hoax in Chicago," *Editor and Publisher* (December 7, 1985), p. 22.

12. Monica Collins, "Ch. 7 Prank Erupts, News Producer Fired," *Boston Herald-American,* April 3, 1980, p. 3.

13. Thomas Sabulis, "Ch. 7 Reacts, Cans Jokester," *Boston Globe,* April 3, 1980, p. 1.

14. John R. Cockran, "Deli Journalism," *Columbia Journalism Review* (September-October 1979), p. 13.

15. Christopher Jones, "In the Land of the Khmer Rouge," *New York Times Magazine,* December 20, 1981, p. 70.

16. Robert G. Kaiser, "Journalist's Interviews with Khmer Rouge Officials Questioned," *Washington Post,* February 18, 1982, p. A6.

17. James M. Markham, "Writer Admits He Fabricated an Article in *Times* Magazine," *New York Times,* February 22, 1982, p. 1.

18. "A Lie in *The Times,*" *New York Times,* February 23, 1982, p. A22.

19. Daniel Burstein, "I Dreamed I Saw Pol Pot Last Night," *The Quill* (May 1982), p. 18.

20. *Ibid.*

21. "Running Down a Rumor," *Time* (February 3, 1975), p. 6.

22. "The Stand-In," *Time* (February 3, 1975), p. 37.

23. Debra Gersh, "Call Him Mr. Hoax," *Editor and Publisher* (June 14, 1986), p. 48.

24. "Rescuers Snatch Human Baby from Renegade Ape," *Weekly World News,* June 26, 1984, p. 19.

25. "Earth Woman Has Alien's Starchild," *Weekly World News,* July 12, 1983, p. 5.

INDEX